A TIME FOR REFLECTION

A TIME FOR REFLECTION

AN AUTOBIOGRAPHY

BY

WILLIAM E. SIMON

WITH JOHN M. CAHER

Since 1947
REGNERY
PUBLISHING, INC.
An Eagle Publishing Company • Washington, DC

Library of Congress Cataloging-in-Publication Data
    Simon, William E., 1927–2000
    A time for reflection: an autobiography / by William E. Simon; with John M. Caher.
    p. cm.
    Includes index.
    ISBN 0-89526-170-7
    1. Simon, William E., 1927–2000. Cabinet officers—United States—Biography. 3. Statesmen—United States—Biography. I. Caher, John M. II. Title.
    E840.8.S5446A3 2004
    336.73'092—dc22

                                        2003023329

ISBN 0-89526-170-7

Published in the United States by
Regnery Publishing, Inc.
An Eagle Publishing Company
One Massachusetts Avenue, NW
Washington, DC 20001

Visit us at www.regnery.com

Distributed to the trade by
National Book Network
4720-A Boston Way
Lanham, MD 20706

Printed on acid-free paper
Manufactured in the United States of America

10 9 8 7 6 5 4 3 2 1

Books are available in quantity for promotional or premium use. Write to Director of Special Sales, Regnery Publishing, Inc., One Massachusetts Avenue, NW, Washington, DC 20001, for information on discounts and terms, or call (202) 216-0600.

To my children and grandchildren, and America's, so that they may fully appreciate and cherish and guard their most precious inheritance—freedom. —William E. Simon, May 2000

To two great American families, Bill Simon's and my own, to whom this torch shall be passed. —John M. Caher, December 2003

ABOUT THE AUTHORS

William E. Simon was also the author of *A Time for Truth*, published by Reader's Digest Press/McGraw-Hill Book Co., 1978; and *A Time for Action*, published by Reader's Digest Press/McGraw-Hill Book Co., 1980.

John M.Caher is coauthor with his brother, James P. Caher, of *Personal Bankruptcy for Dummies*, published in 2003 by John Wiley & Sons; author of *King of the Mountain: The Rise, Fall and Redemption of Chief Judge Sol Wachtler*, published by Prometheus Books, 1998; and coauthor, with James P. Caher, of *Debt Free! Your Guide to Personal Bankruptcy Without Shame*, published by Henry Holt and Company, 1996. Mr. Caher, former state editor of the Albany, New York, *Times Union*, is currently Albany bureau chief for the *New York Law Journal*. He lives in Clifton Park, N.Y., with his wife, Kathleen, and their three daughters, Erin, Kerry, and Norah.

CONTENTS

FOREWORD

by President Gerald R. Ford

The Bill Simon I knew was a man of absolutes—absolute integrity, absolute conviction, absolute candor.

When he was in my cabinet, Bill never shied away from the tough decisions and could be counted on to articulate his position with his trademark passion, vigor, and persistence. Yet when a decision was made, even one with which he disagreed, Bill supported the administration with every ounce of his seemingly boundless energy. No president ever had a more loyal or creative or trusted advisor.

For Bill Simon, service came before self, and his life story is an object lesson of the American spirit and the patriotism that lies at its foundation. Everything Bill did in his life, he did in a big way, and this memoir is certainly no exception. It is an extraordinary work by an extraordinary American.

Bill gave up the security of the private sector, where he was earning millions, to join the Nixon administration in a time of national trauma. He accepted the duties of America's energy czar in the wake of the Arab oil embargo and endured death threats. He became secretary of the treasury just as a recession loomed on the horizon and years of governmental excess threatened American prosperity.

And when the world's greatest city, New York, found itself on the brink of bankruptcy, Bill Simon practiced his own brand of tough love, for which he was denigrated by the tabloids and portrayed (inaccurately) as a cold-hearted numbers-cruncher. The plain truth is that Bill loved the people of New York too much to sacrifice their future to the politicians, which would have been the easy thing to do. Rather, his vision and courage and insistence that New York City get its house in order, no matter how painful in the short term, helped ensure not only that the city would survive, but that it would recover and prosper and become the gleaming metropolis that it is today. New York City returned to greatness in no small measure because of Bill Simon.

Bill was as compassionate as he was competitive, and if he could be demanding—and he surely could—he made his greatest demands on himself, in his most public and his most private capacities. His work ethic as a government official, entrepreneur, and Olympic Committee president was legendary and well documented. Less known is how hard he toiled, often anonymously, for the downtrodden in our society.

Every Christmas morning, Bill and his entire family rose early and quietly headed to Covenant House, where they celebrated the birth of our Savior with runaway and throwaway youths and unwed mothers. He recognized that wealth is not measured in bank accounts or stock options, but in lives rescued and families restored. I can't think of anyone who better embodied the old maxim that while we make a living by what we get, we make a life by what we give. By that standard, Bill Simon lived an exemplary life.

What has always struck me most about Bill is his commitment to the cause of freedom—and that commitment, and its source, is the hallmark of this memoir. The freedom he cherished was the freedom to strive, to foster a climate of incentive, with opportunities to create, to invest, and to expand the frontiers of knowledge. Bill understood implicitly that liberty was not a permissive grant from government, but a natural right bestowed by God, and a right to be revered and cherished and nurtured as the divine gift that it is.

I am delighted, both as a friend and as a fellow citizen, that Bill Simon was able to complete his autobiography prior to his untimely and unfortunate death on June 3, 2000. His inspiring life story is one that should be read and understood and appreciated by Americans of all walks of life for generations to come—for in the great defining struggle of the twentieth century, liberty had no greater champion, and freedom had no greater friend, than Bill Simon.

———

President Gerald R. Ford
August 2000

FOREWORD

by George P. Shultz

Bill Simon is vividly alive in this book. Reading his memoirs, we learn how many Bills there really were.

I knew him first when, as secretary of the treasury, I recruited him to be my deputy. I wanted him for many reasons, among them his knowledge of finance. He was a fantastic trader who obviously understood financial markets by instinct as well as by intellect. I thought we could use a little of both in the government.

But I quickly discovered how much more there was to Bill Simon. We can see him through the many images from his boyhood included in this book. We see him as a soldier in occupied Japan, able to fall in love with a young Japanese girl. We see him as a trader par excellence on Wall Street. I remember when checking him out, I asked my friend, Walter Wriston, who was then head of Citicorp, what he thought. Walter replied, "I hope you get him to go to the Treasury. Then maybe someone else can make some money in the bond market." What an accolade!

We see him in the Northwest Passage, locked in ice and going on with the Simon elan. We see him as a figure in Washington and in politics, as a writer, and as a businessman with a golden touch who spent a good part of his life giving away the money he made. We see him as a man consumed by sports and leading our country in the Olympics. We see him as a man capable of love and caring and a man of deep faith.

Let's pause and look at a few of the things we can learn by reading this book and thinking about Bill Simon.

Bill spent his life taking risks. He was always known as someone who was willing to make decisions and be accountable for them. But as I worked with Bill and watched him, I could see that risk wasn't something you just took. On the contrary, you studied the risks, you learned what their characteristics were, you figured out how to mitigate risks and guard against extremes. So for Bill, risk was not an adversary or chance; risk was an intellectual challenge. I believe this attitude was one of the reasons Bill was so successful: He took risks that other people shunned because he understood better than most how to take at least some of the risk out of risk.

There's also the matter of loyalty. Bill, for example, can be put down as a "Nixon die-hard." His admiration for President Nixon never flagged, although Nixon's imperfections in action are documented by Bill in this memoir. Nevertheless, Nixon's immense positive attributes are what stayed with Bill and what inspired him to lead the effort to fund the Nixon Library. Bill's accounts of many of his experiences with Nixon, particularly with events toward the end of the Nixon presidency and in subsequent years, are most revealing. But you could see in the life of Bill Simon and in the way he writes about his legion of many friends, not just Nixon, that he placed great value on loyalty. He also believed that loyalty was a two-way street.

Along with loyalty came the willingness to speak directly and frankly, often in tense and difficult situations. There is that old saying, "He told it with the bark off." With Bill, the bark was hardly ever on, but he often startled people with his candor which he used to jolt them into clearer thinking. His comments went to the heart of the matter without a lot of detail to fuzz things up.

Bill understood the importance of being able to learn. He was always looking for new ideas. The biggest favor I ever did for Bill was introducing him to my friend Milton Friedman. Milton's brilliance as an economist is well known but perhaps as important and less exalted is his capacity as an expositor. He has a gift of clarity and the patience to work a subject over and over when he thinks the person on the other end of the conversation is worth the effort. Bill was a star pupil, with a voracious appetite for learning.

Bill and Milton were soul mates in their deep veneration for the value of freedom. Freedom was at the center of Bill's life. It was the basis for the policies he fought for as a government official. His advocacy, in his actions and in his writing, of freedom in economics and politics was powerful. He named his beloved boat "Freedom." One of the fascinating aspects of his memoirs is the way you can trace the influence of his reverence for freedom through his life.

It was this belief in freedom that identified Bill with the Olympics. Here were athletes from all over the world competing freely with each other. The contests, fairly run, were the ultimate in accountability. He understood very well that freedom and accountability go together. You are free to lose as well as to win.

Bill and I went through some tumultuous times together, grappling with problems at the Treasury, confronting the energy crisis, trying to work our way out of the maze of ill-considered wage and price controls, coming to grips with the implications of the "Saturday Night Massacre," and many others. These were experiences we shared that created a bond of enduring respect and friendship. So, I am delighted to have this memoir, so full of detail and so full of the real Bill Simon. Like so many other Bill Simon fans, I welcome this opportunity to celebrate the life of this man of many and diverse interests and talents and to learn what I can from the renewed exposure to the life, the views, the battles, and the exhilaration of Bill Simon.

———

George P. Shultz
August 2000

SHIRTSLEEVES
TO SHIRTSLEEVES

My early life was one of luxury and privilege. But the Simon family was living on the coattails of a fortune that would be soon be gone. Shirtsleeves to shirtsleeves, in this case, took only two generations.

My father inherited a couple of silk mills in the 1920s, which he promptly sold, realizing a profit of roughly $2 million—the equivalent of over $16 million today. It was an incredible opportunity coupled with an awesome responsibility. Yet, having all the money he could ever envision needing, my father basically retired at the age of twenty-two and enjoyed living the illusion of perpetual prosperity. By the time he died in 1964, the money was virtually gone. The wake of affluence and the delusion of unending opulence carried the Simons throughout my childhood.

As a child growing up with a fading fortune in an old industrial city—Paterson, New Jersey—during the Depression, I witnessed poverty without having to live it. What I saw was branded on my memory for all time: Families of eight living in a single room, supported by a father struggling on a few dollars a week; people sleeping in boxcars, traveling from state to state looking for work of any kind, begging for meals, searching for hope, and not expecting to find it; desperate men appearing at our back door, pleading for food and clothes; a friend of mine receiving as a Christmas present a comic book—a *used* comic book—that his unemployed father had salvaged from the city dump.

By comparison, the Simon family had a chauffeur and a 16-cylinder Cadillac to take me in style to a Catholic grammar school. I was so embarrassed to be living in wealth when many people were poor and struggling that I often had my driver drop me off out of sight of St. Joseph's School in Paterson so the other kids wouldn't see me.

My parents were a couple right out of *The Great Gatsby*. Dad—Charles Simon—was a dapper, five-foot-eight, 230-pound *bon vivant* with slicked-back hair and an eager expression behind his spectacles. His roots were in the sixteenth century Alsatian village of Soultz, which today is a part of France near the German border. My father was a jovial, good-hearted, generous-to-a-fault gentleman, and a wonderful father. He was considerate and understanding and, above all, fair and just. My mother, Eleanor Kearns, was of Celtic descent. A beautiful, slender girl with misty, soft Irish eyes, Mom was a very nurturing woman: loving, kind, and warm. After their wedding in St. Joseph's Church in November of 1922, Charles and Eleanor had four children: Charles, Mary Ellen, myself (William Edward), and Madeleine Sophie.

Dad was high society, a big man in town, a "Who's Who" in New Jersey. Like most people we knew, he was a marginally active Democrat who paid lip service to FDR's New Deal, the supposed antidote to the Depression.

But my father really didn't give much thought to politics, policy, or philosophy. He was the quintessential, well-to-do product of the Roaring Twenties—living like a nobleman, spending rather than saving, consuming rather than investing, blissfully estranged from the effort and the ideology that made his wealth possible. We had a beautiful home in Allenhurst, and a Victorian mansion on Broadway in Paterson that my grandfather had purchased in 1898. It was a grand home, complete with a staff of seven to attend to our every need. Up the street was the chauffeur's residence, and behind that was a huge garage, a converted stable that must have had room for a dozen cars. Later, my father bought a residence in the New Jersey resort town of Spring Lake, where we eventually lived full-time.

Like many of their class, my parents traveled frequently, taking elaborate and exotic trips to Europe and often leaving the children in the care of nannies. Shortly after my birth, my parents retained a young German immigrant named Hanny Wagner to watch over me and, a few years later, my younger sister Madeleine. We called her "Schatzie"—"sweetheart" in German but "saint" to me. Schatzie was a guardian angel and would become a formative figure in my life.

Hanny Wagner emigrated in 1928, when her homeland was devastated by hyperinflation and civil unrest, and worked briefly for another prominent family before joining the Simons. She fell in love with us, and we with her. In short order, Schatzie was as much a part of our family as any blood relative. So it was without hesitation that she promised my mother that if anything happened to her, she would take care of the Simon children. I can't imagine that either had any inkling how quickly Schatzie would be called upon to assume that responsibility.

On July 29, 1936, I came home from day camp one afternoon, surprised to find many of our relatives at the house at Spring Lake. When I greeted them happily, they just looked at me, biting their lips and not sure what to say. I realized something was amiss, but was far too young to figure things out for myself. Finally—after what seemed an eternity but couldn't have been more than a few uncomfortable moments—my father slowly walked over, knelt on one knee, held me in his arms, and looked me in the eye. I was eight years old and utterly unprepared for the first great shock of my life.

"Son, your mother died."

My mother was only thirty-four years old and had always seemed the picture of health. But a recent affliction of appendicitis had weakened her and an infection killed her.

I threw my arms around my father, buried my head in his chest, and we both wept uncontrollably, clinging to each other for comfort and support. I couldn't contemplate life without my mother, nor could my father imagine going forward without his wife.

I was aware of the beauty of a mother's love, and understood, intuitively, what a special bond that was for both of us, and what a tragic thing it was that she was gone. Some child psychologists speculate that the loss of one's mother at an early age fosters internal fears of desertion and loneliness. I don't know how accurate that theory is, but I do know that since my earliest memories I have always preferred company to solitude. I have also retained a childlike reverence and devotion for the Blessed Mother, perhaps a result of losing my own mother.

With the resiliency of youth, my immediate grief was not terribly prolonged and I very quickly picked up where I had left off and went about the business of being a child. For my father, however, the death of his beautiful, young wife was devastating. Dad looked to Mom as his anchor, his stability, and once she was gone, frankly, he wasn't very stable. He spent money with increasingly reckless abandon, seemingly with no inkling that his wealth was neither infinite nor self-perpetuating.

The few investments Dad made turned out badly, and when the lingering Depression exhausted a substantial portion of his already dwindling reserves, we relied on my grandmother for support. Eventually, Dad went to work in the insurance business, but whatever small measure of self-sufficiency he was able to attain was due mainly to the fact that he was a good salesman with a lot of friends and several wealthy relatives who became steady customers. By the time I was ten, there were no more chauffeurs or servants in the Simon household, and Schatzie was no longer collecting a salary. Yet, she stayed on and continued to watch over me and my siblings, just as she had promised my mother. I'm afraid I proved to be quite a handful.

In 1921, a wonderful silent film was made from George W. Peck's popular stories of a lovably mischievous little boy with a heart of gold but an unending knack for getting into trouble. That was me—the original "problem child." People called me a cutup, a hell-raiser, but mainly I was just a good-natured prankster, a "Peck's Bad Boy." My antics were impish, mischievous, and I seemed predisposed, as the Frank Sinatra song goes, to "do it my way." As a child, I certainly did not ponder freedom in any abstract manner, but I did resent encroachments on my liberty, and naturally rebelled against any infringements. I never considered "because I said so" a valid argument to do—or not do—anything. Most adults bored me to tears with their arbitrary rules and slavish devotion to custom, and I spent an inordinate amount of time concocting what I thought at the time were ingenious ways of breaking their rules, of tweaking the establishment just a bit, of rebelling against regulations.

This was the beginning of "William the Terrible"—as the press would dub me decades later.

———

Sister Julia Agnes Cronin, second grade teacher, February 15, 2000

Whenever there was activity in the schoolyard, whenever there was laughter, whenever there was mischief, there was Billy Simon. And if there was some sort of "trouble" and Billy was involved and you asked who was responsible, his hand would go right up, even if he was going to get into trouble. The other youngsters would wait to see who was going to admit being part of the trouble, but not Billy. He was very, very honest, and very courageous.

Even in second grade, things just didn't move fast enough for him. He liked things to move along and would get frustrated when they didn't. He was very impetuous, and quick, very quick.

I remember once we were discussing First Communion and he called out, with his seven-year-old voice, "Sister, how do they know the Blessed Virgin didn't have Original Sin on her soul?" He needed an answer, and there I was, a twenty-eight-year-old nun. I had never questioned the Blessed Mother's immaculate conception in my life. Just then, another little boy, shouted out, "They x-rayed her, of course, that's how they know there was no Original Sin." Well, that satisfied Billy—and I could have given a great big kiss to that little fellow who said they x-rayed her!

Later he wrote a book—A Time for Truth—and my immediate response was, "Well, Billy Simon always told the truth." He sent me the book and I knew it would displease the politicians, and I asked him, "Aren't you afraid of that book getting you into trouble?" He said, "No, Sister, you can't get in trouble if you tell the truth."

———

Dad never did remarry after my mother died, although he was a debonair ladies' man and great dancer. He once dated a wealthy widow whom he hoped to wed. However, she apparently had little interest in instantly becoming stepmother to four children, especially a little rascal called "Billy," so the relationship came to an end. After that, Dad spent much of his spare time playing pinochle, bridge, and gin with his friends.

My father's card-playing buddies treated me as a plain, ordinary, commonplace kid destined for mediocrity, or less. I suppose they expected that I would spend my life as a clerk of some sort.

Even at an early age, I was offended by their presumptuousness and arrogance. After all, these were men who inherited their money (or married rich) and spent their days in idle pursuits; they were not producers. The men who presumed to pigeonhole Billy Simon were perfectly comfortable with their butts in the air and their heads safely hidden in the sand. I decided to prove them wrong, to prove that Bill Simon could make it, and could make it on his own.

Work appealed to me; school did not. I was a disinterested, bored student. Additionally, I had very bad eyes. I was cross-eyed and had astigmatism. Despite an experimental operation, I still couldn't see very well and couldn't really read the blackboard, which was frustrating and a little embarrassing. But I could read the writing on the wall. I knew what I liked, and what I liked I generally excelled in—history and English. What I didn't like, I simply didn't do, or did just enough to get by. So, while other children were socializing at the Bath and Tennis Club—a perfectly natural and acceptable thing to do in our social strata, or what had been our social strata—or concentrating on their studies, I went to work just after Mom died.

My first job was selling magazines like the *Ladies Home Journal* and the *Saturday Evening Post*. One potential customer asked if I sold *Reader's Digest*. I said I did, even though I didn't, and proceeded to deliver him Dad's copy. Later, I took a job at Lyon's Fish Market, delivering fish for thirty-five cents an hour. My boss cheated me, paying half of what he had agreed to, coldly telling me to take it or leave it. I left it, and that incident was an early lesson in the mechanics of the Golden Rule—treat others the way you want to be treated; it's the right thing to do, and it's good for business. After that, I got a job as a caddy at the golf club, and later worked as a lifeguard at the ocean—a position open to a thirteen-year-old kid only because the older boys were off fighting World War II. As my brother and boys just a few years older than I went off to war, I stayed home, worked hard at my menagerie of odd jobs, and waged my own personal battle with the educational system. The allure of education, I'm afraid, quite escaped me.

I attended four high schools in four years. To be honest, the change in schools wasn't always my idea. I started at a Catholic school, passed some time at a public school, and then entered a New Jersey boarding school called Blair Academy, an exclusive school so tethered to tradition that it proved far too rigid and stagnant for a boy with my restlessness. There was no shortage of arbitrary rules at Blair, and no limit to my knack for breaking them. After a year or so, the headmaster made it abundantly clear that he and the institution would be quite happy to bid farewell to Billy Simon.

My father formally "withdrew" me from Blair Academy, which was the genteel way of avoiding inevitable expulsion. From there I went to another prep school, Newark Academy, where my behavior and my academic performance improved, a little.

———

T. CHANDLER HARDWICK III, HEADMASTER, BLAIR ACADEMY, OCTOBER 18, 1999

You could make the argument that it was a healthy thing for Bill to leave Blair, because it was a firm and clear dose of reality that his behavior was unacceptable to a good educational institution.

When I first came to Blair, Bill was not at all interested in the school. He was still angry that the school had thrown him out and had not supported him. But the class of 1945 never forgot that he was part of their class and constantly told me, "We've got to get Bill back. He was such a great guy. The year we were here with him was one of the greatest years of our lives." It was amazing.

I didn't know Mr. Simon, but I called him and said, "Gee, Mr. Simon, if you'd be willing to meet with me, I'd like to tell you a little bit about how the class of '45 feels about you, and also get a sense of what happened during your experience."

I went down to see him and we met in his office. It was supposed to be a fifteen-minute meeting, and it turned into three hours and lunch. We just sat and talked about education, what his year was like, the fact that the school did a lot of good things for him, and that he certainly has relationships and associations among our alumni that he feels good about. That led to another meeting, phone calls, letters....

Eventually, I said, "Bill, it would mean the world to the class of '45 if you would come up and speak at our sesquicentennial, our 150th anniversary, in the spring of 1998." He said, "I'll do it...."

The class of '45 insisted that we give him a diploma, a real diploma, not an honorary diploma. So, technically speaking, Bill Simon is a member of the class of '45 with a diploma from Blair Academy. We even have a scholarship in his name.

———

Newark Academy was a tough, old-style school, a day school two-and-a-half hours from my home, and I'd occasionally stay with friends in the Oranges rather than make the daily commute. At Newark Academy, I was struggling, really struggling, to make the grade. I certainly didn't have my nose buried in the books all the time, and I definitely hadn't shed my mischievous streak, but at Newark Academy I was beginning to take school at least somewhat seriously. So there was a semblance of balance, an equilibrium of sorts, that had been lacking in my prior educational experience.

Still, I got a D in math, not exactly great, but passing. I was carrying a B-minus in English and history. But Latin was an utter menace, and I was failing that course and fearing that I was, once again, in danger of being asked to leave. So, when a letter from Newark Academy arrived at the Spring Lake house for my father, I nervously steamed it open. It said, in substance, that I was either unwilling or unable to do the work at the academy and should find another school. My God! I stuffed the letter in my pocket and called Mr. Tom Shields—a demanding headmaster, a tough taskmaster, and one of the most honorable men I've ever encountered—and requested an appointment. When I went in, I was terribly nervous.

"Mr. Shields," I said, "I really want to graduate from Newark Academy. I guarantee you, I give you my word, that I will go to summer school. I'll work hard, and I'll pass everything. I know I can do it. Please give me a chance."

We spoke for over an hour. I told him about my work ethic, how I had held a job since I was eight years old. We spoke about my religion and values, my hopes and my aspirations. We talked about the carnage in Europe and the Pacific, and my patriotic desire to contribute to the noble battle for freedom.

"Simon," he said, "did you take that aptitude test?"

"Why, yes," I responded, wondering where in the world this conversation was leading.

"Well, what did it say you ought to be?" Mr. Shields inquired.

"A salesman."

"That's what I thought," Mr. Shields said, a slight smile cracking the stern exterior. "As far as I'm concerned, you just sold me. I believe you. Am I making a mistake?"

"No, sir!" I pledged.

"Bill," he said softly but firmly, "I know you won't let me down, and more importantly, I know you won't let yourself down. Now, get to work!"

"Yes, sir! Thank you, sir!"

Mr. Shields took the time and effort to understand me, and when he gave me an opportunity for redemption, it was a seminal event in my life to that point. My honor was at stake and I was determined, with a passion that would later mark my career, that I would not further hurt my father, that I would not let Mr. Shields down, that I would never let myself down, that I would begin to restore my own reputation and prove that Bill Simon was worthy of a Newark Academy diploma.

After spending the summer of 1945 in school, I returned to Newark as a senior and passed everything, even math and Latin. My rather inauspicious high school career concluded successfully when I graduated (albeit near the bottom of my class) from Newark Academy in June of 1946.

After graduating from Newark Academy, I was afflicted with a bad case of wanderlust, and a good dose of patriotism (and remained similarly afflicted throughout my life). I was quite eager to experience something of the wide world outside New Jersey, and equally anxious to serve my country in the military after having missed out on the "adventure" of World War II. So I joined the army at the end of my senior year, along with several friends. Dad would have preferred that I go right on to college—the natural progression for a Newark Academy graduate—but he understood that I wanted and needed a diversion before enrolling in college. And I suspect that in the depths of my heart I knew I needed to mature a bit as well.

I went for my physical at Fort Dix, New Jersey, and when I couldn't read the eye chart without my glasses, "REJECTED" was promptly stamped on my application. Undeterred, I put my glasses back on, memorized the 20/20 line on the eye chart, and told the officer in charge that a terrible mistake had been made, that there was nothing seriously wrong with my vision. He took my glasses, told me to try again, and I simply recited the eye chart from memory and was proclaimed physically fit and sent to Fort Bragg, just outside Fayetteville, North Carolina, for basic training and assignment to an infantry battalion in Japan.

Although the war was over, it wasn't over by much. We could not forget that the conquerors were living in the country of the conquered. We were there to be infantrymen, always ready to fight, and half expecting to be sent to Korea, where it seemed another conflict was inevitable. It was obvious that Korea was a powder keg that could blow at any time, so it was essential that the "peacetime" army in Japan maintain a state of readiness.

One day, I was out on maneuvers—we were firing dummy shells, making a lot of noise, and creating a lot of smoke, but causing no damage—when a Japanese woman rushed out of her house atop a hill and confronted me in perfect English.

"Young man, just what do you think you are doing!?"

"Ma'am, I'm terribly sorry to disturb you, but my platoon is carrying out maneuvers."

"Well, you are on my property! How dare you come on my property!"

I was thinking to myself: Gosh, we won the war, lady. We are occupying your country. You don't have any goddamned property! But I responded respectfully, "I'm really sorry, ma'am, but I have my orders." She relaxed and said, "You seem like a nice young man. Would you like a glass of milk? Real milk. I get it from the hospital."

I accepted her generosity and enjoyed a glass of real milk for the first time in ages.

"You sound American," I noted.

She explained that she was Japanese-American, a graduate of UCLA, who had come over to visit her family in December 1940. When the war escalated, she couldn't leave, and was still awaiting security clearance to return to the U.S. She was maybe thirty-five years old, and worldly by my standards. I was eighteen, and somewhere between boyhood and manhood. I started visiting her on Sunday afternoons. We would chat, and she'd treat me to milk and cookies. One day, she said to me, "I know a young girl you would like. Her father, however, despises the American invader and he would kill his daughter if he knew she went out with you."

Now, that sounded intriguing and I eagerly accepted her invitation to arrange a secret liaison. The next Sunday, she introduced me to a delicate, beautiful girl and told me her name was Yoshiko Ishikawa. Yoshiko was younger than I, but matured beyond her years by the rigors of wartime. I was immediately infatuated with this lovely flower, with her comforting, knowing smile and silky black hair. She spoke no English; I spoke no Japanese. Despite the differences in language and culture, and largely because of the circumstance of war, our friendship quickly blossomed into a pure and beautiful love affair.

The downside, however, was that she had a father who would kill both of us—literally—if he found out she was consorting with an American soldier.

Yoshiko's father, as explained to me by the woman on the hill, was a leading doctor in Otsu, an old samurai physician. The samurai, I learned, were the knights of feudal Japan, an elite warrior class rooted in the twelfth century and dedicated to a moral code called "bushido," which revered bravery, honor, and personal loyalty above life. Samurai would commit ritual suicide by what the Japanese call "seppuku" (and we called "hara-kiri")—disembowelment—as a respectable alternative to dishonor. Now, if Yoshiko's father was willing to do that to *himself* to avoid losing face, there's no telling what he would have done to *me*!

Obviously, Yoshiko and I had to be terribly careful. We communicated only through the woman on the hill. We'd meet on Sundays and go for long walks in the mountain mist, nurturing a wonderful and enchanting, if destined to be brief, affair. We knew our relationship would be fleeting, and made the most of it. There was no discussion of marriage, although we loved each other deeply and passionately. We were both too young and subconsciously aware that our relationship was destined to be both special and short-lived.

My time in the service was winding down and the American presence in Japan was beginning to diminish as troops were reassigned or sent home. On my last night, Yoshiko tearfully presented me with perhaps the grandest gift I have ever received: the sword, flag, and helmet of her brother, who had been killed in Guam. I was deeply touched by the gesture as we embraced for the last time. However, my possession of those items, like my relationship with Yoshiko, was not meant to last.

I was ordered back to Yokohama to board a ship for my next assignment, and had carefully packed my souvenirs. One night I was sleeping in a former Japanese barracks when I heard the fire bell. They were staging fire drills all the time and I didn't think much of it. Groggily, I mumbled to the guy in the bunk below, "Say 'here' when they call my name, would ya?" and dozed off.

Suddenly, I was jolted awake by the crackling of fire. I jumped out of bed and ran down the hall, which was filled with billowing smoke. I returned to my room, frantically looking for a way to escape, and ultimately wrapped myself in a blanket and ran for safety. No sooner was I safely outside than the entire barracks collapsed in flames. If I had not gotten out when I did, I wouldn't have gotten out at all. But everything that Yoshiko had given me—and all my other souvenirs, mementos, and photographs—were lost in the fire, perhaps fittingly. My life in Japan was over.

I learned a great deal from Yoshiko about myself and, on a certain level, love her to this day. I sent several letters to her via the woman on the mountain, but none were answered. Years later, while traveling in Japan, I tried to track her down, but could not find a trace. Yoshiko seemed to have faded away, like soft morning dew. It has been suggested to me that, despite our love, she never revealed her real name, and that "Yoshiko" was merely a pseudonym to shield her identity, and our lives.

I was formally discharged in January 1948, and returned to New Jersey with $2,000 in my pocket—poker winnings—and a new outlook on life. I came home a much wiser person, a better person in a lot of ways. If I had gone directly from Newark Academy to college, I question whether I would have finished. But I came out of the military as an adult, a grown person with a focus and an aim. I had matured immeasurably in eighteen months, and was ready to begin taking a more serious look at life and my future.

While overseas, I had received a letter from Schatzie, enclosed with a magazine article about a girl named Carol Girard, whose sister Gail was the best friend of my little sister, Madeleine. The article noted that Carol was a young model, and, if she had not been underage, would have been a finalist in the Miss Rheingold contest. She was a beautiful and elegant young lady and I was enamored, and mindful on at least some level that my relationship with Yoshiko was ephemeral. I carried that article and the picture around for months, and showed it to a pal, "Browny" Brownfield from Oregon, while we were in Japan.

"Browny," I said, pulling out the picture, "this is the girl I am going to marry."

"Pretty good-looking lady," Browny remarked, ogling the picture of Carol. "Does she happen to know that she's going to marry you?"

"Nah," I said. "In fact, she hardly knows I exist."

I asked Carol out as soon as I got back and we dated through the winter and spring of 1948. I quickly concluded that she was a spoiled brat, and told her so. We broke up, and I directed my energies, really for the first time in my life, toward obtaining a formal education.

However, with my high school record, college admissions officers were not exactly beating a path to my door. Princeton rejected me out of hand. I thought I had a shot at getting into Georgetown University because a family friend and benefactor of the university vouched for me. But Georgetown was unwilling to take a chance on me. Finally, my father called a close friend who happened to be a trustee at Lafayette College in Easton, Pennsylvania. With his help, I was admitted to Lafayette.

To me, college represented total freedom, a stark contrast to my days in boarding school. If I didn't feel like going to class, I didn't have to, and to a large extent I was left free to do things my way, to succeed or fail on my own.

I remember taking a public speaking course and being very nervous about the prospect of delivering an address in front of my peers. In fact, I was scared half to death. The only way I was going to get through the ordeal was to have some fun and talk about a subject I knew well. So when it came my time to talk, I gave a demonstration on how to make the perfect Manhattan cocktail. I went into exhaustive detail about this brand of vermouth and that kind of whiskey, and explained the difference between bourbon and Canadian Club. Then I demonstrated how to mix the drink. I spent the rest of the class sipping my drink, which I thought was a hoot since we weren't allowed to drink on campus. My demonstration was a rousing success, and did a great deal to get me over my fear of speaking in public. Most of my college courses, however, were not nearly as refreshing.[1]

The spring of my freshman year, Carol Girard started dating a fellow named Peter Fleming, a true gentleman with whom I was acquainted. Although I had thought Carol a spoiled brat, she was, in addition to being gorgeous, intelligent and sensitive. In short, I knew that she was far too good to pass up. I couldn't get her out of my mind and figured I had to act quickly or forever hold my peace. So, in June of 1949, I crashed Carol's high school graduation party and asked her to go out with me again.

"If you could, if you would, I'd like to take you out," I said.

Carol wouldn't commit herself then, but I was persistent and called back the next day. Carol's mother, who held me in very low regard, was apoplectic. But for whatever reason, Carol agreed to go out with me. Soon, we fell in love. Peter Fleming, who had been away for a short period, was crestfallen when he returned.

———

Peter Fleming, May 24, 1999

During the war, I worked as a soda jerk in a place called the Carleton Sweet Shoppe. I was sitting there one day when I was a freshman in college, chewing the fat with the guys I used to work with, and in comes this young woman in a Red Bank Catholic High School green jumper: Carol Girard. Carol was very special. She was my first girlfriend. She was a very attractive woman of seventeen or eighteen, and a great person. She was a lot of fun, just a terrific, terrific young woman.

It was the summer of 1949, and I began going out with Carol. At the end of June after my freshman year in college, I went up to a summer camp to play baseball for a month. I drove back nine hours through the Pennsylvania mountains and went to open the door [at Carol's house], and it wouldn't open all the way. Billy was behind the door!

———

That fall, Carol enrolled in Manhattan Marymount College while I was in my sophomore year at Lafayette College. Every weekend was spent commuting to New York City so we could be together, and on November 27, 1949—my twenty-second birthday—I asked her to marry me. Carol agreed readily, but her family objected stridently.

Carol's parents wanted her to wed someone rich and famous, and I was neither and seemed to have no prospects for becoming either wealthy or notable. Carol's mother completely wrote me off, making it clear that, in her opinion, I'd never amount to anything. Her father thought I was something of a ne'er-do-well and didn't hold out much hope for me either. Neither of them was exactly thrilled that their cover girl daughter was leaving school to marry a seemingly aimless fraternity boy with thick glasses and only the faintest ideas of what he wanted to do with his life. They insisted that I was too young and immature, that I'd never be able to support their princess.

I didn't utter a peep in argument; I simply went to work to prove them wrong. I took every menial job I could find, and supplemented wages from my physical labors with some very profitable mental work: poker. I managed to save enough of my poker winnings for us to plan a modest honeymoon at Sea Island, Georgia.

Carol and I were married on September 9, 1950, at St. Catherine's Church in Spring Lake, with my brother Charlie by my side as best man and Schatzie beaming happily with the rest of the family. Unfortunately, I lost virtually all my money playing cards a week before our wedding and had to borrow some cash to cover the honeymoon. I returned with a grand total of fifteen cents in my pocket. My dad gave us fifty dollars to tide us over until my first GI check arrived. Carol and I left for Easton, Pennsylvania, where we rented a little apartment.

We were counting rather desperately on the sixty dollars an hour Carol could make modeling—but within two months of our marriage, Carol was pregnant, and her modeling career was over. On Tuesday, June 20, 1951, my namesake—William Edward Simon, Jr.—came into this world. Suddenly, a twenty-three-year-old college student was shouldered with the joys and burdens of fatherhood.

I went to work with a frenzy—washing windows, making beds, doing whatever it took to keep us afloat, and simultaneously taking summer courses so I could finish school early. By the time my senior year came around, I needed just two more courses to graduate, so I took only six hours a week of classes and spent most of my time working. Carol and Billy remained in Spring Lake while I attended college a hundred miles away, commuting every weekend. We were a typically harried, but happy, young family.

I graduated from Lafayette College in 1952 with a degree in government and law. I wanted to be a lawyer, but we didn't have the money and I had too many bills to pay. Necessity being the mother of invention, out into the world I went, grateful to Lafayette for giving me a chance, and eager to earn a decent living and provide for Carol and our growing family.

And somewhat to my surprise—not to mention that of a lot of other people who had endured my youth—I did quite well.

OUT ON THE "STREET"

After leaving college, I was as poor as a church mouse and $5,000 in debt. Billy needed a hernia operation and we were uninsured and expecting a second child.

For a short while, I worked for Carol's father, an inventor who ran a tire business and made couplings, but it wasn't anything I wanted to do for very long. My own father was out of touch with the business community and lacked the type of contacts that could help his son. So I was on my own. I set out to make a living in the advertising business, which at the time was paying about $35 a week. But I found myself in the not-atypical catch-22 of a recent grad: I couldn't get a job because I didn't have experience and I couldn't get experience because I couldn't get a job.

On our second wedding anniversary in September 1952, Carol and I were treated to dinner at the Homestead Restaurant in Spring Lake when we bumped into a friend of mine, Chris Devine, whose father ran a famous investment firm, C.J. Devine and Co. Chris was a trainee at another company, Union Securities.

"Do you want to work on Wall Street?" Chris asked.

At the time, I would have worked anywhere at all.

"I would love to work on Wall Street."

"Be in my office at 65 Broadway at nine o'clock Monday morning."

First thing Monday, I made my appearance at the reception desk at Union Securities.

"I'm here to see Mr. Christopher Devine."

The receptionist told me to have a seat. I waited around for hours, wearing the one suit I owned, until 4 p.m., when Chris finally came out and said somewhat apologetically, "We are in the middle of one of the biggest deals in history"—an exaggeration of mammoth proportions, I learned later. I agreed to come back on Tuesday.

The next morning, once again I took the train up to New York from Spring Lake and sat in the reception area for the entire day. Various staffers, noting my presence, stopped by to chat every once in a while. Again I left lacking employment and encouragement, but gaining resolve and determination. On Wednesday, I was back waiting, with Chris Devine popping out every once in a while to tell me how busy they were. Finally, on Thursday, the personnel manager approached me in the reception area.

"Is there something I can do for you?" he asked.

"I've been sitting here because Chris Devine thought he could help me," I said. "I'm looking for a job."

"Look, I'm sorry, but we just don't have any openings for you." The personnel manager scribbled the names of some other firms on a piece of paper—Blyth, Dean Witter, Merrill Lynch—and suggested I give them a try.

"Sir, I really want to work for Union Securities." After investing the better part of a week in the firm, I was starting to feel a bit proprietary.

The personnel manager shrugged and went back outside, and I sat down. A while later, he reemerged.

"Mr. Norman Downey, who heads the municipal bond department, would like to interview you," he said, and escorted me into a conference room, where Mr. Downey and a couple of other gentlemen began a friendly inquiry.

"Where'd you go to school?" Mr. Downey asked.

"Lafayette College, sir," I responded.

"Were you in a fraternity?"

"I pledged Delta Kappa Epsilon, sir."

"Well, I was a Beta."

"That's a great fraternity, Mr. Downey!" I said, immediately deciding against debating the relative merits of DKE vs. Beta.

"I presume you take a drink now and then?" he asked, eyes twinkling.

"Well, Dekes do have a reputation for that, and I guess you could say I've contributed my part to the reputation."

Mr. Downey, a reserved but warm man, cracked a smile and chuckled.

"All right, Bill," he said. "I could use a trainee. I can't pay you very much, but I'd be willing to start you off at seventy-five dollars a week."

I was so happy that I choked up and tears started to well in my eyes. Seventy-five dollars seemed like all the money in the world.

"Mr. Downey," I said, "I'd work for nothing. I'll work hard and you'll never be sorry you hired me."

I didn't know a thing about municipal bonds, but when I joined the trading desk I immediately felt right at home. I went from the fraternity of Delta Kappa Epsilon to the fraternity of Wall Street—and found similar camaraderie.

Wall Street in those days was a wonderful place to work—truly a brotherhood and a place where honor and integrity counted, where your word was your only marketable commodity. I was young, primed with drive and confidence, and enjoyed amazing success at a very early age. Much of the success, however, can be attributed to being in the right place at the right time.

After the Depression and World War II, Wall Street was virtually a ghost town, haunted by the grim nightmares of the crash and stuck in a time warp. There was a handful of young men like me, a handful of veteran traders thirty years older, and virtually no one in between. I was part of the first wave of a new generation of Wall Street financiers and investment bankers, eager young men (virtually all were men) who were far too energetic and impatient to heed the warnings of their elders. We were full of life and energy, ambition, and mischief.

The country was ready to move forward and so were we. The suburbs were beginning to develop, so there was a need to finance public works projects. Municipal bonds, which are offered by state and local governments, offer investors the benefit of tax-free income. The tax-free feature enables municipalities and states to raise money to build schools, roads, bridges, sewers, dams, and other projects at interest rates below those on taxable bonds. Bonds provided funding for scores of municipal projects, including massive highway projects like the New York State Thruway, the New Jersey Turnpike, cross-state highways in Texas and Ohio, that otherwise might not have been built, and certainly wouldn't have been built as quickly.

In the expanding economy of the 1950s, all a person of reasonable intelligence had to do to succeed on Wall Street was work hard, and I was certainly willing to do that. At Union Securities I threw myself into my work with the discipline and commitment that I had always demonstrated in employment and only rarely displayed in school. Years later, I would come to appreciate, abstractly, the importance of productive activity to the mind and soul of both an individual and a nation. In the early 1950s, all I needed to understand was that I was a young man with a growing family and growing responsibilities.

———

DICK CHAPDELAINE, CHAIRMAN OF CHAPDELAINE & CO. MUNICIPAL BOND BROKERAGE, JULY 28, 1999

The market was growing [in the 1950s] and the staid way of doing things wasn't necessarily the right way. Bill caught on to that and did things differently. He was innovative. He did things that other people wished they had done. He took what some might view as greater risks. He was very precise, quick as you could possibly be with numbers. He was a leader. Bill was one of the best, he really was.

I traveled with Bill all over the country, visiting different cities. He was never, ever one to hang out in a bar or womanize . . . We were tied into politics in a way because we were dealing with municipalities. . . .

and that is what sparked Bill's understanding of the political arena....
He was always conservative, and he loved talking politics, sometimes
until two or three in the morning.

————

That fall we moved to Orange, New Jersey, taking up residence in a tidy rent-controlled basement apartment on Central Avenue. The apartment, located in one of the poorest sections of town and right next door to Orange High School, cost me seventy-five dollars a month, considerably more than the fifty-eight dollars a week I was bringing home after taxes and deductions.

We were so financially stretched that Carol used to snip off the tails of my shirts to make patches for the elbows. Occasionally, my father would come to visit, often bringing me a case of beer and the mixings for a Manhattan. We were still living in the two-bedroom apartment when my second son, John Peter, whom we call Pete, arrived on May 27, 1953, and when our first daughter, Mary Beth, was born on December 9, 1954. The quarters were, to say the least, confining for a family of five. Like most young families in pursuit of the American dream, we longed for a house of our very own and began searching for one we could afford.

I had become, temporarily, politically active in New Jersey, and after supporting a successful candidate for the U.S. Senate and winning election as treasurer of the Young Republicans of Essex County, I was offered an opportunity in the early 1950s to become surrogate of Newark. Although I would have had to run for the job, with the backing of the party powers, my election was virtually assured, and the position was a real plum with generous benefits. I was offered a home, a $25,000 annual salary, and the promise of greater rewards, such as an insurance broker's license and commissions on virtually all municipal contracts generated from Newark, a perk that could have easily doubled my salary. I bounced the proposal off Carol.

"Bill," she said, "they are trying to buy your soul."

Neither of us wanted to be beholden to anyone, so I rejected the offer and, for the time being, separated myself from politics.

Meanwhile, Carol and I continued searching for a new home. We eventually settled on a little $20,000 three-bedroom, one-bathroom development home at 21 Townsend Drive in Florham Park, a suburban community a short distance from Madison, New Jersey.

My sister, Mary Ellen, loaned us $2,000 for the down payment and I borrowed the rest from a bank—the first and last time I had a mortgage. For a young couple—Carol was twenty-three and I was twenty-six—that little house with one bathroom and a den we converted into a bedroom seemed downright palatial. We were the very picture of a happy middle-class family on the rise.

On Wall Street, I was working extraordinarily hard, striving to learn what to me was still a foreign culture, and spending a great deal of time on the Street, absorbing all I could from the great market men and traders of the day.

By the mid-1950s, the young bond traders on the Street were becoming more and more of a fraternity. We organized informal luncheons every Thursday in an effort to educate financial writers, who knew next to nothing about municipal bonds. Later, we formed the Municipal Bond Study Group—we called it the "Thursday Club"—which became an institute where young Wall Streeters learned about the bond market and shared their experiences. Eventually, the upstarts like myself, John Fitterer, Chet Viale, Ned Shean, and Danny Whitlock became the new guard. We were a close-knit brotherhood, and developed a mutual respect and loyalty that continues today.

I found that I not only tolerated taking risks, I loved it. And it paid off: Three years after starting, at the age of twenty-eight, I was named assistant vice president and manager of the firm's Municipal Trading Department. I became the youngest officer in the history of Union Securities, and my income was raised to the princely sum of $6,200 per year. The following year, I was making $10,000, which seemed like all the money anyone could ever possibly want or need. I had arrived on the Street, and landed in the municipal bond department at an opportune time. Nobody, and certainly not I, realized at that juncture just how profitable municipal bonds would become—for those who were willing to take the risks, position securities, and carry inventory.

Aside from providing what seemed a celestial salary, the world of finance fascinated me, and appealed to my risk-taking, poker-playing nature. Do I feel lucky today? What are the odds? What is my opponent up to? Imagination, ingenuity, hard work, and luck determined whether you won or lost. I, of course, subscribe to the maxim that the harder I work the more luck I seem to have. But you have to be willing to take a risk. Even a turtle makes progress only when he sticks his neck out.

If you take prudent risks and understand the risk-to-reward ratio, you are going to succeed in the long run. The market provides an opportunity for a more than adequate return, if you can recognize all the important elements that are involved—the number of buyers that exist, the number of sellers that exist, whether comparable securities are about to hit the Street—a whole host of factors and variables that have to be considered and evaluated in an instant.

People who operate in the marketplace can actually feel a tempo and attempt to anticipate the next move, much as basketball legend Michael Jordan or hockey immortal Wayne Gretzky just seem to know where the ball or puck will be a couple of plays down the line. The "Great Gretzky" has often said that the secret of his athletic success was that he always strived to be where the puck was going to be—not where it was or where it has been.

The secret of business success is precisely the same: You have to be where the action is heading. You have to anticipate and prepare and be there when the risk/opportunity (words I often use interchangeably) presents itself, even if—especially if—the crowd is focused elsewhere. You have to know when to count your blessings, take your profits, and avoid greed. My son Pete often jokes that the secret to my success is that I always sell too early, and in a way he's exactly right. You never go broke taking a profit.

———

MICHAEL STOTT, COUSIN, BROKER, DECEMBER 17, 1997

When I first came in the business after I was hired by Easton Dillon Union Securities, I was assigned to work for Billy on the municipal

*bond desk where he was the head trader. I had some of the greatest
times of my career working for him. Bill would take me to all kinds
of lunches, cocktail parties, and dinners. This was better than the fraternity house! Because of this socializing, I got to know everyone, and
it sure put my career on the fast track.*

*Having worked with many traders over my lifetime, I would have
to say that Billy was the best I ever saw. He understood markets,
rates, and when to pull the trigger.*

––––

Family life during these years was both immensely fulfilling and typically hectic. I was still a young man, though, and the growing pressures of work and family were sometimes daunting for both Carol
and me. Thankfully, Schatzie would stay with us for months at a time,
helping to bring up my children the same way she helped to mold me.
Occasionally, I would get home late at night, but I always, always
went home. The weekends were reserved for the family. I enjoyed
doing the fatherly things, although I was not always the most patient
husband or father.

Once, I recall, Billy had a friend over, and they did something or
other to annoy me. I confronted them angrily.

"Go to your room!" I shouted.

Billy took off like a bat out of hell and ran to his room as I glared
at his little friend, who was frozen in terror. "But Mr. Simon," he said
pitifully, "I don't have a room here."

"That's no excuse," I responded. "FIND ONE!"

Meanwhile, my family was continuing to grow. Our third son and
fourth child, Timothy Charles, was born on January 18, 1956.

Tragedy, however, struck four months later. While Carol was on a
Catholic retreat and I was caring for the other three children, my
mother-in-law graciously offered to watch the baby for the weekend.
One evening, I got a call that shook me to the core: Overnight, very
peacefully, little Timmy had died in his sleep of what they now call
Sudden Infant Death Syndrome (SIDS).[1]

It's often said that there is no more difficult or painful ordeal for the parent than experiencing the death of a child, and I can attest to that. Carol and I were completely heartbroken. We were utterly devastated and, for a time, I drank more than was appropriate until we were able to regain a sense of balance and equilibrium. God helped us out of our depression with a blessing in the form of a little girl we christened Carol Leigh (we've always called her "Leigh") on July 13, 1957. Schatzie was her godmother.

———

WILLIAM E. SIMON JR., SON, MAY 4, 1998

I have wonderful memories of my childhood. Mom and Dad were different, but they complemented each other well. Dad was tough, no question; he could be demanding and he could be volatile. Dad definitely went off like a Roman candle on occasion. But with Dad, he'd get mad at you, send you to your room. Ten minutes later, he would call for you and ask, "Are you sorry?" and you'd say, "Yes," and that would be the end of it. Mom would never send you to your room until the last minute, but once she did, you were there for the duration.

Dad was, curiously, very understanding about the bigger stuff, and sometimes not so understanding about the smaller stuff. If you didn't say "thank you" he'd get madder at you than if you cracked up the car. If you got into a scrape where you were the underdog, Dad would naturally take your side and encourage you. On the other hand, he was real good at kicking you in the butt if he felt you needed it, but he well understood that it does no good to kick someone when they are down.

When I was growing up, one of the things I remember clearly is that Dad had a lot of understanding for people who weren't getting good grades, because he himself hadn't gotten good grades. And he had a lot of understanding for kids who got in a little trouble, things that you might characterize as innocent pranks, because he too did those things. . . . Dad had a really good sense of what mattered and what didn't matter. And if you got into trouble, as we all do on occasion, Dad was right there. He definitely went to bat for you and you always felt as if you had a strong ally in your corner. But you always felt that you were accountable to him, too—and you'd better be worthy of his support.

He taught us a sense of independence, a sense that we've got a great deal of freedom in our lives and should make the most of it. He taught us that human relationships are very important, that friends and family are very important. And he taught us a respect for the underdog. Dad is driven by a number of things that relate to freedom and fairness, traditional American values, religion and family....

I vividly remember when we got the news [that Timmy died]. We were all sitting in the kitchen at Florham Park and Dad all of a sudden gasped, "Oh my God!" He ran out to the living room, fell down on his knees, threw his hands toward the sky, and pleaded, "Dear God, help me! Help me!" I will never forget that as long as I live.

———

Union Securities was a terrific firm and I was delightfully happy there. In 1957, however, Union merged with Eastman Dillon & Co., a "stock shop" or brokerage firm with a brokerage mentality, as opposed to an investment banking firm with an investment banking mentality.

Eastman Dillon & Co. was very risk averse and seldom took major positions in underwriting or trading. They were interested in serving as an intermediary—as a firm that takes an order and executes it—not in trading. I, of course, was a trader, and I wanted to remain a trader. They made it clear that I—at the age of thirty—would be a full partner within two years. Still, I resigned, a move my peers viewed as downright stupid. But I knew that I could do better elsewhere and that it was time to move on to new challenges.

Weeden and Co. had been after me for a long time and, with the Eastman takeover of Union, I accepted an offer (with a somewhat lower salary, but the possibility of a bonus if I did well) in 1957 and became vice president a year later. Alan Weeden, a warm, intellectual, and eclectic gentleman, ran the firm.

Alan was a character and a champion swimmer (he had been a member of the Stanford University team) who introduced me to snorkeling and diving. In those days, we didn't have computerized diving apparatus, and venturing into the depths of the sea with the relatively primitive equipment available then was a dangerous and thrilling experience.

The business side of our relationship was equally exhilarating, and I ran my small department with military-style discipline.

Trading demands total concentration and the ability to do several things at once while instantly recalling trading prices from the day, or week, before. I understood that every bond trader has to have the right to be wrong, the freedom to make judgment calls that turn out to be errors—an attitude that was not prevalent at Eastman Dillon. I didn't get overly upset if my traders made a mistake and lost money (depending, of course, on how they lost it) on any particular deal, but I did care about sloppiness. If my traders lost money because they hadn't done their homework or hadn't paid attention or weren't using their head, I came down hard, very hard, and I made them realize that mistakes could be very costly, to everyone. Nobody at Weeden was on commission, so our compensation depended on how the firm as a whole did in any particular year.

———

ROBERT F. TIGHE, TRADER, SANDLER O'NEILL & PARTNERS, AUGUST 18, 1999

I started working with Bill in 1954. He was the number two man on the trading desk, but there was no doubt that he really ran the trading desk. He was definitely the dominant person and did almost all the trading. The man who was the head trader was more of an administrator, so Bill was really in charge—or, more accurately, took charge....

It was Bill who taught me the bond business, sometimes very harshly. He has a pretty good temper, but at the end of the day, he'd say, "Let's go have a beer," and we'd talk it over. Yes, Bill shouts. Yes, Bill loses his temper. But at the end of the day, all his colleagues really

*respected him and really liked him. He is always willing to help peo-
ple out.*

*When we were first in the business, and he had a little house out in
Florham Park, guys sometimes needed money and he would lend
them money even if he was having trouble paying his own bills. Some
guys never even paid him back.*

*I've had some ups and downs in my life, and he never deserted me.
Once, I had a problem, a pretty serious problem, and went to see him
in Washington when he was secretary of the treasury. He took two
hours out of his schedule to talk with me in his office. He is always
willing to help people out. He is the kind of guy who always finds
time for people.*

*We combined hard, intensive, pressure-laden work with boyish
mischievousness—which I now view as a safety valve that let out the
steam and allowed us to function collegially in a rough-and-tumble
environment. Our imaginations were fertile, and in New York City
there was an abundance of opportunity to nurture our, well, let's say
creativity. Whenever someone made partner, we would celebrate
appropriately with a luncheon or dinner, and often the occasion
inspired some shenanigans.*

———

There used to be a store down on Liberty Street in Manhattan,
Traflichs, where you could rent or buy just about any kind of animal,
which of course created all manner of potential for aspiring
pranksters. Once, we considered getting a little elephant and bringing
it to a restaurant, but there would have been no way to get it up the
stairs. Another time, we thought about renting a chimpanzee and
sneaking it into an office function, but suspected a primate could get
out of hand, literally. We wanted something a little more manageable,
and asked the manager at Traflichs for some advice.

"I've got just what you want, a six-foot python."

He explained that since it was wintertime, the cold-blooded reptile would be quite docile, and offered it to us for $70—a $35 rental

fee and a $35 deposit, which we would get back if we chose to return the snake. Otherwise, it was ours to keep.

Chet Viale, Danny Whitlock, and I plunked down $70, and walked out of Traflich's with a sluggish, lumbering reptile coiled in one of those travel boxes people use when they bring their cats on airplanes, and hailed a cab. We put the box in the front seat with the cabbie and climbed into the back.

"What's in the box?" the cabbie asked suspiciously.

We all kind of looked at each other, and finally Danny said, "Why, it's a pussy cat. Here, let me show you."

Danny opened the box and the startled cabbie drove right up on the sidewalk.

Later, we smuggled the reptile into the Banker's Club bar, where I gave a little speech about Ned Shean, who had just made partner, and commented on how he was jumping into a real snake pit. With that, Danny, who was behind Ned, draped the snake around his neck. Ned turned white and the room cleared out. Some people, it seems, just don't want to be in the vicinity of a six-foot python. So we put the snake back in the box and went down the bar.

"Guess what's in the box?" Danny asked the bartender as he set the box on the bar.

"An elephant," responded the bartender, in a "screw-you-I've-seen-it-all" tone.

A handful of people at the bar put up wagers on what was in the box. Some bet it was a puppy, others a kitten. When we opened the box and stretched the snake out on the bar, panic broke lose. That was so much fun that we brought it back to Weeden & Co. and let it loose on the trading desk; not a single trader flinched. But Alan Weeden wandered over curiously, and fell madly in love with the reptile.

"Gee, what a beautiful snake," Alan cooed. "Oh, can I buy it from you?" I just shook my head and sold Alan the python for $35.

Now, Alan's wife, Barbara, was this sweet and proper lady who wasn't exactly thrilled about the prospect of living with a snake. I guess she was afraid it would eat her cats, and it would have if Alan ever ran out of his supply of live rodents. In any case, Alan's snake was banished to the basement, where he would bring friends after dinner to show off his prized python.

One evening, Alan brought his guests down to the basement, where he proudly draped the python around his neck, a great big, happy smile on his face. A python, of course, is a constrictive snake, which kills by wrapping itself around the victim and tightening its coils until the prey asphyxiates. And by that time, it was spring, and the python was no longer the groggy creature that Alan had brought home a few months earlier. It was starting to get pretty frisky.

Slowly the python started to wrap itself around Alan's neck. Alan's smile turned to gape-mouthed terror and his eyes started to bug out and his ears turned purple as the guests watched in horror as, apparently, the life was being squeezed out of their host. Was this for real? Nobody could believe their eyes. Wall Street has been called a jungle, but this was a little extreme. Meanwhile, Alan's wife knew just what to do. Shaking her finger at her apparently soon-to-be-asphyxiated husband, Mrs. Weeden delivered a stern scolding.

"See, Alan, see! I told you something like this would happen! I told you. I told you. I told you...."

The absurdity of the situation shook everyone out of their trances, and together the guests pried the snake from Alan's neck. It took three men to unwind the python. After that, Alan donated the snake to a zoo.

We seemed to have more than our share of animal mishaps, long before "stupid animal tricks" became a staple of late-night talk shows. In honor of my fortieth birthday, which coincided with an Investment Bankers Association convention in Hollywood, Florida, Danny Whitlock arranged for dozens of live chickens to be delivered to my room in what was then the Hollywood Beach Hotel. You can imagine my surprise when I walked into my room to be greeted by a horde of cackling, scurrying, loose-bowelled fowl running around like, well, chickens with their heads cut off, and crapping on every-thing in sight. Lord! It was like a zoo with no cages, or perhaps a sub-urban shopping mall full of teenagers on a Saturday afternoon.

"Bill," Carol said, "would you please GET THESE CHICKENS OUT OF THE ROOM!"

"Gee, I didn't put them here, sweetheart."

"GET THEM OUT OF HERE!!!!!"

I grabbed a pillow and started swatting at the chickens, and the more I swatted the more they pooped. I finally got them out the door and called the front desk. "Hello, I'm on the ninth floor. My wife just came in and told me there are a lot of chickens in the hall."

The chickens were racing up and down the hall and all of a sudden the elevator opened. Four bellhops jumped out, and a bunch of chickens jumped in, riding the elevator to other floors. Days later, they were still finding chickens all over the hotel.

Another year at the convention, I came back to the hotel late one night and found a dead barracuda protruding from the toilet, wearing a bowler and a bow tie. But it wasn't all fun and games.

Although the investment bankers on the Street were a close-knit crew, there was also fierce, yet fair, competition. Most of us were family men, and Carol and I continued to do our part to contribute to the baby boom.

My daughter Aimee Girard was born January 29, 1961, followed by "Melissa" (or at least that's what we called her for the first few months) on November 2, 1963. I never liked the name "Melissa," and, after a while I persuaded Carol to change our baby's name to Julie Ann.

"What are we going to tell people?" Carol protested.

"We'll just tell them that I wanted to name her after my favorite spud, 'julienne' potatoes," I joked.

————

RITA (MRS. CHESTER) VIALE, FAMILY FRIEND, NOVEMBER 29, 1994

He's probably the most dedicated friend I know. He's never out of touch, no matter where he is or what he's doing. There isn't a person I know who devotes so much time to maintaining friendships. Bill shares. Other men who have achieved success like he did might not have.

He's a man that bore everything well—including the tragedy of losing a child. That was a terrible chapter in their lives.

Later, somebody gave Peter a lollipop and he pulled it off the holder with his teeth; and was literally choking to death. Bill turned him upside down and punched him until it popped out. We were just frozen but Bill was in control of the situation. He saved the boy's life. Then, he took the box of lollipops, threw them across the room and said, "I've told everybody I know, I don't like lollipops! They are child killers! He almost choked to death!" He was shaking. He was ashen. He knew his son could have died on the spot.

Bill and Carol were wonderful parents. They brought up their kids properly. They taught them values, manners, and to wear the right clothes. They went to good schools. They were hooligans, at times, but they had to toe the line, because if they didn't pay attention to Carol's first words, Bill's voice would be heard, like a gentle lion.

———

With six children underfoot, we were more than ready for a larger home. I bought a big, beautiful old house on Prospect Hill in Summit. It cost me $48,000. I borrowed $25,000 from Weeden and paid it off with my year-end bonus.

My father had contracted cancer a few years earlier, and the disease that started in his colon spread to his liver. He was in and out of the hospital repeatedly, and it was evident by the winter of 1964 that the end was near. Pop suffered terribly and endured four operations during his final two years. After one of them, his stomach virtually exploded, spewing bile about the room. He died June 3, 1964, leaving a terrible void in my life.

Dad was a good and decent man, a big-hearted gentleman who shaped me in ways it took years to understand. Although the Depression forced him to moderate his expectations somewhat, Dad was very much a product of inherited wealth. The German poet Goethe once said, "What you have inherited from your forefathers, earn it over again for yourselves, so that you may truly possess it." I sometimes think that the only person fit to inherit wealth is the person who doesn't need an inheritance—the person who would create his own fortune no matter what his start in life—and have come to view inherited wealth as an affliction. In retrospect, it was a blessing that I was unable to ride my father's coattails or live off the wealth created by my ancestors.

Yet, while Pop lived his life in comfort, he was always generous to the less fortunate. I have never forgotten how he shared his declining wealth with the downtrodden of Paterson. He taught me a great deal about life and how to live it, and how the measure of a man is what he's got in his heart and soul. Pop taught me respect for my fellow man and reverence for my God. He taught me the importance of family and religion. And he seemed to know intuitively how to deal with a mischievous son—when it was necessary to lecture or punish, and when it was wise to simply dismiss my shenanigans with a "boys will be boys" smile. There's not a day that goes by when I don't regret that he's not here to see how his son, grandchildren, and great-grandchildren have maintained his values.

After Dad's funeral, I began to assess my own life and career. Personally, I was extremely happy. I had a wonderful wife, beautiful, healthy children, a nice home—in short, everything one could ask for. Professionally, I was also happy and productive. Yet I was growing restless and bored at Weeden & Co., and feeling that I needed a new challenge.

At the same time I was taking an inventory of my life, Salomon Brothers & Hutzler was looking to become the major force in the municipal bond business. Bill Morton of W. H. Morton recommended me to the chairman of the firm, William "Billy" Salomon. Billy Salomon offered me the chance to run his firm's municipal bond department, and I jumped at the opportunity.

No one could understand why anyone in his right mind would give up a $125,000-a-year job at a comfortable and respected firm like Weeden to take a $50,000 position—with the promise of "consideration of partnership," but no guarantees—at a house like Salomon Brothers, a big leaguer in general but a minor player in my specialty, municipal bonds.

But then, some people just don't understand risk.

AT SALOMON BROTHERS

Salomon Brothers was a scrappy, bare-knuckled, risk-taking firm, well outside the Wall Street clique, with a genesis in a family feud.

The Salomons, who had been money brokers in Alsace-Lorraine, first stepped on American soil in the late nineteenth century when Ferdinand Salomon emigrated with plans to continue the family trade in the New World. His sons joined him in the business, but Ferdinand, who was an orthodox Jew, insisted on observing the Sabbath even though business was routinely conducted on Wall Street on Saturday mornings. Ferdinand's sons, reluctant to relinquish an opportunity to expand the firm, even if it meant violating their religious tradition, insisted on working Saturdays. In time, the dispute became irreconcilable and, in 1910, the sons formed their own firm.

The new firm was founded by brothers Arthur, Herbert, and Percy Salomon, and a clerk named Ben Levy. The partners gathered together $5,000 from their personal savings, took out a small loan, and opened a tiny business in the days when Wall Street was dominated by a small handful of large financial institutions (mainly, J.P. Morgan & Co., First National, National City, and Guaranty Trust), standoffish blue tie firms. They soon joined forces with Morton

Hutzler, a man of some status *and* a seat on the New York Stock Exchange; Hutzler was the progeny of a Baltimore department store family.

The Salomons and Hutzler tapped the talent of people with little formal education and no business or social connections—people who would normally be far removed from the financial elite.

Salomon Brothers & Hutzler[1] was opportunistic from the start, partially because it had to be. It was among the few houses to immediately recognize the potential offered by the new Federal Reserve System, and promptly registered to become an active participant. That foresight enabled the firm to share in the government securities market during the World War I expansion and to grow into an increasingly significant player during the Great Bull Market of the 1920s. With the passage of the Securities Exchange Act of 1934, most investment houses joined a "capital strike" in protest; Salomon Brothers & Hutzler served as the agent for a bond offering for Swift and Co., and broke the logjam.

The firm had a small stock business in the 1920s, mainly to service clients attempting to profit during the bull market, and to take advantage of Morton Hutzler's NYSE seat. But Arthur Salomon refused to allow the firm to operate on margin.[2] With Arthur's dictate, the firm focused instead on doing business only with institutions—banks, pension funds, corporations, insurance companies—where the volume was high and the competition extraordinarily fierce. Throughout World War II, the Salomon firm traded heavily in bonds issued by the U.S. government to bankroll the war effort.

But by the late 1950s, Salomon Brothers & Hutzler was somewhat stagnant under the leadership of Rudolf Smutny, who developed a base of large institutional clients, led primarily by Equitable Life Insurance. Smutny had served as a marine in both world wars and his management style tended toward the dictatorial. Everyone, apparently, was afraid of Rudy Smutny.

Everyone, that is, except Billy Salomon.

Billy, the son of Percy Salomon, had come to the firm from prep school in 1933. His career as a salesman was unremarkable. But by the late 1950s, Billy saw the family firm floundering under Smutny, and proposed a much more dynamic, aggressive posture. Rudy resisted Billy's efforts to expand the firm's boundaries beyond the comfortable cradle of institutional clients that had been Salomon Brothers's meal ticket.

In what amounted to a power coup, Billy elbowed him out of the way, orchestrating a buyout of Rudy's 12.5 percent and banishing him from the partnership; a brief in the *New York Times* on April 20, 1957, noted Rudolf Smutny's "retirement."[3] In 1964, just before he hired me, Billy took the title of managing partner, formalizing the role he had played since Rudy's exodus and confirming the status he had long held in the firm and the industry.

Billy was a gentleman of the highest order—a suave, dignified man and natural leader who, incidentally, made the best paper airplanes in the trading room and was deadly accurate with a spit ball. We hit it off immediately.

As a manager, Billy was firm and fair and gregarious. He'd bring me out with him, his hat literally in his hand, and we'd call on every major bank in New York City to give them our financial statement. Salomon Brothers was not a public firm, but Billy disclosed every-thing—what we had, what we were long, what we were short, the money we made—and created a tremendous reservoir of respect and credibility. Nobody else did that, but nobody else was Billy Salomon and nobody else functioned like Salomon Brothers.

Salomon Brothers was an institutional firm; it did not do business with individuals. When an institution came in to buy and sell, we accommodated them, even if we didn't have the securities. If neces-sary, we would short them to the client, disclose what we were doing, and then, on the other side, sell them something else, and make a profitable trade for the firm (assuming the short was covered prop-erly, but that's the risk you take).

From the start, Billy gave me the freedom and autonomy to run the municipal department—one of the major sections of the firm—in my own way. Still, the first year was among the toughest of my pro-fessional life.

Some of the long-timers resented the fact that I, a newcomer, was upsetting the status quo, taking positions that were aggressive even for a firm like Salomon Brothers, and nudging the partnership toward the type of cooperative ventures that it had shunned under Rudy Smutny.

I was as tense as I've ever been that first year, so much so that I wore my teeth down by grinding them in my sleep, but determined that the naysayers would not wear me down as well. Billy Salomon, however, was completely willing to let me sink or swim on my own merits and, within a year, made me a full partner.

———

WILLIAM SALOMON, FEBRUARY 22, 1994

Certainly at the time we were the largest risk-takers in the business. That wasn't always necessarily out of choice. It was due to expediency. We didn't have many people working for the firm who were members of the "right" clubs. Years ago, the old-time firms that became our major competitors had built-in business through family connections and college acquaintances. They were tied in because of who they were, while we were somewhat of a Johnny-come-lately with no Ivy League background and no tennis or other club memberships. We weren't part of the "in" group in those days . . . So we had to fight our way in. The only way we knew how to fight was to take more risks than somebody else would take.

The important thing on Wall Street, in a competitive environment, is to get the first call . . . The long-time firms . . . got the first calls because of their friendships. Those friendships were built by their fathers and grandfathers and were handed down to the Morgan Stanleys, to the First Bostons, to the Smith Barneys, and to all the great names on Wall Street. But no one handed us anything. We had to make people alert to the fact that we were there. We constantly had to illustrate we would pay more or sell cheaper. Our philosophy was taking chances . . . We were a risk-taking firm. That atmosphere prevailed, and Bill absorbed a lot of that philosophy. I think Bill learned a lot.

But he always had tremendous confidence in himself.

My assignment was to run the municipal bond department, to underwrite and trade securities.

In the bond market, bidders respond to an advertisement, which might say, for example, that a municipality needs $100 million for water and sewer lines. Typically, a big institution would serve as senior manager of a "syndicate," which would include the leader and three or four co-managers. If, for instance, a fourhanded, $100 million deal was reached, every member would be in for $25 million in bonds. However, the senior manager set the terms: If it was a particularly good deal, the senior manager would take the bulk of the action, because it was taking the bulk of the risk. Salomon Brothers wanted a bigger piece of the action, and the only way to do that would be to break away from the safety and security of the syndicates.

Salomon Brothers had a superbly capable partner named John Gutfreund (pronounced "Good Friend"), a pudgy, round-faced, gruff man who barked orders through teeth clenched on a big cigar. A lot of people were put off by Johnny's rough exterior, but I liked him immensely. Before long, we were both considered potential heirs apparent to Billy Salomon.

John was a brilliant man, an English literature major who became partner at a time when most of his colleagues in the firm had never been to college. John, a Democrat who chaired the Wall Street arm of George McGovern's fund-raising effort for the 1972 presidential campaign, worked his way up through municipal bonds and syndicates and became a partner at the age of thirty-four. John Gutfreund revolutionized the corporate business by forming what eventually came to be known as the "Fearsome Foursome," an alliance of Salomon Brothers and three other firms: Lehman Brothers, Blyth (later Blyth Eastman Dillon and now Paine Webber), and Merrill Lynch. The "Fearsome Foursome" united to challenge the Old Guard and shook the Wall Street establishment to its core.

Shooting for a high percentage of every deal, the foursome could afford to bid at a lower rate of interest than the big syndicate-lead groups. Because the cadre was shooting for volume, it was extremely active, and truly sparked a revolution in the corporate bond business.

We did the same thing on the municipal side with what we called "Guerrilla Groups." We'd break away from major syndicates, where we would take large positions in underwriting.

An unsuspecting visitor on a peak trading day during my time at Salomon Brothers would find up to three hundred traders and salesmen scampering through the trading room in barely controlled mayhem, shouting orders and trading at a frantic pace as tickets representing buys and sells were shuffled around the room. I would be standing at the corner of my desk downing glass after glass of ice water—the ice water kept me cool, literally; the coffee drinkers tended to get hot under the collar and nervous, and they had to run to the bathroom all the time—exchanging shouted information with my traders, working the phones, and making instantaneous decisions.

The trader and salesman would work together in a state of perpetual natural tension. The salesman was always trying to take care of the institution he represented so it would buy more bonds. The trader was always trying to make a profit on his position so the firm would make money.

We traded in a long, narrow trading room that was the pulsing epicenter of the Salomon operation at 60 Wall Street. A long board ran about half the length of the room and as trades occurred, trainees would scamper around, shoving updated numbers into various slots on the board. But for the most part, we communicated via "hoot and holler"—in other words, we shouted updates, often offering editorial remarks. It was, "Are you out of your goddamned mind?" rather than, "I respectfully beg to differ," and the decibel and adrenaline levels were usually high. Trading required total focus and the ability to switch gears instantaneously, and it fostered an environment that was intensely, brutally competitive, and, simultaneously, warmly friendly, even fraternal.

We used to play a game called "Liar's Poker." The game consists of a group of people, each holding a dollar bill close to his chest, and trying to bluff and call the bluffs of the others in guessing the serial numbers. The object is to psyche out your opponents, and to avoid being psyched out. We were professional gamblers; and Liar's Poker, as well as other games of chance, fit in perfectly with our corporate culture.

Our futures, as well as the success of the firm, were intertwined. Billy Salomon had wisely structured a unique compensation system. Salaries were actually quite low,[4] but at the end of the year Salomon Brothers would distribute bonuses, based on how the firm as a whole had performed. However, we could draw only 5 percent of our capital, which meant the bonus money was invested with the firm. Consequently, the fate of the partners was directly linked to the success of Salomon Brothers, which fostered a clannish connection within that boiling cauldron of activity. It was understood that apart from our homes, insurance policies, and bank accounts, we didn't have interests separate from the firm's and we didn't make investments outside the firm. All for one, one for all.

———

Al Shoemaker, December 8, 1993

Bill is tough and he scares people when he shouts. But he is also the kind of guy to whom you can stand up and say, "Listen! Bullshit!" and he'll stop and listen. If you're right, he'll say, "Yeah, maybe." He might not admit it right away, but the next day he'll say, "You know, I think maybe you're right." If you're wrong, of course, he'll wipe you out....

But there is a fun side to Bill that a lot of people don't see. One story I'll never forget: I was sitting in a dentist chair, having a tooth drilled early one morning. The dental assistant came in and said, "There's a phone call for you." I couldn't think of anything so important—with my mouth stuffed full of cotton—that someone would need to get me out of a dentist's chair. I get on the phone and hear, "Hey, pally! We've got tickets for the Knicks game tonight. Wanna go?"

———

In 1966, Girard Spencer, who headed the government bond department, was ravaged by Parkinson's disease and decided to retire. Billy Salomon was looking to take a more aggressive, less risk-averse position in government bonds than Gerry had maintained, and asked me to take charge of that department.

The United States dollar is the reserve currency of the world. Treasury bills, notes, and bonds are internationally traded, and the market is huge. The need to finance huge budget deficits makes the federal government the biggest borrower in the long-term market. Running a government bond department at a firm like Salomon Brothers is an enormous responsibility.

"Sure," I said instantly.

"Wonderful," Billy replied.

"As long as I run *both* municipal and government departments."

"What? Both!" Billy said. "You can't do both. Municipal is big; government is big. It's too much for one man!"

"I can do it," I said confidently. "They are related to each other. They trade equally. What affects one affects the other. I really believe they belong together."

"But who's going to run your municipal business?"

"I'll run it," I said, "with Dale Horowitz." Dale was my assistant. Eventually he became executive vice president of the firm and chairman of the Securities Industries Association. "Don't worry. We'll do fine. And we'll make money."

Billy Salomon gave me the opportunity that led to a revolution on Wall Street.

For institutional political reasons as much as anything else, the governments and municipals departments were separated by a historical gulf, exacerbated by the fact that they didn't understand each other, didn't talk to each other, and didn't trust each other. When he allowed me to run both departments, Billy built a permanent bridge between those two cultures and changed the way our firm, and subsequently others, did business.

As the first summer wore on, I sensed that the Federal Reserve was about to reduce interest rates and increased the firm's capital into intermediate and long-term bonds, buying at every sign the market was softening. A couple of the senior partners were clearly uncomfortable with my aggressive position, but Billy Salomon gave me his support and confidence. The first year we made $50 million dollars on government bonds.

———

WILLIAM SALOMON, JUNE 10, 1999

We were having problems in our government bond department which, at that time, was the most important department in the whole organization. Fortunes rose and fell with the performance of the government bond markets and how they interpreted the government bond market . . . Some were trading shorts and some were trading the agencies. They were doing a rotten job, and obviously the thing that impressed us most was they weren't making any money. I concluded we needed a new head of that department. I went, one by the one, to the heads of other departments—proven traders: the head of the industrial bond department, the head of the utility bond department, the head of the stock department. These were all good, established fellows who had good records of trading. Not one of them wanted it or would even accept the assignment because it looked like a dead end to them.

I called Bill in. He was our latest acquisition; that's why I went to him last. I said, "Bill: Government bond department. How would you like to go in there and head that for a while, see if you can make a go of it?"

He said, "Sure, why not."

He was in sole charge, and could fire anyone, no matter how long they had been with the firm. He did not fire anyone. He did not hire anyone. Inside of a few months, the department was pulling together and making money. He had a way of ingratiating himself with the people who work with him . . . He was extremely liked in his department and the government desk once again was a successful and profitable area.

———

The game, of course, is to "make the market," and to make the market, you have to be in the market, and sometimes you are going to lose. But one thing is absolutely certain: You can't hit so much as a foul ball, let alone a grand slam, unless you are willing to step up to the plate and face whatever is thrown your way. You've got to be in the game to play—an obvious observation, but one that bench warmers fail to grasp.

Example: Let's say I own $100 million in bonds and you don't. If I break even or lose a little bit of money, guess what I know that you don't? I know who is buying the bonds and at what price. The next week, when a new offer comes up, I am ahead of the game and in a position to turn it around.

My theory in bond trading was that a trader should always own bonds, because if you do you are in the flow—people are calling you for information and you are calling them for information. Even if your position is not a profitable one, it may become profitable because you are in the loop. To profitably "make a market," a trader has to know the attitudes of both the sellers and the buyers.

As my reputation grew, the market would move, at least to some degree, in response to what I was doing—with an emphasis on *what* I was doing, not *why* I was doing it, regardless of whether there was a rational basis behind my activity. When I was in the marketplace, whether I used brokers or not, people would guess that it was me cleaning the market. They would try to figure out if the market was moving on its own momentum, or if I was causing it to move. Either way, there would be a reaction.

Good bond traders have quick minds and unlimited stamina. When I ran the trading desk at Salomon Brothers, what I looked for in traders was that rare blend of attributes that would enable them to keep their head when everyone around them was losing theirs: integrity, energy, confidence, instinct, discipline. College graduates were rare, and I would often tell my traders: "If you guys weren't trading bonds, you'd be driving a truck. Don't try to get intellectual about the marketplace, just trade. Most of the time a market moves, nobody really knows why. So, don't worry about it, just react!"

At the time, Salomon Brothers was one of the largest borrowers in the United States, needing approximately a billion dollars a day to carry its inventories. Most of the loans, since they were secured by the inventory that must be available for trading, were very short term, and Salomon Brothers' daily entry into the market often caused a ripple in interest rates. Timing, of course, is everything.

One day in 1969, I instructed one of my bankers, Bob Dall, to "buy" (borrow) $50 million to finance some bonds I would be buying the next morning. But Bob, who had come to Salomon Brothers after working several years as a commercial banker, was stymied. Every effort he made to buy that sum of money at the rate I required—5.25 percent—led to a further tightening of the market and an increase in interest rates. The market had reacted to the apparent entry of a major borrower. Bob was terribly frustrated and didn't know what to do.

"I can't buy at five-and-a-quarter," he said, exasperated. "Every time I try, the price increases."

"Then you be the seller," I told him. "And as the rates go down, sell some more, and keep selling."

So, Bob sold $50 million, lending money he didn't have at 5.25 percent which, as I had guessed, caused the market to collapse within a matter of hours. Everyone assumed money was plentiful, and therefore cheap, and the rates fell to around 4.5 percent.

"Buy it back now," I instructed Dall.

He bought the $50 million I needed at 4.5 percent—considerably less than I was willing to pay—and the firm took a handsome profit on the money he sold at the higher rates. Bob learned a crucial lesson in the difference between making a market and being a casualty of it.

Was there a chance that our little gambit would backfire? You bet. Whenever you take a risk, there are going to be those doubts that haunt you at 3 a.m. and the voices around you saying, "Better not take a chance." A good trader trusts his judgment, and doesn't allow his failures to shake his confidence.

————

BARBARA JENSEN, FORMER SECRETARY FOR WILLIAM E. SIMON, SR., MAY 17, 1994

The great gift that Bill has for people is he instills in them the faith in themselves that they can do something. Whether they can do it or not, they're going to learn how to do it, because they think they can do it. And nine times out of ten, they can do it. I know he did that to me many times. He'd give me something to do that I thought, I can't possibly do this—and then did it. And he must have thought I could do it or he wouldn't have given it to me. I've seen him do that throughout his career. He's very good at it.

———

On July 17, 1970, Salomon Brothers[5] moved from 60 Wall Street to One New York Plaza, a spectacular new home at the tip of Manhattan, just across from the Staten Island Ferry terminal with a spectacular view of the Statue of Liberty, Ellis Island, and the Verrazano-Narrows Bridge. It quickly became famous for its two-story-high trading room. Running the entire length of the building, "The Room"—as it was called—extended from the forty-first to the forty-third floor, with a balcony where visitors could watch nearly two hundred traders and salesmen engaged in what was often frenetic activity.

Beneath the balcony was a ninety-six foot long telex board, where the moving prices of the most heavily traded debt instruments were perpetually updated. At the north end of the floor was the municipal bond department, and next to it was the government bond department. At the south end were corporate bonds and equities. For anyone who loves constant activity, as I do, it was paradise.

What was it like? Let's say that in a given week the state of New York announces that it wants to sell $150 million in bonds, to be auctioned at 11 a.m. on Wednesday.

On Monday of that week, the salesmen from the various firms start hitting the phones, garnering what are known as "pre-sale" orders and feeding that information to the traders, who are responsible for setting a price on the "state" bonds.

The firms start forming bidding groups, or "syndicates," based upon historical relationships. (At a time when syndicates were frequently massive undertakings, with dozens and dozens of firms splitting proceeds and mitigating individual risk, Salomon Brothers was known for establishing small, highly competitive and aggressive bidding groups—the aforementioned "Guerrilla Groups" modeled after the "Fearsome Foursome" that John Gutfreund put together. Since there were only a few firms involved in any given "guerrilla" operation, each had a larger participation—which meant a much higher potential return, and much more risk.) Perhaps Salomon Brothers aligns with Morgan Guaranty and Bear Stearns and ends up bidding against Chase and First Chicago.

From the beginning of the week on, the dealing is incessant. Salomon might get "pre-sale" orders and be willing to bid more aggressively. Chase might have fewer orders and be badgering their salesmen constantly for more business. Simultaneously, salesmen are hustling orders to give to the trader, so the trader can figure out the pricing to buy the bonds (an obviously crucial judgment call since the firm only makes money if it wins the bid).

The day before, and the day of, the bid opening, the syndicate members meet again to set the bidding price, based, of course, on the interest in the bonds. Salomon might feel good about a deal, and want to press the price. Someone else may have bad vibes, and drop out of the syndicate. Meanwhile, maybe there is a rush of orders, so perhaps the syndicate lowers the interest rate. This give and take continues until literally the last minute with everyone trying to get orders up to the deadline.

Moments before 11 a.m., the bids would be delivered to the auction site and opened. And when the Federal Reserve came into the market at 11:30, all hell would break lose.

Whenever the Fed came in, it would signal to the market that they were either tightening or loosening credit. If the Fed wanted to take money out of the market, it would sell bonds. If the Fed wanted to loosen the market and pump money into the system, it would buy bonds. In either case, it was a signal to the market that the Fed wanted credit conditions to either ease or tighten. Consequently, our position would either be worth more or less.

Keep in mind, that the above describes just a portion of what might be occurring on the Salomon floor. Simultaneously, there might be a government auction going off, and a corporate bond underwriting underway, and perhaps a block trade going down at the equity desk. It was boiling cauldron of barely contained chaos, and I loved every minute of it.

Meanwhile, I was meeting regularly with Treasury Department officials, advising them on government financing for Fannie Mae (Federal National Mortgage Association) and Ginnie Mae (Government National Mortgage Association)—and had taken an active role in helping construct the enabling legislation, the Housing Act of 1968.

In addition, in my capacity as the Salomon Brothers partner in charge of the government and municipal bond departments, I helped negotiate financing with the state treasurers as well as corporations and commercial banks, creating financing packages tailored to their specific needs. I became chairman of the Technical Debt Management Committee of New York City.

The more I worked with government and the more attention I paid to matters of politics and public policy, the more I became interested in political philosophy and the roots of the freedom that most of us take for granted. Still, I didn't take seriously the collectivists and assorted academics who clamored endlessly for more government and less individual autonomy. To me, they and their philosophy was akin to the Tooth Fairy: Lots of people talk about the Tooth Fairy, but only children and imbeciles take it seriously. I assumed it was the same with leftists and did not yet fully appreciate the danger and threat that their ideas represented.

Yet my increasingly frequent encounters with government and bureaucracy during the administration of President Lyndon Johnson suggested that America was drifting away from its economic moorings and infringing on the freedoms that had made our prosperity possible. I was growing increasingly concerned about the direction in which the country was heading.

In 1967, I started the William E. Simon Foundation, which is dedicated to helping those in need by providing the means through which they may support themselves. It began with modest means and a lofty mission—to strengthen the free enterprise system and the moral and spiritual values on which it rests.

In truth, my philosophical views were just beginning to jell, and when I established my foundation my thoughts on economic freedom were more intuitive than intellectual. I had a code of values, but I didn't fully understand the philosophical and pragmatic implications and ramifications until after my arrival in Washington several years later.

Salomon Brothers encouraged its employees to participate in charitable work, and in the late 1960s I began to devote more of my time and resources to other endeavors, especially the Olympic movement. I'd always been a sports nut and supporter of the Olympics. I began taking an interest in the financial backing of the games and the athletes after receiving a call from a friend, Ed Mosler. Ed ran the Mosler Safe Co. and was very dedicated to helping potential Olympians reach their goal.

"Bill, I assist athletes and I wonder if you'd like to help, too. I've got my eyes on a particular skater and I'd really like to help her out, but I'm helping so many others that I just can't do it," Ed said.

I said I'd be delighted to help and contributed something like $500 a year toward an aspiring Olympian's skates and ice time. It wasn't until much later that I learned the name of the promising young skater: Dorothy Hamill, the gold medalist at Innsbruck, Austria, in 1976.

At the same time, I was becoming increasingly aware of how under-funded our athletes were. I felt that many American athletes were lacking the support necessary to even take part in the games, and thought perhaps I could help. I became a very active member of the United States Olympic Committee.

Since 1950, when the United States Olympic Association (precursor to the USOC), was granted a federal charter under Public Law 805, the organization had the authority to solicit tax-deductible contributions as a private, not-for-profit corporation. However, fund raising was a decidedly casual activity, and our athletes and our athletic programs were often left wanting, particularly in relation to the lavish facilities and programs available to athletes in many other countries.

Don Miller, who would become executive director of the USOC in 1973, and I started the first organized U.S. Olympic national fundraising program to address the imbalance and inequity. We wanted to provide a level of financial security for our athletic programs, without getting the government involved. Government funding inevitably brings government control, and Don and I felt strongly that the Olympic movement could, and should, be funded totally with private dollars.

Don and I had a dream—that we could establish a U.S. Olympic Committee Foundation to raise funds for America's future generations of athletes. As part of that effort, we would lead a great national drive to support our coaches and athletes, and to provide them with the finest facilities in the world. It took three decades to fully realize our dream.

————

COL. F. DON MILLER, FORMER EXECUTIVE DIRECTOR OF THE UNITED STATES OLYMPIC COMMITTEE AND PRESIDENT OF THE U.S. OLYMPIC FOUNDATION, APRIL 19, 1994

In 1964, the World Fair was in New York and the United States Olympic Committee held its trials there, prior to the 1964 Olympic games—trials for boxing and several other sports. Ed Mosler [of Mosler Safe Co.] and Bill Simon—Mosler, a multimillionaire, Simon, earning several million annually—were there hawking Olympic pins for a dollar apiece to raise money for the Olympic effort. That's how money was raised in those days—bake sales, car washes, everything under the sun....

Candidly, at that time, the U.S. Olympic Committee was nothing more than a glorified travel agency. Once every four years, it would bring athletes together, after they had been selected by the national governing bodies, and send them to the Olympic and Pan Am games... There was little foresight given to the needs and interests of the youth of the country in developing their athletic skills or in assisting them in accomplishing their goals. Bill and I talked about this at great length....

When Bill and I took on the job [of fund raising], they increased our fund-raising goal. It had been $3.4 million, but they increased it to $5.6 million. A lot of them were saying, "They'll never do it." We raised $8 million.

————

Carol and I had our last child, Johanna Katrina—"Katie"—born on July 25, 1967, and we were the epitome of the prosperous, happy suburban family. It was a magical time in our lives. All seven children were at home, the younger ones still enchanted by Santa Claus and the Easter Bunny, the oldest well into adolescence, with all the wonder and chaos those years bring.

I was a not-quite-forty-year-old millionaire with a beautiful wife and seven wonderful children. Within a year, we would own an idyllic sixty-four acre parcel in New Vernon, New Jersey, where, over the course of four years, we gradually built our dream home. My children wanted for nothing, yet they were taught to want little and to appreciate that which they had.

Little did I know at the time that my growing interest in political matters, and nagging concern over the misdirection of President Johnson's "guns and butter" economics, would shortly take us all away from the life we envisioned and cast us into the hurricane of government.

————

J. PETER SIMON, SON, SEPTEMBER 26, 1994

We had a typical upper-middle-class life. We were always encouraged to take responsibility. We were taught the value of a dollar, and we were expected to understand what that meant. We were taught to be grateful for what we were given, and to be aware of what other people didn't have. We were expected to make our beds. We were expected to pick up our room. Since I was fifteen, I've held a job. Once, I took the car out and crashed it. I think it cost my father $400 to get me out of it. I had to pay him back the $400....

You didn't mess around with Dad. You never talked back to him. If you did, it didn't last long. We soon learned that arguing with him was a losing proposition. Dad was an authoritarian. He would describe himself as a benevolent dictator, which he is. Yet he loves the underdog.

I think one of the wonderful things about America is that we always love the underdog. We root for the underdog. That's Dad in a nutshell. He loves the long-odds play. He loves to invest in entities that are down and out. He loves to bet on the team where he can get the odds. He feels a lot of compassion for the loser.

––––

Like many Americans, I was not aware of the extent of the economic and political problems in the country. I was critical of Johnson's liberal and statist policies, and profoundly disturbed by the total disintegration of values that seemed to have afflicted our young people. But still, my political activity was peripheral, although my interest in politics was growing.

In 1968, I supported Richard Nixon and was among seventeen Salomon partners who donated a total of more than $100,000 to his presidential campaign. I personally pledged $15,000 myself to help him defeat Hubert Humphrey. I had never met Mr. Nixon; although we were both on Wall Street—after losing the 1962 California gubernatorial race, Richard Nixon moved to New York and became a partner in a Wall Street law firm—our paths had never crossed.

I was, however, very close to a man who was very close to Richard Nixon: John N. Mitchell, without question the best bond attorney in the nation. There is probably no state, and few cities, which today boast a hospital, or a school, or a public housing facility that doesn't owe its existence to John Mitchell's expertise. In 1967, after John's law firm merged with Nixon's, the two men became dear friends. The following year, John Mitchell managed Richard Nixon's successful presidential campaign.

Shortly after the 1968 election, I was at a convention in Hollywood, Florida, with John Mitchell and some other pals from Wall

Street at the same time that president-elect Nixon was putting together his cabinet.

The new president would inherit a mountain of problems in taking over the leadership of a country splintered by political controversy over a losing war started by his predecessors, and an economy struggling with a currency devalued by an inflation exacerbated by that war. His difficulties were compounded by the fact that he was the first president since Zachary Taylor to begin his administration with both houses of Congress in the hands of his opposition.

Obviously, every president desires a strong cabinet. But a president whose party was in the minority in both the Senate and House of Representatives simply must have the absolutely best aides and advisors available. John Mitchell fit the description perfectly. It was inconceivable that Richard Nixon would not select for his cabinet a man of John's intelligence and ability.

We were teasing John, asking when he would be joining the new administration.

"I don't want to go to Washington. It is not a place I enjoy. Politics is not my business," he said, perhaps prophetically. "I am not going," he insisted.

I said, "John, do you really think you will be able to turn down the president?"

John sat there, smoking his pipe and seemingly lost in thought.

Within a matter of days, it was announced that John Mitchell would become the next attorney general of the United States. John was neither the first, nor last, to learn that Richard Nixon did not take no for an answer.

Nor was he the first or last to pay a terrible personal price for accepting this president's call to duty.

INSIDE THE BELTWAY

During President Nixon's first term, my work at Salomon Brothers continued to lead me closer and closer to the orbit of national politics.

Frequent trips to D.C. to meet with top officials at the Treasury Department or to provide expert testimony on some aspect or other of government financing gave me a professional perspective on how Washington functioned. My regular visits with Attorney General John Mitchell provided more of a personal perspective. John often said that he would like me to join the administration, but our discussions on that point were casual and never resulted in either an offer from him or a request by me.

By mid-1972, John's life was beginning to unravel.

John had resigned as attorney general in the spring to manage the president's reelection campaign, but left that position on July 1, citing "the one obligation which must come first: the happiness and welfare of my wife and daughter." John's wife, Martha, was an alcoholic who simply could not handle the pressures of Washington political life, and John knew it. In fact, Martha's instability—and John's fear that Washington would exacerbate her problems—was one of the major reasons he had been so reluctant to become attorney general in the first place. The June 17, 1972, break-in at Democratic headquarters at the Watergate seemed to push Martha over the edge.

Just a few days after the burglary and a few days before John resigned as campaign manager, Martha, beset with emotional problems and openly talking of suicide, called Helen Thomas of United Press International and claimed she was a "political prisoner" and that she was going to leave her husband because of "all those dirty things that go on." At that time, however, Watergate was at most a minor distraction. No one in the administration perceived of its future implications that early. Only the press, and Martha Mitchell, seemed obsessed with the matter, and few seemed to be taking either seriously. John, regardless of the embarrassment, stood by his wife, did his best to remain loyal to a woman who he knew was seriously unhinged.

Meanwhile, John's ten-year-old daughter, Marty, was having a difficult time with all the goings-on at home—her mother's increasingly irrational behavior and apparently alcohol-induced delusions, and the daily political and media assaults on her father. Marty desperately needed a respite. When I mentioned to John that I was bringing my entire family and Schatzie to the 1972 Olympic Games in Munich, he asked if I would be willing to bring Marty along as well. I was more than happy to help out.

We sailed to Europe on the *Queen Elizabeth II*. After sightseeing in England and Austria, we met up with my sons, Billy and Pete, who were spending the summer working on a dairy farm in Germany. From there, we continued on to Munich for the Olympic Games, where my sons worked as "runners" in the Olympic Village.

The Federal Republic of Germany touted the XX Olympiad (the first Olympics on German soil since Hitler presided over the 1936 Games in Berlin) as the "friendly games" and put forth an impressive effort to host a magnificent event. From an athletic standpoint, the games were glorious, with a record number of 122 nations engaged in friendly competition in 195 events. Highlights included swimmer Mark Spitz's seven gold medals and seven world records in seven events, Frank Shorter's tremendous victory in the marathon, sparking a national running boom, and the spunk of a tiny Soviet gymnast named Olga Korbut who charmed us all with her skill and grace on the uneven parallel bars, the balance beam, and the floor exercises.

One day, I was walking through a tunnel to the infield where the track and field events were underway and I heard someone call my name.

"Hey, Simon! Simon!"

It was Willie Davenport, America's hope for a gold medal in the 110-meter hurdles. He had won in Mexico City and aspired for an encore performance. Willie reached into my shirt pocket and helped himself to a cigarette.

"Got a light?"

Willie Davenport, on his way to run in Olympic competition, was bumming a cigarette! Just like Jesse Owens,[1] Willie was a chain smoker. The smoke seemed to calm his nerves. However, it apparently did nothing for his speed; Willie failed to place.[2]

––––––

WILLIE DAVENPORT, OLYMPIC CHAMPION, DECEMBER 9, 1998

I met Bill by serving on the Olympic Committee. I started out serving as the athletes' representative with what they called the AAC, the Athletes Advisory Council. From there I went on to the executive committee of the board of directors, during the same time Bill was serving. I think what struck me about Bill was the way he could raise money for the Olympic Committee. He worked extremely hard and was extremely successful. He has a certain foresight; when you are on page six, he's on page eight. We, the Olympians, help people like Bill Simon raise monies, to further the Olympic Movement.

What drives him is what drives athletes: competition. Whatever he goes into, he has to be successful. I think it is a built-in drive for us to have that competitive desire to win, that desire to do more than was expected, to never be satisfied with the status quo, to always, always reach for a higher plateau. Bill is one of us. I love the man.

The Simon family, like much of America, celebrated the performances, by Americans as well as others, and joined in the outrage over the final days of the games, which were marred like none before or since.

On Tuesday, September 5, 1972, the eleventh day of the games, eight Palestinian guerrillas invaded the Olympic Village, where Billy was still working (Pete had flown home early with Marty Mitchell) and where my entire family was wandering around, carefree. An Israeli wrestling referee and a weightlifter were murdered on the spot and the terrorists demanded the release of some two hundred Israeli-held prisoners, plus safe passage for themselves, lest there be more killings.

After twenty hours of negotiation, German authorities transported the killers and hostages to the airport, where sharpshooters attempted to pick off the terrorists. In the battle, five terrorists and all nine Israelis were killed. The violence, while profoundly disturbing, seemed surreal, unbelievable and oddly remote; indeed, I never for a moment felt that my family was in danger, perhaps because of the refusal of the organizers, athletes, and spectators to allow evil to overcome good.

Avery Brundage, then president of the International Olympic Committee, vowed that "the games must go on," and indeed they did, provoking a fury of dissent, mainly among journalists. Avery Brundage, however, was absolutely right. After suspending the games for a morning memorial service the day after the carnage, the Olympics continued—with the full blessings of the state of Israel. The Olympics, and the good that it represents, would not be stolen by a handful of terrorists.

We left the games with mixed emotions: shaken by the violence and bloodshed that had occurred in our vicinity, but gratified that the evil of terrorism could not overshadow the glory of the Olympic spirit. If we had allowed cowardly terrorists to cancel the games, we would have surrendered to them all that the games represent.

COLONEL F. DON MILLER, APRIL 19, 1994

Bill took his entire family to the 1972 summer games in Munich. I was serving as assistant executive director and my time was spent in the village with the athletes, trying to keep everything organized. Bill, almost every day, like clockwork, would come in and sit at my desk with me and keep asking what he could do. When this basketball thing broke [a protest over the gold medal game between the United States and the Soviet Union], there wasn't money to lodge a protest, and no one could find Cliff Buck, who was then president of the U.S. Olympic Committee. Bill had money in his pocket and said, "I'll go over." Not giving it a lot of thought, I said, "Fine. You go over and find Cliff Buck. Give him the money and get things straightened out."

Bill didn't have a pass, so he tried to climb the fence. Keep in mind the Israeli shootings and all the other events that were happening had resulted in tight security. When he got to the top of the fence, Bill tore his trousers eluding the guards, but did get into the building....

As a result of that incident, we had to spend some time dealing with the media....

———

When we returned from the Olympics in Germany, I received a call from E. Pendleton James, special assistant to President Nixon.

For several months, I had been working with Pen and Fred Malek, assistant to the president for executive management, to identify appropriate candidates who could help the administration achieve its goals in the second term. Even though Watergate had yet to become a national fixation, potential recruits were somewhat reluctant to crawl into the snake pit that Washington had become. However, we had managed to recruit top-flight people, and the administration appreciated my efforts.

"We would like to put your name forward for a cabinet post. Would you accept it?" Pen James asked.

"Yes."

"You say that very fast."

"Well, some people might think I'm nuts, giving up a $3 to $5 million job to work in government," I agreed.

At the time, I was a senior partner at Salomon Brothers, one of the leading investment houses in New York. Carol and I were blessed with seven wonderful children. We had just built our dream home in New Vernon, New Jersey.

I looked over at Carol, knowing that the same thoughts racing through my mind were racing through hers. We were a close and happy family. Financially, we had reached the point where we had always longed to be. Professionally, I was at the edge of the big time, ready to break into the ranks of the elite and fabulously wealthy investment bankers.

Certainly I felt pride, excitement, and, above all, gratitude at the prospect of being asked to serve my country, especially during that critical time in our history. Divisive forces from the war in Vietnam and an increasingly unstable economy—the consequence of profligate government spending—were tearing at the fabric of our nation's freedom, prosperity, and goodwill.

Early in this century, the idea began to take hold in the United States that the problems of our society were growing so large that individuals could no longer cope with them. Instead, people began asking the government to assume responsibility for solving their problems—and to do the things for them that they once did for themselves. Government gradually became a beneficent protector against the evils of modern life. That trend accelerated during the 1960s as we were promised through the powers of government that we could fight a land war in Asia, abolish the business cycle, eradicate pollution, and put a man on the moon, all at the same time. The result of President Johnson's "guns and butter" economy, broken promises, and an overbearing government, was predictable.

Young people soured on politics and politicians, and I can't say I blamed them. Washington had become an elitist, self-absorbed city that cared little for the values of everyday Americans who believe deeply in the work ethic and in family, freedom, and faith in God. Behind those majestic monuments in the backrooms of Congress, self-serving politicians were busily spending and borrowing America ever deeper into debt. The country was at a critical juncture and I felt that, perhaps, I could make a contribution.

Regardless, I was far more suited to the freewheeling, rough and tumble business world than the encrusted and too often cryptic cocoon of bureaucratic life in government. I'd had a bird's eye view of the bureaucracy as an investment banker, and the contrast I saw between modern-day Washington and the city built as a proud trademark to the ideals of the founding fathers gave me pause. While my philosophic views were surely not fully formed—although I was well on my way to understanding the link between economic and personal freedom—there was a nagging voice within that told me something was fundamentally amiss. Against that rising tide of corrosive sludge, could I be anything more than a boy with his finger in the dike? But there was really no question, from the first moment, that I would serve my country in any way I could.

"You owe it to the country," Carol said quietly. Like me, Carol was very patriotic.

True, I would be interrupting a successful career, uprooting my family, and giving up a comfortable and relatively predictable lifestyle for the vagaries of Washington. But my country called, and I was raised in an era when if your country called, be it to fight a foreign enemy or serve in government, you answered the call—with pride and honor and gratitude and respect. If you truly love your country and if you fear for freedom, can you stand by and see the battle lost without joining the fight? Inconceivable.

"Nothing would please me more than to spend a couple of years in government serving my country," I told Pen. "I've been a very lucky man and it would be an honor to serve in the second Nixon administration. What post are you talking about, anyway?"

"Secretary of HUD [Housing and Urban Development]," he said. Pen said the administration needed a "financial man" to straighten out the agency.

I winced.

HUD was a viper's nest, hopelessly mired in bureaucratic morass. I had served on the Special Advisory Liaison Committee for HUD (which, by the way, didn't do much of anything. But at least it didn't

do it often; I don't recall a single meeting between 1970 and 1972)
and was all too aware that running it could be like swimming in
manure. But if that is where the president wanted me, that was where
I would go. Mine was not to reason why.

"If anybody can clean it up," he said, "you can."

Maybe. Maybe not.

The president was easily reelected. When I heard nothing from the
administration, I more or less assumed that the HUD position had
been withdrawn. Then, two days before Thanksgiving, Fred Malek
called and said the president wanted to see me.

———

FRED MALEK, FORMER AIDE TO PRESIDENT NIXON,[3] FEBRUARY 3, 2000

*My job was head of personnel for the administration and it was my
responsibility to find really outstanding people, high-energy, intelligent people to bring into the administration, to reach beyond the typical "who-do-you-know?" political circles. We were looking for really
capable people whom we could convince to leave their careers and
join this adventure in government . . . We were looking for someone
who had a track record, but in government it's not enough to just be
successful in business, academia, or law. You have to be able to adapt
to this type of environment, adapt to the body Congress, and do the
kind of collaboration and consensus building that you have to do in
a government position, and put up with the inevitable frustrations.
Bill was a person with strong views, and he expressed those views
with strength and conviction. He is not shy; he is a guy who is eager
to get out there and, with gusto, demonstrate his points.*

———

E. PENDLETON JAMES, FORMER SPECIAL ASSISTANT TO PRESIDENT
NIXON, FEBRUARY 4, 2000

*When Nixon was first elected in 1968, he put his administration
together like previous presidents, paying off his cronies with cabinet
appointments. That is not atypical. Then, in the second year of his first
term, when he was confronting all of these horrendous problems—*

"*Flower Children,*" *Berkeley riots, Vietnam protestors, wage and price controls, a bad economy—those guys were off the reservation. They had their own political careers. They had their own political agendas. They weren't really on the president's team anymore.*

The president wanted to make appointments a little more thought-fully in the second term, and I was brought in to help identify men and women throughout the United States who had the substantive ability to serve in these spots, instead of relying on the patronage system or the political process. Under Malek, we set up a two-tiered appointment process. I headed the recruitment effort and my job was always to look outside the administration. The other side was to look at the political people....

Paul Volcker at that time was undersecretary for monetary affairs. Paul's deputy had left and the assignment came to me to find a new deputy for Paul. So, I got on the phone and called international bankers across the country. I must have made two dozen phone calls and somebody suggested, "You ought to call this fellow Bill Simon in New York because he has a network of bright, talented people and is a good source of talent." Well, I called Bill and immediately had the sense that he was somebody who really knew what he was talking about. Bill gave us some very good ideas....

After the reelection, one of the president's plans was to restructure the executive department. He planned to create four "super cabinet" positions with subcabinets reporting to the super cabinet. My job was to develop a nationwide talent bank of leading businessmen and women in engineering, science, health, finance, agriculture . . . The president had a chart of those he was going to ask to stay, those he was going to ask to leave, and those he was going to ask to stay in another post.

One of the positions on my list to fill was deputy secretary of treasury. I wrote a memo to President Nixon on Bill Simon. It came back and there was a line drawn through it and a big "NO! East Coast Establishment! Other options?" Richard Nixon had a knee-jerk opposition to the "East Coast Establishment." He thought they hadn't supported him and he didn't want anything to do with anyone who came from Wall Street. So, I wrote a second memo about Bill Simon to President Nixon. It came back, "No." But I really thought Bill Simon should be in the administration, and I wrote a third memo. Shortly after that, I got a call from Haldeman's office asking, "Can you get Simon down here?" I called Bill and the next thing I knew he was on a helicopter to Camp David.

––––

The following Monday, I flew to Washington, hopped on the presidential helicopter along with John C. Whitaker, undersecretary of the interior. I was flown to Camp David, where I was met by Chief of Staff H. R. "Bob" Haldeman, and John D. Ehrlichman, assistant to the president for domestic affairs.

We arrived at the president's residence and I walked in with a combination of anxiety and excitement for my first meeting with the President of the United States. Richard Milhous Nixon exuberantly jumped up from his chair and came over to greet me.

"Bill! Welcome! I'm awfully glad to see you! I've heard some wonderful things about you. Come on over and sit down. Would you like an iced tea with pineapple? That's how we drink it down here, you know."

I didn't know, but I gratefully accepted the beverage and readied myself for what I was certain would be a stimulating discussion with the leader of the free world.

I'd rehearsed everything I intended to say, and I was eager to talk politics and public policy and philosophy and economics with President Nixon. What an opportunity, I thought, to discuss such ideas and ideals with my nation's leader, the historical progeny of Jefferson and Lincoln!

I barely got in a word.

Richard Nixon, clearly an introvert who had answered the call of destiny and selected a vocation—politics—suited to extroverts, was simultaneously talkative and remote, delivering a nonstop monologue on various affairs of state, interwoven with erudite musings on history and politics and the balance of power between great nations.

President Nixon had an incredible sense of history and a grand vision for the future, and he enchanted me with insightful stories of different leaders and how they dealt with different crises. The president impressed me as a serious, dedicated, highly intelligent person, but a pragmatist, a person more attuned to the end result than the philosophical means to that end. He was, however, intensely interested in the *political* means to the desired result. I listened attentively, like a student at the knee of a learned teacher, fascinated, hypnotized, and mesmerized by what I was hearing, anxiously awaiting an opportunity to share with the president my views—an opportunity that never came. At times, I felt as though I was the beneficiary of a lecture. At other times, I felt like an invisible observer, and had a strange feeling that President Nixon's dissertation would have continued unabated whether I was there or not.

Even now, I can't remember a single word I said to the president that day in November 1972. But I remember his words exactly.

"I am going to get the best people I can, and you are certainly one of them. I am so thrilled you are going to join my administration!"

President Nixon never bothered to ask whether I wanted to serve in his administration; it was self-evident that his wish would be granted, and I assumed I had just "accepted" his "invitation" to become the next secretary of housing and urban development.

"You know, this is a very important job," the president added. "You realize this is tantamount to running the department."

Tantamount to running a department? I found his comment odd, since I had always assumed cabinet members ran their department. Before I could reply, he added, "[Secretary of Treasury] George Shultz is going to be given other duties. He's going to have a powerful position, secretary of the secretaries. And you will be his deputy!"

At that point, my head was spinning. Is George Shultz going to HUD? Have I been demoted to undersecretary before I even got the job as secretary? What in the world is going on here?

"George Shultz is going to be a very busy man," the president said, "and the deputy secretary of the treasury is going to be a very important job, equivalent to a cabinet position in my government. You are going to be running the department!"

Aside from my befuddlement, I was delighted with the thought of going to Treasury. I much preferred being a deputy in Treasury than a secretary at HUD. I knew the job. I knew the departments. I had lots of friends at Treasury. I had enormous respect for George Shultz, a brilliant man who had previously served as the president's first secretary of labor and then as director of the Office of Management and Budget. It was a good place for a financial professional, a market man, who recognized the fact that economics is, at its essential level, a study of people's behavior in the marketplace. Unlike career bureaucrats, I fully understood that markets function because individuals and corporations pursue, rightly, their rational self-interest. But I also appreciated the complexity of legislation and the need, in the political as well as business world, to compromise and negotiate.

I left Camp David somewhat bewildered, unclear of precisely what I had gotten myself into, or even how I had gotten myself into it. It was only later that I learned the full story of how I had come to be deputy secretary of the treasury. It had its genesis in a debt-management session many months earlier.

I had been a member of the Government Securities Committee of the Investment Bankers Association, one of two major committees that advised Treasury on financings. The committee had come up with some recommendations and George Shultz was looking for an alternative view, and I had one. He quizzed me at length about my ideas.

"Mr. Secretary," I told George Shultz, "I am going to present an alternative to what was proposed by the majority, but I want to preface my remarks by saying that what the majority has proposed will be a success. However, what I would recommend would, in my opinion, be even more successful and it would 'dress up the market' "— meaning prepare the market for future financings while simultaneously providing a debt extension.

The secretary, obviously immensely intelligent and extraordinarily well prepared, questioned me thoroughly and ultimately adopted my position. The financing was a rousing success.

In all honesty, the incident made me appear smarter than I am. Certainly I don't have a crystal ball and, in any circumstance, this one included, the market can beat you. I advocated taking a risk, and Secretary Shultz agreed. We both lucked out, and we both knew it. Regardless, George was impressed and, shortly thereafter, approached the president, seeking approval to bring me on as a deputy.

"Mr. President, I'd like to bring on a new deputy secretary of treasury," George Shultz said.

"It's your department, George, and you run it. If you want to bring new people in, that's fine with me," President Nixon responded. George turned to leave, and the president said: "By the way, who is he? Where is he from?"

"Bill Simon, a New York banker. He's a partner at Salomon Brothers in New York."

"Oh come on, George, I don't want any of those New York Cadillac liberals! Go get yourself a nice conservative Chicago or San Francisco banker."

Shortly after the election, George Shultz was in the White House for a meeting when, by chance, he stopped by the cafeteria for coffee just when Fred Malek and other presidential aides were sorting through documents describing various pending appointments.

"Simon's going to be terrific," one of them said. "He'll do a number on that department!"

George's ears perked up. "What's that?" he asked. "Are you talking about *Bill* Simon? Let me see that."

On the sheet, it said: "Simon: Secretary, HUD." George wrote "deputy" in front of "secretary," scratched out "HUD" and replaced it with "Treasury." The president signed the document as presented, perhaps without even reading it, and all of a sudden I was his nominee for the $42,000-a-year position of deputy secretary of treasury.

Salomon Brothers at that time was one of the biggest dealers, underwriters, and market makers in the field of federal, municipal, and corporate bonds and other debt securities. It was essential now to make abundantly clear that my foremost allegiance was to the betterment of the country.

At my confirmation hearing, I told the Senate Finance Committee that as soon as my nomination was announced, I immediately removed myself from any economic interest in Salomon Brothers. My assets were placed in a blind trust[4] managed by Morgan Guaranty Trust Co. of New York and, per my instructions, restricted far more than the law required (a decision which would ultimately cost me millions). As subsequent events would prove, both integrity, and the perception of integrity, are vital to the smooth functioning of the republic, and I was determined immediately to secure and maintain the confidence of the public and the Congress.

Senate Finance Committee chairman Russell Long, a Louisiana Democrat, asked whether I would have a conflict of interest since, in 1969, I had appeared on several occasions before Congress, testifying in defense of the municipal tax exemption in my capacity as a leader of the Securities Industry Association.

"You have had a great deal of experience in marketing tax-exempt bonds," observed Senator Long, who would later become a great supporter and friend. Russell Long, along with Wilbur Mills, was one of the great statesmen of the era. "If the issue of tax exemption is raised as part of a tax reform bill, do you think you would be in a position to act objectively and in the best interests of the Treasury Department in making recommendations with regard to a measure of that sort?"

I responded: "I do. I hope that my experience of more than twenty years in the investment banking world would be looked upon as an *identity* of interest rather than a *conflict* of interest and that my views as a senior member of the Treasury staff would be determined by the best interests of our country, and not shaped by any parochial view."

I was easily confirmed December, 6, 1972, by voice vote with no debate. United Press International transmitted a story describing my appointment as "one of the least controversial major appointments of the Nixon Administration" (it wouldn't be long, however, before "the controversial" always seemed to appear before "William E. Simon" in newspaper articles). A few weeks later, on December 31, the *New York Times* superimposed headshots of the president's "All-Star Economic Team" on a group photo of a football squad. And there was my mug on the muscular body of some football player, along with such notables as George Shultz; Arthur Burns, chairman of the Federal Reserve; Roy L. Ash, director of the Office of Management and Budget; William J. Casey, undersecretary of state for economic affairs; Frederick B. Dent, secretary of commerce; Peter M. Flanigan, council to the president; Herbert Stein, chairman of the Council of Economic Advisers; and Paul Volcker, undersecretary of the treasury for monetary affairs and eventual Federal Reserve chairman.

It was an exciting moment, but George warned me of what was ahead.

"You're going to have trouble," he predicted. "You are a person who likes to get things done, and when somebody likes to get things done in government, he is going to have all sorts of people sniping at him."

I left my home and, briefly, my family and headed south to a new adventure, arriving in Washington just in time to experience two economic cyclones, an energy plight, and various international crises—not to mention the historic resignation of the vice president and president.

At the time I joined the administration, the president was implementing a major restructuring, something that had been in the works since George Shultz replaced John Connally in a newly expanded role as secretary of the treasury. Secretary Shultz was given oversight over all economic policy, a daunting responsibility with the mission of coordinating the departments of Treasury, State, and Commerce. George had more influence over economic policy matters at the time than anyone in the country. While George was overseeing economic policy, I assumed responsibility for the day-to-day operation of the Department of Treasury, an enormous bureaucracy.

Next to the State Department, the Treasury—the division of the executive branch charged with managing and supervising the nation's finances—is the oldest of the cabinet departments. Its principle functions are to manage the financial and economic affairs of the U.S. government, and that mandate includes both domestic and international responsibilities. Domestically, Treasury collects revenue for the government, disperses funds for approved purposes, manages the public debt, maintains government accounts, oversees national banks, ensures the soundness of the national banking system, and manufactures coins and currency. On the foreign policy side, Treasury is involved in myriad issues involving dollar exchange, trade, the International Monetary Fund, the World Bank, and what is known as G-7, or the Group of Seven.

There was a tremendous amount to learn about economics, energy, imports, exports, monetary policy, and government in general. When I went to government, I thought I was a pretty sophisticated person. Over the next year, I learned otherwise—but I learned well at the knee of George Pratt Shultz.

With the children in school, Carol and I decided it would be best for the family to remain in New Jersey until June. So, George would frequently have me over to his house for dinner, along with guests like Milton Friedman and George Stigler, brilliant economists who would both later win Nobel prizes, as well as a host of other people—scholars, business leaders—who had forgotten more economics than I would ever know. They would engage in the highest level of debate I had ever encountered, arguing points and counterpoints, feeding off each other, playing cat and mouse with each other, playing devil's advocate, but always in a tenor of intellectual inquiry rather than mental combat. For me, it was fun and exciting and inspiring and exhilarating, but also exhausting and, at times, intimidating.

———

GEORGE P. SHULTZ, MARCH 9, 1994, AND JANUARY 7, 2000

I needed a new deputy when I was secretary of the treasury and I wanted someone who knew financial markets and had personal experience in them; I knew the financial markets, but I hadn't been an active participant.

John Mitchell, a person whose judgment I had come to admire a lot, suggested Bill Simon, so I asked around. I remember talking with Walt Wriston, who then was head of Citicorp. He said, "I hope you get Bill. Then maybe somebody else can make money in the bond market." Simon had a sensational reputation. . . .

I found that Bill's capacity for work is infinite. He is always decisive. He is always ready to make decisions, and to take responsibility for them. Bill is a risk taker and, if he feels he can do something, he's not afraid to go do it. Many people are afraid to make a decision because they don't want to stand up to the heat that comes with it, but not Bill Simon. Yes, Bill worked people as hard as he worked himself. He could be tough and abrasive, at times, particularly if people didn't do their work or did it sloppily. But the job got done, and that's what counts. . . .

One of the most important things I did for Bill was introduce him to Milton Friedman. He was a colleague of mine when I was at the University of Chicago, and is a good friend to this day. Milton is not only about as sharp an economist as ever lived, he also has an extraordinary gift for exposition. He can really explain things, and if he winds up talking with someone he thinks is worthwhile he has immense patience, and a willingness to engage and argue. Milton is a great arguer, and we used to say that everyone loved to argue with Milton—when he wasn't there!

Well, Bill Simon loved to argue with Milton Friedman when he was there, and he learned a great deal from Milton.

———

That first year, it turned out for the better that Carol and the children weren't with me because I worked late every night, struggling to stay afloat. On one of my first Fridays, I popped my head into George Shultz's office to wish him a good weekend.

———

"Bill," he said, "good timing. I was just about to call you. We've got a meeting at eight Saturday morning in the White House."

That was that, and the following morning I found myself in a meeting with intellectual giants like George Shultz and Secretary of State Henry Kissinger along with such extraordinarily capable people as Peter Flanigan and John Ehrlichman, and feeling very inadequate. "I don't belong in this league," I said to myself, and redoubled my efforts to get up to speed. I read everything I could get my hands on regarding economics and economic policy, studied the classics from the Enlightenment, listened intently like the privileged student I was—and gradually began to comprehend not only the pragmatic aspects of policy, but the crucial philosophical underpinnings. It was then that I began to fully appreciate that ideas have consequences.

THE ENERGY CZAR

One morning shortly after my swearing in, I was working in my office when George Shultz stopped by.

"What do you know about the oil import policy in the United States?"

"Nothing."

"Well, the president wants you to take a look at it. He decided that you should be the head of the Oil Policy Committee."

"George," I said, "you know I will gladly do whatever you and the president want me to do, but I don't know anything—*anything*—about oil or oil policy."

George Shultz shrugged. "You'll learn. The president and I both feel that what's needed is a man without any built-in prejudices or vested interests. You are a businessman. You know markets. We want you to take a look at the entire oil import program. My opinion, by the way, is that it ought to be wiped out."

I quickly learned that the Oil Import Program had begun in 1955 when substantial amounts of crude oil were produced in the Middle East for the first time. The controls were designed to maintain higher domestic prices and, therefore, as incentives for domestic drilling. As long as we continued to produce oil at a level well below full capacity, we were in a position to control the world price by expanding or contracting production.

Through the early 1960s, the program was moderately successful in maintaining the pace of oil development. But the agenda was fatally flawed, for two main reasons: It discouraged refinery construction; and it encouraged foreign, not domestic, investment by U.S. oil companies.

The federal government established maximum, but not minimum, amounts that could be imported, leaving to the eight largest oil companies, the "majors," as they were called[1]—the decision as to where to purchase fuel. The companies operated under various concessions, paying the host company an agreed upon sum per barrel, but retaining the power to make basic production and marketing decisions. Since the quota system restricted imports of crude oil but encouraged importation of refined products, and environmental restrictions made drilling prohibitively expensive, the construction of refineries in this country slowed to a standstill at precisely the time that U.S. demand for refinery products was increasing. Consequently, by the early 1970s, when energy consumption in the U.S. was growing at a rate of about 4.8 percent annually, domestic energy production had peaked and we were increasingly dependent on imports.

President Nixon early on clearly understood the implications—domestically and internationally—of consuming more oil than we were producing, and warned the nation that the United States could no longer take its energy supply for granted. Shortly after taking office, the president created a Cabinet Task Force on Oil Import Control to review the quota system.

George Shultz, as secretary of labor, had chaired the task force, which also included, among others, the secretaries of state, treasury, defense, interior, and commerce. Pete Flanigan, assistant to the president, was the White House liaison. After eleven months of deliberations, resulting in roughly 10,000 pages of testimony, the task force in February 1970 produced a 400-page report. The report recommended scrapping the import quotas and replacing them with tariffs, so that foreign producers would be free to compete in the American market, subject only to customs duty.

However, a minority view, represented by the secretaries of interior and commerce and the chairman of the Federal Power Commission, prevailed with the president. The minority feared that the proposed tariff system would drive down the price of domestic oil, thereby discouraging domestic production and ultimately creating an unhealthy reliance on foreign oil. The big eight oil companies were extremely powerful and lobbied relentlessly, begging like panhandlers to retain what amounted to a government-contrived monopoly on imports. So, the quotas remained, as did ceilings on American production of oil.

In the early part of 1972, the Texas Railroad Commission, the agency that set the ceiling on U.S. production, panicked in the face of increasing demand and increased reliance on foreign energy. When it authorized full production, it brought to a skidding halt the days when the U.S. could control the world price of oil. No longer was there a question that the U.S. was facing an energy crisis; the only question was when it would hit, and how severely. That year alone, the retail price of a gallon of gasoline rose from 35 to nearly 45 cents, and the average wholesale price of crude oil at the wellhead jumped from $3.40 to $4 per barrel, an increase of 18 percent.

By 1973, President Nixon thought that both the regulators and the American public were willing to listen to what he had been saying for several years, and asked me to take the lead in revamping our oil policy. It was immediately apparent why the president wanted a "neutral" personality. No sooner did the rumor get out that I was to chair the Oil Policy Committee than I was bombarded with advice, demands, and warnings from an astounding number of constituencies—ranging from the fifty-five federal agencies that had been regulating the oil industry to the industry itself to refiners, brokers, dealers, jobbers, and, of course, the eight major oil companies.

My first two-hour meeting with the Oil Policy Committee was appalling, and served to convince me only that it should be the *last* meeting of the Oil Policy Committee. It was abundantly clear that its goal was not to solve problems—that would entail taking responsibility, which was to be avoided at all costs—but to ruminate, incessantly. The committee, like many committees inside government as well as in the private sector, spent so much time discussing, deliberating, and debating that it rarely got around to deciding anything.

So I went about establishing my own private energy school—what I termed my "kitchen cabinet"—and selected as my "professors" the men in the administration who impressed me most with their knowledge of energy: James Akins, a State Department expert who, in short order, would become ambassador to Saudi Arabia; Pete Flanigan; Stephen Wakefield of the Department of the Interior; Duke Ligon and William Johnson, energy advisers in the Treasury Department; and Jack Bennett, a former (and future) Exxon executive.

For three months, we met nights and weekends as my "tutors" generously educated me on energy—oil, gas, imports, exports, shipping, transportation, trucking, pipelines, petrochemicals, thermal energy, water falls, the mandatory import quota policy—and the international implications of the most complex, intricate industry on earth. We survived on greasy hamburgers and pizzas, delivered to my office at 10 p.m. and consumed into the wee hours of the morning. They gave me specific assignments, homework essentially, and I worked harder than I ever had in school, devouring a wealth of information. The more I learned, the worse it looked. And the more I learned, the more apparent that the government, with its controls, regulations, and subsidies, was the prime culprit.

By the time I took over the Oil Policy Committee, we were in the beginning stages of a government-manufactured crisis, and an immediate response was required. We quickly established three general goals: an improved distribution system for import licenses; a long-range approach that would prove both stable and predictable; and a program to stimulate adequate domestic exploration and encourage refinery construction.

We were determined to help the president reach his goal of energy independence but encountered, at first, indifference, and then abject hostility on Capitol Hill. At one of my first appearances before a congressional committee, I found myself the target of a bizarre tirade by then congressman (and later senator from Iowa) John Culver. He screamed and yelled at me, blaming *me* for the energy problem. I quickly concluded that he was insane.

"I've only been in government for sixty days, for God's sake," I whispered to two colleagues who had accompanied me to the testimony. "Even *I* can't do that much damage in sixty days!"

The congressman's staff later apologized to me for the incident, which proved a precursor for things to come: For the next four years, it seemed I was forever delivering to members of Congress the last message they ever wanted to hear: that the government in general and Congress in particular were responsible for both the economic and energy crises. I appeared on Capitol Hill some four hundred times before elected representatives whom I once described in an unguarded moment as "those coconuts on the Hill." Their ignorance and arrogance seemed to flow in reverse proportion to their importance; a psychiatrist might say they suffered from delusions of relevance.

During a rare (at that time) appearance at a cabinet meeting, I grasped the unexpected opportunity to tell the president my views.

While George Shultz was out of the country, I attended a cabinet meeting in his place as acting treasury secretary. Although I was scheduled to deliver a report on the economy, I instead addressed the energy situation, and implored the president to act quickly and decisively. President Nixon, normally bored by such abstract discussions, took interest, if for no other reason than that the Democrats, led by Senator Henry "Scoop" Jackson, were making energy a major political issue; additionally, anything that might get Watergate off the front page was automatically appealing.

The president reacted the way he always did when truly interested in something: Head cocked to one side, he pulled off the top of a fountain pen with his teeth and began writing deliberatively.

He immediately grasped that we were on the brink of an ever-worsening energy problem and, characteristically, took prompt action. By the spring of 1973, the president succeeded in scrapping the mandatory quota system, but much of the damage inflicted by fourteen years of quotas remained. We were heading toward an energy crisis of historic proportions.

Dovetailing the direct domestic problem was, of course, an international problem.

Since the 1930s, international oil companies had functioned much like a cartel to regulate production in the Middle East and refining in Europe. However, the market power of the "majors" began to slip throughout the 1950s and 1960s. Reason: Competition from uncontrolled sources is poison to a cartel, and smaller independent and state-run oil units were beginning to flourish. At the same time, the oil-producing countries from Iran to Venezuela, which had been trying since the end of World War II to exert more control over the oil companies, began flexing their muscle. Venezuela forced companies to accept a 50-50 split on oil profits in 1948.

Three years later, Iran nationalized oil operations, allowing the majors to work their oil fields only under contracts with the government. By the late 1950s, the Arab world, inspired by the Suez nationalization, was stirring with a new sense of power, and searching for the common ground that is essential to a cartel. They discovered that common ground in August of 1960 when Standard Oil Co. (later Exxon Corp.) of New Jersey initiated a wave of price reductions on Middle East crude.

Arab nations were so infuriated that they were able, for the first time, to put aside some of their historic hostilities and territorial disputes and unite, at least to the extent that they could jointly agree at a meeting in Baghdad on September 14, 1960, to establish a cartel. The cartel succeeded in forcing oil companies to rescind most of the price cuts. But there still existed a worldwide glut of oil, so the cartel's collusive power was restricted by the normal market forces of supply and demand. By the 1970s, the demand for oil remained insatiable while production peaked. At long last, the Middle East cartel was in a position to exploit its position of power. All it needed was a pretext.

Concurrently, Watergate, the scandal that began with what the administration had officially dismissed, accurately, as a "third-rate burglary" at the headquarters of the Democratic National Committee, was becoming more of a distraction.

In January 1973, seven of the men indicted for burglarizing the Watergate apartment complex, were convicted—five by guilty pleas and two, G. Gordon Liddy and James W. McCord, by jury verdict. On March 1, 1973, John Mitchell was indicted,[2] along with Bob Haldeman, John Ehrlichman, Chuck Colson, and various others,[3] on allegations of involvement in a cover-up.

On April 30, 1973, the president announced the resignations of Haldeman and Ehrlichman,[4] two of his closest confidantes, and Attorney General Richard Kleindienst (who was John Mitchell's successor), and the firing of John Dean, the counsel to the president.[5]

On May 8, 1973, George Shultz and I were waiting outside the Oval Office for an appointment with the president when General Alexander Haig, Jr., one of our most distinguished military leaders, rushed by us.

General Haig, a four-star general, had been Henry Kissinger's top aide when Henry was director of the National Security Council. He was commander of NATO and a highly respected general. Later, he would serve as President Ronald Reagan's secretary of state.

The evening before, General Haig had received a call from Bob Haldeman, who said the president wanted to see him. The general was, at the time, stationed at Fort Benning, Georgia, and was eager to finish his military career as a soldier.

"Congratulations, General," George said. "You're the new chief of staff."

"I sure hope not," General Haig said. "I've been practicing my speech and I am going to tell the president I don't want it."

I looked over at George and grinned, recalling a similar declaration a few years earlier by John Mitchell, and remembering my own initial meeting with the president at Camp David. It is very difficult to turn a president down when he doesn't ask you if you want a position, but tells you which position you will occupy.

Less than five minutes later, General Haig walked out of the Oval Office with a grim expression and a new title: chief of staff.

Meanwhile, the president initiated the Special Energy Committee, headed by Charles J. DiBona, to coordinate energy analysis among the various agencies, while continuing to stress the importance of establishing an energy department. At the urging of Roy Ash, the director of the Office of Management and Budget, President Nixon established the Energy Policy Office on June 29, 1973. Governor John A. Love of Colorado was responsible for formulating and coordinating energy policies while Charlie DiBona remained the liaison between the new office and the White House. I remained, for the time being, head of the Oil Policy Committee.

Our days were a nonstop exercise in speeches, meetings, interviews, and congressional testimony. The phone never stopped. My appointment schedule spanned at least twelve hours, and was always subject to last minute changes.

But my home life was beginning to stabilize, or so I thought. I had purchased a large stucco house with a swimming pool and stables in McLean, Virginia, and was very much looking forward to the family joining me. Carol moved the family down after school adjourned for the summer, just before I would take on additional responsibilities that would add both excitement and turmoil to our lives.

The first rumblings of a possible Arab oil embargo began in the spring of 1973 and, within months, King Faisal of Saudi Arabia was publicly warning that unless we changed our policy toward Israel, there would be a reduction in oil. President Nixon, in a press conference of September 5, declared that the United States of America was not going to play that game: "We are not pro-Israel and we are not pro-Arab, and we are not any more pro-Arab because they have oil and Israel hasn't," the president said. "We are pro peace...."

The October 6, 1973 (Yom Kippur), the Arab invasion of Israel precipitated the energy crisis that we had long anticipated but tried so hard to avoid. When the United States agreed to assist Israel in repelling the invaders, the Arab countries, under the umbrella of OAPEC the "Organization of Arab Petroleum Exporting Countries (eventually shortened to "OPEC"—Organization of Petroleum Exporting Countries), unanimously decided to place an embargo on their oil sales.

At the time, we were importing one-third of our oil, 6.5 million barrels a day, and of those 6.5 million barrels, 2.7 million came from the Middle East, directly or indirectly; OPEC (which was comprised of Saudi Arabia, Iran, Iraq, Kuwait, Algeria, Libya, Venezuela, Quatar, Nigeria, the United Arab Emirates, Indonesia, Gabon, and Ecuador) sold to other countries and we bought from them, at an inflated price. So, we were indeed obtaining Middle East oil, although not directly from the Middle East. Regardless, the demand was high and the immediately available supply was low, and OPEC took full advantage of its position.

On October 16, 1973, the cartel raised the price of oil by 70 percent, to $5.12. The following day, oil ministers met in Kuwait and agreed to reduce OPEC production by 5 percent to sustain the higher prices. On October 18, Saudi Arabia cut its production by 10 percent. Two days later, the Saudis, in protest of an American airlift to Israel, announced a total embargo of oil exports to the United States. The cartel, finally, had us over a barrel.

Public hysteria, coupled by intense political pressure, ensued. Governor Love advocated a World War II-type, government gas-rationing program, a proposal that ultimately eroded his credibility with both President Nixon and Secretary Shultz. He was clearly on his way out, and President Nixon was not inclined to replace him with Roy Ash.

———

FRED MALEK, FORMER AIDE TO PRESIDENT NIXON, FEBRUARY 3, 2000

President Nixon and I discussed at some length whether Bill should become energy czar. At first, the president expressed some concern of whether Bill had enough experience as a national spokesman. But he was quickly convinced that Bill was the right guy to do it. We thought he had the intellectual understanding of the issue, and he had forcefulness. Let me tell you, when you come over to the White House press briefing room and you are facing the assembled press corps of the United States, it could be a little daunting. It didn't bother him a bit. He had the guts and confidence—even cockiness, you might say— to just come in there and let them have it.

In early December of 1973, President Nixon asked me to assume the responsibilities of "energy czar" as the first head of a new super agency to be known as the Federal Energy Office.

This new agency, the president told me, would oversee all of the government's energy programs and the "czar" would be charged with exploring ways of developing new sources of natural gas, oil, coal, and nuclear energy. I was eager to accept the new challenge, but reluctant to relinquish my position as deputy secretary of the treasury.

"Mr. President, I would be glad to become the 'energy czar,' as you call it, but I'd like to remain deputy secretary of treasury as well."

"Oh, no, Bill," he said, "you can't remain deputy secretary. This is too big a job. It's a full-time job."

President Nixon had indicated that his plan was to assign me the best men from each of the relevant agencies to staff my organization. By then, I was savvy enough about Washington ways to understand that I would be cooked without a bureaucratic base of my own; the agency heads would, understandably, dump on me every piece of Civil Service dead wood that they had been longing to get rid of for years. No thank you.

"Mr. President," I said, "I must have a bureaucracy that I know, and trust—and I know the Treasury bureaucracy and we work well together. They know me, and they are loyal."

"Bill, you've got a point. I agree with you." And so the president appointed me administrator of the Federal Energy Office, and allowed me to retain my position as deputy secretary of the treasury.

President Nixon announced to the cabinet that I was to have "absolute authority" and compared the job he was giving me with the role Albert Speer played in the Third Reich when he was put in charge of German armaments. The president told the cabinet that if Hitler had not given Speer the power to override the German bureaucracy, the Nazis would have been defeated far earlier, and indicated I would have comparable power. I was quite aware of the tremendous responsibility the president had placed on my shoulders and perfectly understood Nixon's analogy, although the informal title of "czar" and comparison to an instrumental figure in the Third Reich were discomforting to say the least.

My deputy, John S. Sawhill, associate director of Office of Management and Budget and former senior vice president of the Commercial Credit Co. in Baltimore, and I drafted personnel from energy offices throughout the federal bureaucracy—the bulk of them coming from Treasury. We also obtained the staff from four offices at the Department of the Interior: Petroleum Allocation, Energy Conservation, Energy Data and Analysis, and Oil and Gas. I recruited Frank G. Zarb, a wonderful man who was then associate director for the Office of Management and Budget for Energy and Natural Resources and had previously acted as an assistant secretary in the Department of Labor.

Frank, who would later serve in various private sector capacities and public positions (he was an advisor in one capacity or another to every president from Nixon to Clinton), took on a temporary assignment as acting assistant administrator of the Federal Energy Office, which became the center for energy policy and planning.

Within a matter of days, Frank Zarb and I established a comprehensive allocation program including everything from gasoline to lubricants to petrochemical feedstocks, and drafted a plan to overhaul the fuel allocation program to the states to ensure that rationing measures (which both of us viewed as less than a last resort) could be introduced, if absolutely necessary, within ninety days of a crisis alert.

Congress had passed a mandatory allocation program—an abomination—for oil and gas: No government, and no individual, can reasonably micromanage an industry as large and complex as the oil and gas industries in the United States. That, of course, did not stop the bureaucrats from trying. It was an absolute mess, an utter, and utterly predictable, disaster. And some politicians were eager to impose a government rationing program, which I considered disastrous.

Who's to decide which persons "need" more and which need less of gasoline or petroleum products? Allocations would have to be changed every time someone was born or died or moved or got married, every time a business was started or merged or sold. And some government officials would have to approve it.

What would the bureaucracy do about a poor family that heats a small, poorly insulated house with oil while a wealthy neighbor heats a large, well-insulated home with gas? Or the Montana rancher who drives 600 miles a month versus the Manhattan apartment dweller who drives less than 100? Or the family that moves from New York to California and uses several months' worth of coupons in making the trip? And how do we cope with collusion, counterfeiting, and the black-market activities that would surely develop?

In short, I refused to believe that the American people would be willing to trade their basic freedoms—in perpetuity—for 10 or 20 cents a gallon. I opposed rationing with every fiber of my being, and so did the president, or so I thought.

One day I was sitting with President Nixon in the Oval Office when the press was invited in for a photo-op. The president leaned forward in his chair, as if to emphasize a point.

"About gas rationing," the president said as if we had been discussing the topic, and we hadn't. "We'll do that as a last resort. But I want to tell you something, we're going to seriously consider that."

I was stunned, speechless, utterly flabbergasted. Months earlier, I had told a nationwide audience on The Today Show: I "absolutely do not consider rationing even a possibility."[6] And here was the president, within earshot of the media, saying that gas rationing was very much a possibility.

When the press left, President Nixon chuckled.

"We're not going to have any gas rationing," he said, "but I want to scare people into conservation." The president went so far as to have rationing stamps printed up, although he had no intention of using them.

"Maybe that will shut them up," he said.

It didn't.

Every day, Frank Zarb and I confronted increasing reports of mass hysteria. There were no tankers to deliver oil and gas. Lines at gas stations were a block long. Panic-stricken citizens were perpetually "topping off" their gas tank with a quarter or 50 cents worth of gas, taking every opportunity to keep tanks full at all times. Businesses were exasperated because it was impossible to predict what the government would do next. Politicians besieged by infuriated constituents demanded that I do "something," although they rarely suggested a solution of their own. When they did, the solution was usually worse than the problem.

One night I was summoned to a hearing on Capitol Hill where an angry congressman from Oklahoma demanded to know why bee farmers in his district could not get fuel for their trucks, which transported bees from site to site to pollinate.

I tried to explain that the main culprit was the bureaucracy. The government in its effort to mandate allocation had assured only that there would be geographic pockets that received fuel, and geographic pockets that did not, with little rhyme or reason to explain why. However, the congressman didn't want to hear about markets and regulations; he wanted fuel for bee truckers, and he wanted it now. The man could not be reasoned with and seemed convinced that I, like some wizard at his disposal, could simply wave a magic wand and grant his wish.

On the way out of the hearing, I quipped to an aide: "I've got a solution. Why don't they let the bees fly down?" The remark, overheard by a reporter, wound up on the evening news, which made me none too popular with the congressman from Oklahoma.

The energy crisis would get worse before it got better.

At an OPEC meeting two days before Christmas in 1973 (which I celebrated at home with my family and my friend Alan Greenspan, the brilliant economist and eventual Federal Reserve chairman who was about to join the administration), the shah of Iran successfully pressed for the most radical price increase ever. Over the objections of the Saudis, the per-barrel price was raised to $11.65 from $5.12, an increase of 128 percent coming on the heels of a 70 percent increase two months earlier; between October and December, the price of oil had risen 387 percent.

The implications, worldwide, were enormous: With the top six OPEC nations controlling over half of the world's oil reserves, yet consuming relatively small quantities, the cartel was providing over 85 percent of the world's trade in oil. Since the cartel had (limited and temporary) control over the supply of oil, our immediate remedy to force a cut in prices was to decrease the demand.

On January 10, 1974, Secretary of State Henry Kissinger and I held a joint press conference to announce the Washington Energy Conference, a gathering of consuming nations (Canada, France, the Federal Republic of German, Italy, Japan, the Netherlands, Norway, and the United Kingdom) eager to present a unified consumer challenge to the oil producers. At the conference, I attempted to remove some of the terror of the crisis, by analyzing its causes, effects, and remedies and urged the consuming countries to cooperate in the development of new energy sources as well as conservation. With the United States consuming enormous resources, it was important for us to set an international example.

However, our effort was undercut sharply by the shah of Iran. Out of the blue, the shah announced to the world that the United States was importing more oil than ever before—an utterly false absurdity that sparked a reaction of demagogic ignorance on Capitol Hill.

The day that the shah made his pronouncement, I was meeting with several lieutenant governors when I received word that Congressman Al Ullman, chairman of the House Ways and Means Committee, wanted me. I rushed out to my government-issue compact Chevrolet, a vehicle that had been confiscated from a drug dealer (I had previously grounded government limousines to conserve fuel). While walking backward as I spoke to two lieutenant governors, I cracked my head open on the upper edge of the door. With blood pouring from my head, I returned Ullman's call.

"We want you up here immediately to answer the shah of Iran's charges," the congressman demanded.

"I've just split my head open. I'll have to see the nurse first," I said. The Treasury nurse informed me that I needed half a dozen stitches to close the wound on my scalp, information that I relayed to the congressman.

"No! Get down here now! We'll keep you for only a half hour," he promised. I spent the next five hours in considerable pain and discomfort, bleeding profusely as various congressmen screamed at me, demanding to know why we were importing more oil. I tried, *ad nauseam*, to explain that we were not importing more oil than ever before, and that the shah of Iran was clueless.

"Are you telling me the shah of Iran, the world's most renowned oil expert, doesn't know what he's talking about?" demanded Congressman Charles Vanik of Cleveland, Ohio, incredulously. I was beginning to feel a bit like the little boy in *The Emperor's New Clothes*.

"That's what I'm telling you," I replied.

The shah, in my opinion, was not only an uninformed, misinformed, irrational megalomaniac given to hallucinating, he was also duplicitous. Additionally, I was friendly with the Saudi oil minister, Sheikh Ahmed Yamani, and favored a closer relationship with Saudi Arabia than with Iran.

Once, I made an impolitic, and off-the-record, remark to a reporter for the *American Banker*, describing the shah as "a nut about oil prices"—in the same way I might describe someone as a nut about golf or tennis. The reporter violated our "off-the-record" agreement and reported, out of context, that I had called the shah "a nut." The remark made news around the world.

While flying to Saudi Arabia, I received an urgent cable from the secretary of state: "I am besieged by queries about you calling the shah 'a nut.'"

I quickly wired a brief note to Henry Kissinger, noting that the quote was "taken out of context." Henry, who has a marvelous sense of humor, promptly cabled back a tongue-in-cheek retort: "Just exactly how do you call the 'King of Kings' a 'nut' out of context?"

Although Henry and I differed on occasion—rare occasion, actually—we enjoyed and respected each other so much that our infrequent differences were inconsequential. Henry sometimes referred to

himself as the "good cop" and me as the "bad cop," a characterization that wasn't altogether inaccurate.

On one occasion, Henry publicly commented about our relationship and our respective roles in the administration: "I have a treaty of
nonaggression with Secretary Simon. I will not speak about economic
matters, he will take over foreign policy only slowly."

———

GENERAL ALEXANDER HAIG, MARCH 22, 1994, AND OCTOBER 26, 1999
*As the Watergate situation was evolving, they [Simon and Kissinger]
had clashes, but the clashes were the natural clashes that occur between
the fellow who is responsible for politics and national affairs and the
guy who is responsible for America's economic interests. That is a natural area of periodic clash and difference . . . They are both two strong
guys. Henry isn't a direct guy like Bill. Just the opposite. He goes about
everything from the rear. But he has a point of view and he knows
where he is going, the problem is just finding where it is. Bill is not difficult—you know where he is. You can say what you will about Nixon,
but he assembled, in my view, the most impressive cabinet that I had
seen before or since . . . Everybody was very carefully handpicked.*

———

Since progress on the international front was obviously going slowly,
much of my focus as energy czar was on the domestic problem of
encouraging conservation. We had become a nation of energy wastrels.
In 1973, with 6 percent of the world's population, we were consuming 33 percent of the world's energy. And studies showed consumers
were so addicted to oil that even a 100 percent increase in the price of
crude would lead to only a 15 percent reduction in consumption.

As a nation, we had to face the facts. We had a choice between
turning down thermostats or closing our schools and businesses. We
had a choice between fueling the economy or simply filling the tank
of every car we could get on the road. We had a choice between keeping our farms and our factories in production or inconveniences at the
gas pump.

I knew the American people would eventually rise to the occasion, as they always do, but I also knew we had a difficult sales job ahead of us. The simple fact of the matter was that Americans did not did not trust the government—partially a consequence of growing concerns over Watergate and a suspicion that the energy crisis was a hoax to divert attention from the political scandal.

We spent an outrageous amount of time trying to convince people that the crisis was real. Critics found it easier, and more fruitful, to attack the messenger rather than the message, and I seemingly became a staple in the repertoire of comedians and comics.

———

RICHARD M. FURLAUD, FORMER PRESIDENT, BRISTOL-MYERS SQUIBB CO., AUGUST 16, 1999

I first met Bill when he was the energy czar, and he was put in charge of energy allocation, and I was chairman of the [National Association of Pharmaceutical Manufacturers]. My job was to go and see him and request an adequate supply of fuel. If we couldn't get the necessary fuel supply, we would have had real difficulty distributing antibiotics and other pharmaceutical products. Knowing Washington, I was prepared for weeks, if not months, of red tape, hassles, forms, questionnaires, and so forth. Bill said, "Of course you need these energy supplies, and you'll have them." He made it happen right way. I was terribly impressed by his decisiveness, and we've been friends ever since....

Bill is obviously very decisive. He makes up his mind quickly. He has a very distinct set of beliefs. He believes in the free market economy, in individual freedom. He has a lot of energy and is very motivated to do things to carry out his beliefs. He is a unique person because he is so passionate about what he believes in, and so energetic about pursuing his beliefs. Bill is not a person who compromises easily.

———

The press dubbed me the "Prince of Darkness," and called Carol the "Czarina." Some dismissed me as a hip shooter. On one occasion, the *Wall Street Journal* called me "incompetent." Kaskat Music published a tune called "That's What Simon Says," ending with the refrain: "Don't leave on any lights. That's what Simon says; Don't drive too much. That's what Simon says." Bob Hope, in a comedy special of January 24, 1974, quipped: "William Simon is putting in twenty hours a day in his office because he can't get enough gas to get home." The *New Yorker* published a cartoon on February 11, 1974, depicting a couple at the breakfast table, with the wife saying to the husband: "William E. Simon says you cannot continue to live your wastrel ways." A "Berry's World" cartoon in the February 26, 1974, edition of the *Washington Star-News* shows me standing next to President Nixon and the president inquiring: "Say Bill! Pat and I were wondering if you and the Czarina could come over for dinner next Thursday night?"[7] The *Denver Post* printed a Pat Oliphant cartoon in which labor, business, Congress, Nixon, and I are preparing to evacuate from a plane. Everyone but Nixon and I are wearing parachutes. The caption: "Keep flapping, everyone, it's all under control." I was regularly caricatured in Garry Trudeau's "Doonesbury" comic strip as a pipe-smoking energy czar who doled out gasoline like medieval popes distributed indulgences (which, by the way, I considered hilarious). I was even hanged in effigy in Waltham, Massachusetts. It seemed people were paying more attention to the comics than the news columns.

MARY SIMON STREEP, DAUGHTER, AUGUST 12, 1999

I had an (National Outside Leadership) instructor who put me through hell when my father was the energy czar. The instructor found out that I was the "energy czar's" daughter. One night he went on and on about what a horrible man my father was, that it was his fault that we were in the state we were in. He was relentless. It was awful for me. I was nineteen years old. I was upset, and I was embarrassed.

Meanwhile, my life was further enriched by constant death threats, and over my objections, George Shultz ordered round-the-clock Secret

Service protection for me and my family. Our home in McLean had multiple points of ingress and egress, and the Secret Service had every one of them covered. It was hard to believe that I warranted that level of concern, and it seemed unimaginable that only a year earlier I had bounded into Treasury known only as a daring bond trader with a passion for creamed spinach.

One time, a stalker who had issued various threats followed me to a football game at Lafayette College. There I was, sitting with my family in the stadium, while a guy who planned to do me in sat a few rows back. What he didn't know was that there were Secret Service agents all around, ready to take action if he made a move against me. I enjoyed the game immensely, and while there was never any interaction between the stalker and the Secret Service, he never bothered me again.

———

KATIE SIMON MORRIS, DAUGHTER, JULY 27, 1998

I remember the Secret Service being very present in our lives. I remember the Secret Service taking me to McDonald's one day before school. And I remember my father getting fed up with them following us everywhere. It became an after-dinner game to try to lose the Secret Service agents in our car. My father would drive all over the place to try to lose them! I remember the hysteria in the car. I also remember seeing my father for the first time in tails. He started walking like a penguin. To this day, whenever I see anyone in tails, I think of my father mimicking a penguin.

But I definitely lacked a father figure for four years . . . I know I had a very, very different upbringing from my older siblings. We often talk about the differences and the way we grew up. I know my older siblings spent a lot of time with my father and that he spent a lot of time with them at night playing backgammon and dominoes and they would have a lot of fun. I did not have those experiences with him at all. When he came home there would be paperwork to do and phone calls to make. I don't ever recall playing dominoes with my father. It is hard to get close to a child when you were absent for four years of her life, but he tried to make up for lost time, tried to create as good a bond as any.

He is incredibly gentle and generous. He is as soft as they come, but can be as fierce as a lion. People who don't know what they are talking about piss him off to no end, and he can't stand laziness. Patience has never been one of his good traits. But he can be as gentle as a lamb. One minute he is as soft as a pussycat and the next he might be roaring like a lion. But he is incredibly generous, and gentle, and spiritual.

———

The notoriety and fishbowl existence was stressful for the entire family, but it also provided some fun and interesting times. We all learned a lot, and occasionally traveled together.

Once, I brought the family with me on a trip to the Middle East and we were invited to the home of the Saudi oil minister. I read the children the riot act and told them to be particularly conscious of the cultural differences they would encounter. The last thing I needed was for the Simon family to commit some international faux pas.

"Whatever you do," I told them, "do not, under any circumstances, compliment any of the minister's personal possessions. If you do, he will feel obligated to give it to me. So, if you like a painting on the wall or the silverware or the carpet or his pencil or his shoes, just keep it to yourself, okay?"

They all assured me they would behave.

Well, as soon as we walked in Billy gets this mischievous grin on his face and says, "Gee, we sure love your camel!"

Instantly, I was the less-than-pleased owner of a dromedary, with visions of the hump-backed beast invading our suburban neighborhood ("Hey, Simon, get your camel out of my driveway. I gotta go to work!"). I could have killed Billy, and was tempted to make him ride our camel back to the United States.

It took two days, considerable effort, and some deft diplomacy to convince the oil minister that it just wouldn't be appropriate for

a member of the United States government to accept such a generous gift as a camel. That escapade remains a matter of family lore
to this day.

––––

LEIGH SIMON PORGES, DAUGHTER, SEPTEMBER 8, 1998

*My father was very much a family man. We took family vacations
every summer. Pretty much every night he was home by six o'clock
and we used to play cards or dominoes and he spent a lot of time with
us. He used to say that he would rather have us spend time with him
than even do our homework; [actually] he wanted us to get our homework done before he got home. We were able to spend a lot of time
together. He was a real jokester, and there was lot of love and laughter. It was a wonderful household. We always had all the neighborhood kids over to our house. My father was just fun to be around.*

*When we went to Washington, he wasn't around very much. So we
were like two different families, the oldest four and the youngest
three, and I think it was hard on my younger sisters.*

*My father is incredibly complex. He is a wonderful leader and a
loving father who has made his mark on this world. He is always
looking to help other people; he has always considered himself a
very lucky man and wants to give back for everything he has been
given. But he is very quick tempered. He'll react to a situation very
quickly, without all the facts. Sometimes he can say things that
aren't particularly nice, and while it stays with you, he's forgotten it
five minutes later.*

––––

Although each and every one of my children was proud and supportive, it's never easy on an adolescent or young adult to have their father
caricatured and pilloried in the national press, nor for that matter is
it a prescription for marital bliss.

I was preaching a message of conservation, and insistent that my
own family practice what I preached—which didn't always make me

the most popular person in the Simon household. The romance of candlelight dinners quickly lost its novelty, particularly since I usually wasn't home to share them with Carol. The children were no longer driven to school, but walked to the bus stop. We unplugged all but one of our several televisions. Carol starting making casseroles for dinner because they require less cooking time than roasts—and then left the oven door open after cooking to help warm the kitchen. We combined errands into a single trip to save fuel.

One time, I came home at midnight after one particularly grueling day, wanting only to sip a Manhattan and hit the sack, when I was confronted by Carol. That normally cheerful, loving, upbeat woman sprang at me like a cobra, and advised me that because of my widespread unpopularity she had stopped going to our regular gas station. She said she didn't want to be recognized as the wife of the energy czar.

"Do you know how long I waited in line [for gas]?" she screeched. "You have to do something!"

Egad! The mania had finally hit home, and I was very concerned the national hysteria was getting out of hand. Near the end of January 1974, I had lost whatever patience I had with the silly allocation program and on a Sunday morning called Frank Zarb and my executive assistant, Gerald Parsky.

"I want to over allocate oil and gas to every area of the country. I want to flood the market. And I'll take full responsibility."

I understood the risk—namely, that we would exhaust reserves and create a larger crisis and bigger panic in the spring and summer—but I also understood the need to take a risk, as did Frank. For a day and a half, we worked the phones, contacting every governor in every state where there were problems, talking to every oil company.

The oil companies were, to say the least, nervous, and there was some question whether I had the authority to change the allocations. Well, as President Nixon had said earlier, I was to have the power of Albert Speer. I used it, in what was probably my most dramatic act as energy czar. The first reaction of the oil executives was to suggest that I'd taken leave of my senses and was behaving like a riverboat gambler. But when I explained what I was up to, they came on board without (much) hesitation.

"We're going to break the back of this crisis," I told them, "and I'm asking you to help us."

We oversupplied the market, and while we certainly didn't resolve the energy problem, we were able to stifle the hysteria. All of a sudden there were no more lines, no more screaming, and no more hoarding. The clamor from Capitol Hill subsided, and Carol was once again willing to show her face at the local gas station.

————

FRANK ZARB, JANUARY 11, 2000

We decided to demonstrate to the world that we weren't going to take any shit and would use all the resources at our disposal, politically and economically, to break the crisis before it became unmanageable. We agreed that inflation was whipping us badly, that we didn't have a strong economy, and that it was time to do something to break the back of this thing. Congress made us print ration stamps, which never would have worked. The idea of continued allocation controls was not going to work and was only making matters worse. Price controls certainly hadn't helped. The only leverage we had at our disposal was the threat of flooding the market and expressing to the world that we were not going to be bullied. Whether we had the ability to really carry through on our threats is another matter, but people believed us, and it worked....

————

The embargo continued for another six weeks, essentially ending on March 18, 1974, when seven of the nine Arab states finally agreed to lift the oil embargo.

Suddenly, I was never more popular. Opined one commentator: "The new U.S. energy chief is a rarity in government." But ultimately, the laws of the marketplace—not Bill Simon or any other individual—resolved the problem. In the final analysis, there was no real shortage of oil, just a supply and demand imbalance caused largely by the allocation program, price controls, and various burdensome regulations.

SUCCESSOR TO HAMILTON

President Johnson's "Great Society," based on the fallacy of Keynesian economics, had assured an entire generation that they could have their cake and eat it too.

Throughout the 1960s, politicians promised that we could wage war on foreign soil, control pollution, rebuild our medical system, overhaul our transportation network, guarantee the good life to the poor and elderly, provide a college education for everyone, feed the world, improve our weapon systems, and continue to increase everybody's disposable income—all at the same time.

It was a fool's paradise, and the Nixon administration was determined to do everything humanly possible to break the crazy cycle of boom and bust that had begun with the decade that encompassed the Great Society and led to steadily worsening inflation, recession, economic dislocations, and instability.

Chronic deficits, coupled with President Johnson's irresponsible spending, had weakened the dollar terribly. Once the world's most highly valued currency, the dollar, by the time President Nixon took office, had become a glut on the market and a threat to international trade.

In August 1971, Secretary of the Treasury John Connally and, to a lesser extent, Federal Reserve Chairman Arthur Burns, had convinced the president to impose a ninety-day freeze on wages and prices. George Shultz, then secretary of labor, argued strenuously that the controls were a terrible mistake. As usual, George was right on the money.

———

PETER M. FLANIGAN, INVESTMENT BANKER, FORMER AIDE TO
PRESIDENT NIXON, JULY 14, 1999

All of us in the Nixon administration had a free-market orientation, except John Connally, who really was not a philosophically dedicated free marketeer, and Arthur Burns. Arthur would always claim he was not for wage and price controls, but he wasn't comfortable letting the market manage itself, saying we needed a wage "regime." However, he never defined the term "regime."

The president was, philosophically, a free marketeer. He just didn't think it was important compared to the political advantage he could get from things like wage and price controls, limiting soybean exports, slamming the gold window.[1] That's not to say the people who did them liked them. There was a political need, and they were done, and it was a mistake....

Bill was a voice in the wilderness, a strong voice for free enterprise and markets. He is a good leader. He has strong ideas and he advocates them forcefully. The nation owes him a debt of gratitude for what he's done.

———

Controls are the most structurally damaging thing that can be done to an economy and amount to nothing more than political window dressing that allows government leaders to present the image that they are doing something constructive, when they are actually exacerbating the problem. They distort the economy by eliminating natural, and necessary, price and wage fluctuations, which respond to the allocations of resources. The end result of controls is that competitive relations are disrupted, which causes domestic shortages and a concurrent increase in demand for exports. Government intervention merely suppresses underlying wage and price pressures; it does not in any way alleviate the normal market pressures. The moment the controls are eliminated, as eventually they must be, the mounting pressures push through the surface—not unlike volcanic action—and a surge of further inflation follows.

Although the president's initiatives—both the wage and price controls and the removal of the gold standard—were domestically popular and seemed to remedy the immediate economic flux created by the irresponsible spending by President Johnson's Great Society, they were extremely unsettling to the international economy, and particularly troubling to the oil market.

Around the world, oil sold in dollars, so the health of the dollar was vitally important to exporters. Without the gold standard, the dependability of the dollar was suspect, and it lost purchasing power—its value—on the world market. Since the dollar was worth less, inflation ensued: It took more dollars to purchase goods because each dollar had less value.

The oil embargo aggravated the inflationary stress, which led to increased unemployment, decreased real incomes, and a decline in manufacturing output. Inflation hit 11 percent, which had not occurred since the Civil War, and we were simultaneously in the midst of a recession—a strange and dangerous combination (a stagnant economy combined with severe inflation: "stagflation") since the cure for each was ruled out by the presence of the other. A bear market, defined as a decline in the Dow Jones Industrial Average of 20 percent or more from its peak, began in January 1973 and continued for a painful 694 days, until December 1974.

In early 1973, the president was considering reimposition of the wage and price freeze that had been so popular and, on the surface, successful, when he first did it in August 1971. His motive was the same in 1973 as in 1971: political expediency. The president simply wanted to respond to the political clamor from Congress that he "do something" about inflation. George Shultz saw clearly that the controls were nothing more than a political cosmetic, and he wanted nothing to do with them. The last of the original cabinet members tendered his resignation, igniting an internal turf battle over who would succeed him as secretary of the treasury.

Roy Ash was lobbying for the job, claiming that he had been promised the cabinet position by Haldeman and Ehrlichman, which, even if true, was irrelevant since they had resigned in the wake of Watergate. Walt Wriston, chairman of Citibank, was under consideration, as was David Rockefeller of Chase Manhattan Bank. But a groundswell of support emerged from both houses of Congress on my behalf. Ultimately, it was Al Haig who convinced the president that I should be the next secretary of the treasury.

———

GENERAL ALEXANDER HAIG, MARCH 22, 1994, AND OCTOBER 26, 1999

We had to rebuild the Nixon administration following the departure of Ehrlichman and Haldeman. There were over ninety vacancies—top appointees, agency heads, cabinet members. The government was virtually at a halt. It was being run by unconfirmed professionals, and it wasn't being run well because in general technocrats are afraid to take a risk.

At the same time, risks were terribly high for any official in that administration, dangerously high. Your name, your reputation, your family, and maybe even your freedom were in jeopardy. The opposition was out to jail everybody. Whether you knew anything about Watergate or not, you were subjected to reckless insinuations of criminality.

Bill Simon did not cringe from the risks that were associated with being one of Nixon's key people, and thank God he didn't. Bill was in there slugging away every day and doing the best he could in a most difficult situation. Bill was a loyalist who stayed a loyalist, because that is the character of Bill Simon.

So, when we were looking for a replacement for George Shultz, I went to Nixon, who always liked Bill, and said, "We can't just go out and get a new secretary of the treasury. We need a proven commodity, and it should be Bill Simon."

It was a very difficult decision, only because we needed Bill where he was—running the Energy Department. But it proved to be the right decision, and I never regretted it. Bill is a feisty guy. You don't sail on a ship with Bill Simon and find everything hunky-dory every day. You have an agitator and a doer and a conceptualizer, but the results are far better than having some safe-sider who wants to get along with everybody while avoiding risks.

———

Word of my designation was greeted warmly by the press. In his April 17, 1974, commenting for the ABC Evening News, Howard K. Smith said: "When they write the history of the Nixon administration, they'll have trouble finding one single generalization that explains the president's judgment in making staff appointments. He's put into office some of the worst we've ever had... Yet in his darkest year, which is this one, Nixon has filled the one, two, and three jobs in his cabinet with men who may well equal the best ever to hold these positions: Henry Kissinger as secretary of state; Kissinger's Harvard classmate, James Schlesinger, at Defense. And now, for secretary of treasury, William Simon, who combines qualities of open-mindedness about options, yet the ability to make quick decisions, skill at handling money, which is his new job, and, yes—somebody's got to have it—candor towards the press and the public...."

The next day, David Brinkley for NBC proclaimed me an "interesting character... a new kind of bureaucrat" (I know he meant it as a compliment, but to be called any kind of "bureaucrat"—even a "new kind of bureaucrat"—made me cringe!). Said Brinkley: "It may be because he made millions in Wall Street before he came to Washington and doesn't need the work... But whatever it is, he's been exceptional in that he's been outspoken, accessible, and on the radio and television about as much as those of us who work here... And so far as I know, nobody's caught him in any lies, which is not always the case."

During my confirmation hearing on April 24, 1974, I was questioned on everything from oil company profits and gas rationing to tax cuts and interest rates.

Senator Walter F. Mondale, a Minnesota Democrat who would become vice president in less than three years, took issue with the administration's economic policies and accused me of taking a "typical old-fashioned big banker [read: conservative] approach to this nation's economy"—apparently an indictment of my opposition to government controls.

I calmly reminded the committee that free enterprise "has provided us with the greatest standard of living of any country in the world...We have veered away from these fundamentals, and I am just suggesting that it is a good idea now to come back to them."

On April 25, 1974, the day after my confirmation hearing, the Roper Organization Inc. released a poll reporting: "The power of the media and the rapidity with which fame can come is shown by the recognition of William Simon, recently federal energy administrator and now secretary of the treasury-designate, who after a few months in the public eye is known by 48 percent of the public, nearly as famous as TV interviewer Barbara Walters (54 percent), after ten years of exposure in the media."

Congress quickly confirmed my nomination on April 30, 1974, and I was sworn in on May 8. Supreme Court Justice Potter Stewart administered the oath of office, with Carol proudly holding the Bible, in the East Room of the White House. Of course, the entire family, including Schatzie, who was eighty-one years old and often living with us, was present. What a country—a Peck's Bad Boy from Paterson, New Jersey, can grow up to serve in the cabinet of the president of the United States!

Serving as George Shultz's deputy was the greatest privilege and finest personal, as well as intellectual, experience that any man could have. His brilliance, his analytical mind, his reasoning, his patience, his thoughtfulness were incomparable. It was an enriching experience and I emerged from it a much better man.

But it was time for me, a forty-six-year-old investment banker, to step up to the plate as the sixty-third secretary of the treasury and successor to Alexander Hamilton, the first secretary of the treasury and, coincidentally, the founder of my family's hometown, Paterson, New Jersey.

· ____

PRESIDENT NIXON, PRESS CONFERENCE OF MAY 8, 1974

George Shultz is a fine man; he is a good man. He, I am happy to say, is my friend, and he is a man whose shoes are hard to fill. And so, as we looked for a man to succeed him, our search was very broad. There were a number of splendid individuals who could perhaps, we thought, fill that position. But the man who we thought, by what he had done both in the private sector and in government, had demonstrated that he had the capacity to step into the shoes, big shoes, that George Shultz had filled so well [was William Simon]. William Simon's record in business is well known. He was successful. Like so many who came to Washington, he came here at great personal sacrifice.

When he came to government, he demonstrated his capacity as an administrator as the deputy secretary of treasury. He had good training, on-the-job training, under a very great secretary of the treasury. And then when we had the energy crisis, we had to turn to an individual in government who understood the problem, and here he demonstrated not only to his colleagues within the government but to the whole nation that he was a man who could not only inform the nation in a very effective way of what the problem was about and gain cooperation of the people as well as government officials in a program to deal with that problem, but he also developed those programs with the assistance of others, those programs that have moved us through that crisis.

It is not yet something that we can say is not a problem; it is, and will continue to be, but we are on our way to solving it, and the fact that we have moved through what could have been a desperate crisis and what is a desperate crisis for many countries abroad, that we have moved through it so successfully, is due, in great part, to the leadership of Bill Simon... We had a very long economic meeting yesterday,

over two hours, and Bill Simon came down very hard for keeping
government spending down, for austere policies in terms of govern-
ment spending...recognizing, of course, that the final answer is pro-
ductivity of the economy.

———

The secretary of the treasury is the chief financial officer of the federal government. As the second ranking cabinet member, he is also
the president's chief economic spokesman and chief architect of the
administration's economic policies. The treasury secretary works
with the Council of Economic Advisors, the Office of Management
and Budget, and the Bureau of Economic Analysis in the Department
of Commerce to develop forecasts for the administrations' budget
projections.

Under the secretary is the undersecretary for monetary affairs[2] and
the IRS commissioner, who have equal status in the hierarchy, followed by five assistant secretaries and the counsel for the department.

For a financial man like myself, becoming secretary of the treasury is akin to a lawyer becoming Chief Justice of the United States,
and I was eager to get to work on the most troubling economic issue
facing the administration: inflation. Our economy was reeling from
the ravaging effects of double-digit inflation (it soared as high as 12.2
percent in 1974) and the energy crisis was still looming in the background.

In the autumn of the administration, Alan Greenspan was brought
in as chairman of the Council of Economic Advisers, and our joint
mission was to get America off that disastrous economic roller
coaster. Alan, like me, had achieved success in the New York financial markets. But our personal styles were markedly different; he is
scholarly and reserved while I am more impulsive and outspoken.
Although we are philosophically alike, we did not always agree on
policy matters. For instance, Alan thought that my concern over the
immediate threat of federal borrowing was overstated. But, as a rule,
we spoke in a unified voice in favor of checking government spending and reducing the role of government in the economy.

Bringing inflation under control is an extraordinarily difficult and complicated problem, precisely because it is a political as well as an economic problem resulting from myriad, interconnected factors.

The energy crisis was a contributor, certainly, but the underlying momentum had been built up by the excessive economic policies of the federal government for more than a decade.

Deficit spending forces the Federal Reserve to increase the money supply, which decreases the value of the dollar, leading to higher and higher prices and lower and lower purchasing power. The tragedy of the misguided policies is that they were sold on the mistaken notion that they would help the poor, the elderly, the sick, and the disadvantaged. Yet when those policies trigger inflation and unemployment, it is the poor, the elderly, the sick, and the disadvantaged who suffer first, most, and longest. Ironically, inflation is foremost an attack on the poor, because it means that their few dollars can buy less and less. And, ultimately, an attack on the freedom of the marketplace becomes an attack on other civil freedoms, under the end-justifies-the-means bromide.

By the time President Nixon took office in 1968, the federal government had become the single largest employer, the single biggest consumer, and the single biggest borrower. When government exercises such enormous authority over our economy, it also exercises enormous control of many of the economic decisions of its citizens—and when economic freedom disappears, you can be certain that personal and political freedoms are not far behind.

I urged the president to cut taxes by $20 billion, accompanied by a $20 billion reduction in federal spending, a proposal which ignited a frantic response: White House aides were scurrying to party leaders, furiously arguing the political consequences of budget cuts; Roy Ash argued that nowhere in the budget could significant cuts could be made; and the president retreated to San Clemente to decide between my position and Roy's. With Watergate monopolizing his time and energy, President Nixon never did come to a decision on that issue.

During that entire period, I felt as if I were in an endless race requiring the speed of a sprinter and the endurance of a marathoner.

By 7 a.m., I'd be in the office reading the daily newspapers and an advance copy of the Treasury Department's news digest. Within forty-five minutes, I would have gulped my coffee, smoked a few cigarettes, met with staff, and issued the day's marching orders. The rest of what was often a sixteen-hour workday was consumed responding to the crisis of the moment, and it seemed there was a crisis every moment.

I sustained myself on beer and pizza, delivered to my office late at night. I kept three secretaries frantically busy, and required that every single call be returned every single day, insisted that every single letter be responded to promptly and courteously—a policy I maintain to this day. The *New York Post* observed that I spent "more time talking to the White House than to his wife and children." I'm afraid there was some truth in that.

J. PETER SIMON, SON, INTERVIEWS OF SEPTEMBER 26, 1994, AND JULY 14, 1998

Throughout my high school days and into my college years, we had many, many late night conversations. But that changed when Dad went to Treasury. Life changed dramatically.

He was working terribly, terribly hard—home no earlier than ten o'clock at night and out the next morning by six. It changed our life as a family. My younger sisters, Aimee, Julie, and Katie, didn't have the influence of my father's good side. Previously, he would overreact to something I did. I was sent to my room a million times. Then he'd come in and give me a cuddle and say, "Come on. Let's make up. Tell me what's wrong and we'll set this straight." I'd always end up feeling pretty good about it. My father was very big on the "get out of my sight" philosophy. But he never forgot to bring you back and explain why he was mad at you and why it was wrong to do what you did.

I don't get the sense that he was around long enough to do that with my sisters. He'd have just enough time to race in, overreact the way he characteristically did, and then, unfortunately, have to leave. He had so many demands on his time that he wasn't there to follow through and smooth out the situation.

But we always were, and remain, a very close-knit family. Dad is a busy man, but he is always available if we need him. There is a lot of love, common sense, and basic, fundamental decency in our family.

————

Meanwhile, it seemed every day brought more troubling news regarding Watergate. By April of 1974, one conservative ally, Senator Barry Goldwater, was bluntly questioning the president's judgment, and another, Senator James L. Buckley, was openly calling for his resignation.

On the evening of April 29, 1974, the president told the nation that he would, at long last, release transcripts (edited, it turned out) of several of the conversations recorded in his office by means of a electronic taping system, similar to those used by his recent predecessors. President Nixon, the student of history, had recorded most of his important personal and telephonic conversations, and those discussions—which the president obviously presumed were confidential—became perpetual fodder for his enemies.

The release of edited transcripts, however, had the effect of giving a shark a taste of blood, and ultimately resulted in a full-fledged political feeding frenzy. The cabinet viewed the crisis as a call to arms and struggled, with great success, to continue the administration's policies and initiatives and keep the government functioning.

But outside the White House, the mood was hostile and ugly, with Congress behaving more like a lynch mob than the dignified body it ought to be, and with politicians eagerly interrogating anyone from the administration they could get to appear before a committee. Everything and everyone in the administration seemed ripe for investigation. From my perspective, I had work to do and couldn't be bothered with occurrences with which I had absolutely no connection or control.

The closest I came to direct involvement in Watergate was when an aide informed me in the spring of 1974 that piles of tapes had been discovered in a broom closet at the Treasury Building. I immediately ordered a Secret Service agent to guard the closet and called Al Haig and told him about the tapes.

"Holy shit!" General Haig said. "Did you listen to them?"

"Absolutely not, and neither did anyone in Treasury as far as I can tell."

I didn't want to listen to the tapes. I didn't want to touch the tapes. I didn't even want to be in a room alone with the tapes. The tapes were delivered to President Nixon's lawyers. To this day, I don't know what was on those tapes, and I have no idea how they ended up in a broom closet at the Treasury building.

———

EDWARD C. SCHMULTS, FORMER GENERAL COUNSEL OF THE TREASURY/ FORMER UNDERSECRETARY OF THE TREASURY, JULY 26, 1994, AND JANUARY 24, 2000

I remember when the Watergate people were interested in Treasury, and they wanted to talk to Simon about an IRS audit of President Nixon's tax returns. We really didn't know much about it since it had been handled by the IRS. I went over to inform Bill and said, "They want to come down and interview you." He said, "That's fine, fine." They were sending over Terry Lenzner, one of their toughest prosecutors.[3]

Well, it was August and it was extremely hot and Lenzner was scheduled to arrive at 2 p.m. Around one, Simon called me over and I went to his office and he said, "Let's build a fire." I said, "A fire?! Bill, it's 105 degrees!"

So, he has the maintenance people start a big fire in the fireplace and we take a long conference table and turn it around so that one end is near the fireplace. At 2 p.m., Terry Lenzner and a court reporter arrived and the first thing they notice is this roaring fire and Terry said, "A fire in August? Isn't it kind of hot for a fire?" And Bill replied, "Not at all. It makes the office warm and cozy, gives it a nice feeling, don't you think?"

Terry and the court reporter sat down at the end of the table near the fire, and the perspiration was just pouring off their faces. It must have been 130 degrees at that end of the table! They took off their coats and loosened their ties, and after about a half hour they went out the door. Simon and I roared! Bill really enjoyed practical jokes and pranks, and this sort of thing really tickled him.

Watergate was becoming more and more of a distraction.

On Tuesday, July 30, 1974, I was scheduled to meet with the president at 11 a.m. along with some of his other top advisors (Lt. General Brent Scowcroft, deputy assistant for national security affairs, and former deputy secretary of defense Kenneth Rush, who had just been appointed to the cabinet-level position of counselor to the president for economic policy).

At 10:30, we were advised that the president was still sleeping. The meeting was rescheduled for 3 p.m., but when we returned the president was sequestered by himself in the Lincoln Sitting Room, listening to tapes that would ultimately lead to his resignation, including the so-called "smoking gun" conversations of June 23, 1972, between himself and Bob Haldeman.

The "smoking gun" tape revealed that President Nixon and Bob Haldeman had discussed a plan, just a week after the Watergate burglary, to have the Central Intelligence Agency impede the FBI's investigation, indicating that the president was at least aware of a potential cover-up on June 23, 1972. Two years later, after the Supreme Court ordered the president to turn over sixty-four tapes—including the one involving the conversation of June 23—impeachment was imminent. The White House publicly released transcripts of the tapes on August 5, 1974; four days later the president resigned.

To people who knew the president, and the way he worked with Bob Haldeman, the discussion a few days after the Watergate break-in was neither surprising nor significant.

President Nixon would on occasion overreact to some events, and when he did, he was prone to rash judgments.

Bob Haldeman, and later Al Haig, understood the president, and knew that Richard Nixon had a tendency to think out loud (perhaps forgetting that the tape recorder was running, perhaps supremely confident that the recordings were confidential) and, in the heat of the moment, say and propose things that were less than advisable. Invariably, when the crisis abated, cooler solutions would prevail. Bob and Al were generally expert at knowing which presidential decrees to undertake immediately, and which to procrastinate on until the president calmed down.

For example, once after someone in the Philadelphia office of the Internal Revenue Service leaked inaccurate information suggesting that the president had manipulated the IRS, I received a call from General Haig.

"Bill," he said, "the boss is up the wall over this. He wants you to deal with it immediately. Immediately."

Promptly, I called the commissioner, Donald C. Alexander. It was obvious that the chances of finding the leaker were minuscule and I instructed Don to administer a stern warning to his staff, hoping that would be the end of it.

Two hours later, Al was back on the phone, informing me that the president wanted to subject the entire Philadelphia staff to a polygraph—a lie detector—test. It was a terrible idea, particularly since a large proportion of the staff was African-American; the political fallout would have been disastrous.

Still, the president issued an order, and I was prepared to carry it out. It took half of a Saturday to locate a polygraph machine, and I was ready to put it into action when the president rescinded his order. To say I was relieved is the understatement of the century.

———

GENERAL ALEXANDER HAIG, OCTOBER 26, 1999

Listen, the president ordered things like that pretty regularly, but when I was chief of staff, it never happened. I'd always go back to him the next day and say, "You don't really mean this, do you?" And he'd say, "No, I really didn't, and I'm glad you didn't do it."

You have to understand the nature of the presidency. I've worked for seven presidents, four at close range. They all had different personalities, interests, temperaments, and skills. Nixon was certainly not lacking in skills. He was probably the most skilled of them all. But he liked to play macho in front of his staff. You listen to these tapes now, and they sound outrageous. Anyone who knew President Nixon knew that he was just letting off steam, and what you had to do is say, "Wait a minute, let's sleep on it and discuss it again tomorrow," which I said many, many times. The next day the steam would be gone and he'd be ready to march in a more sensible direction.

The mistake of Watergate was precisely that some of President Nixon's people who didn't have the necessary maturity and judgment took him too seriously. They executed what they knew were wrong orders or even erroneously anticipated what they thought the president wanted. That did not happen on my watch. (Haldeman also reeled the president back quite often. The press portrayed him as a fascist or Nazi, and with that brush haircut and square jaw, he fit the mold—but it was an entirely inaccurate characterization.) The great tragedy was I don't think the president fully realized the impact that some of his off-hand remarks might generate....

Some of the Nixon loyalists were mad at me for "urging" him to resign. I didn't urge him to resign at all. I knew it was a decision he alone had to make. What I did do was assemble the facts and provide the environment under which he could make such a decision, one way or the other. Had he not decided to resign, he would probably have been impeached, but it would have consumed a year or more of a crippled nation facing urgent problems at home and abroad. He might have even gone to jail. Actually, that possibility didn't bother Nixon; in fact, in some ways he even wished for it. He was a tough, disciplined individual with far more courage than his critics care to recognize.

———

Just as President Nixon called off the IRS interrogation before it occurred, I suspect he would have curtailed any actual effort to have the CIA impede the Watergate probe, notwithstanding his remarks on the "smoking gun" tape.

In any case, the same day transcripts of the tapes became public, the House Judiciary Committee passed the third and final article of impeachment, accusing the president of obstruction of justice in attempting to cover-up Watergate.

Late that afternoon, when President Nixon met with Henry Kissinger, Brent Scowcroft, and me, he was as strong and confident and focused as ever. It was as if he could pull down a screen and utterly separate his professional duties from his political problems.

The end of his presidency, however, was plainly in sight.

On Sunday, August 4, 1974, I received a call from Al Haig, who had just come from a meeting with the president's lawyers, in which they discussed the impact of the June 23, 1972, tape, a transcript of which would be released the following day.

"I've got bad news," General Haig said. "It may be fatal to the president."

Despite what must have been incredible pressure and stress, I never, ever saw any evidence that Richard Nixon was breaking down, and I never found him incoherent, regardless of some accounts to the contrary. The president was, however, in a state of denial toward the end, as evidenced by the final cabinet meeting held under his presidency—a session held on Tuesday, August 6, a day after the transcript of June 23, 1972, was released to the public. The meeting was tense and subdued.

"I would like to discuss the most important issue confronting the nation, and confronting us internationally, too," President Nixon said as we all anticipated an announcement that he planned to resign. "Inflation. Our economic situation could be the major issue in the world today."

Inflation?! Good God, I thought, the president is acting as if this was just any ordinary cabinet meeting! Can he fail to see the walls tumbling down around him?

The president spoke about the economy and an economic summit of business and labor leaders that had been proposed by Vice President Ford (which occurred a few months later under the Ford presidency). Abruptly, he shifted to the topic on everyone's mind.

"I have a very loyal, competent cabinet," the president began. "I want to say at the outset that major problems plagued us . . . If I resign, it would change the Constitution. Some of you may disagree, and I respect that. But I've made my decision . . . I will go through this with my head high, right up to the end, if it comes."

I had the distinct impression that the president sought and expected a vote of confidence from the cabinet, a rallying cry to continue the fight. But the room was silent, and the silence was deafening.

Everyone knew, in his heart, that there was but one course of action, for both the president and the presidency—resignation—but no one was prepared to accept that inevitability. Certainly, no one was going to suggest such a drastic step to the chief executive. That was his decision, and his decision alone, to make.

Finally, Gerald Ford spoke up.

"Mr. President," he said, "with your indulgence, I have something to say."

The president nodded solemnly and the vice president, clearly aware of the historical gravity of the moment, continued:

"Everyone here recognizes the difficult position I'm in. No one regrets more than I do this whole tragic episode. I have deep personal sympathy for you, Mr. President, and your fine family. But I wish to emphasize that had I known what has been disclosed in reference to Watergate in the last twenty-four hours, I would not have made a number of statements I made either as minority leader or as vice president. I came to a decision yesterday and you may be aware that I informed the press that because of my commitments to Congress and the public, I'll have no further comment on the issue because I'm a party in interest. I'm sure there will be impeachment in the House. I can't predict the Senate outcome. I will make no comment concerning this. You have given us the finest foreign policy this country has ever had. A super job, and the people appreciate it. Let me assure you that I expect to continue to support the administration's foreign policy and the fight against inflation."[4]

I was impressed at the time, and remain impressed today, that while Vice President Ford at that moment disassociated himself from President Nixon, he steadfastly stood by the administration's policies and its agenda. He would neither exploit nor exacerbate the situation. Classic Gerald Ford.

The president, however, seemed to hear nothing that the vice president had said, save for the remark about inflation. "I think your position is exactly correct," President Nixon said, and then turned to me. He started to question me about an upcoming economic summit. I was virtually speechless, but answered as best I could.

The cabinet meeting adjourned abruptly at 12:30 p.m. I was designated by President Nixon to face the throngs of media gathered outside the White House. The rest of the cabinet scooted out a back exit.

"The president sincerely believes he has not committed any impeachable offense," I said as I was besieged by reporters on the White House driveway. "President Nixon said he has no intention of resigning. He intends to stay on."

I told the media that President Nixon was totally committed to addressing the problems the nation faced, especially inflation. Reporters, however, continued to hurl questions about Watergate.

"Did the president seek a vote of confidence from the cabinet?"

"No, he didn't have to ask for our support. Of course he has the support of the cabinet," I responded.

"Do you think he is going to resign?"

"The president told me to tell you that he has no intention of resigning."

"Yes, but do *you* think he is going to resign?"

"The president told me to tell you that he has no intention of resigning."

"Yes, but. . . ."

"Look," I said, "We've got a country to run. Let's not have this tragedy obscure the fact that we have a lot of determined people at work."

Two days later, on Thursday, August 8, I received a call from an exhausted Al Haig. "It's all over, Bill. You'd better get Carol down here right away."

Carol was at our summer home in East Hampton, Long Island, and immediately made arrangements to fly to Washington.

That evening, I was sitting in my office at Treasury, right across the street from the White House, waiting for Carol to arrive and staring out the window in a state of shock. The telephone rang. It was Ken Rush, the president's economic advisor.

"Bill, what are you doing?"

"Ken," I said, "I'm really not capable of doing much of anything right now. I'm looking out the window at the park, watching an old woman feed the pigeons, which she does every evening. It's a funny way to amuse myself, don't you think, on the night the president is going to resign?"

"Come on over and have a Scotch."

I walked over to the White House, where Ken and I proceeded to consume a bottle of Dewars. A half hour before the president's address, we walked over to the Oval Office.

Shortly before 9 p.m., the president came out, cleared his throat, mopped his brow, and delivered his resignation speech in the East Room. President Nixon told us that stepping aside from a fight offended his every fiber, but that it was the right course of action because it would save the nation from a long and agonizing experience of watching its president stand trial. He did not apologize for his conduct; Richard Nixon believed to the end of his life that he had acted in the best interests of the United States of America.

President Nixon completed his brief address and walked toward Ken and me, tears streaming down his cheeks, his mouth set in a quivering frown, and when he was a few feet from us he abruptly turned right and headed into the residence.

I was frozen in my spot, overcome with grief and disbelief. Do we know, I wondered, do we *really* know what we have done? Just a week earlier, King Faisal of Saudi Arabia had predicted to me: "The American people are too wise to get rid of a great president because of something as insignificant as Watergate." Perhaps not.

The following morning, a very emotional President Nixon bade farewell to his staff in the East Room of the White House and then walked the red carpet to the helicopter pad on the South Grounds. I will never forget that moment, when President Nixon turned at the door of the helicopter, choked back the tears, and gave that final wave. We waved good-bye to Richard Nixon and the First Lady as he was whisked away by helicopter, and then gathered in the East Room.

"Mr. Vice President," inquired Chief Justice Warren Burger, "are you prepared to take the oath as president of the United States?"

"I am, sir," replied Gerald Rudolph Ford, an extraordinary man thrust into extraordinary circumstances. Abruptly, and remarkably, a man who had never sought the office took the oath and became the thirty-eighth president of the United States. Over the next 865 days,

President Ford would adhere to the letter and spirit of his oath in every way—preserving, protecting, and defending not only the Constitution, but also the moral fabric of a nation wounded by Watergate and Vietnam.

In retrospect, it is incredible how smoothly and gently the executive branch changed hands. In many other countries, a dozen despots would have literally been killing each other to assume the throne of power. But in the United States, the transition, although painful, was virtually seamless, and a tribute to our democracy and our Constitution.

Richard Nixon, no matter what his sins, deserves credit for his achievements, and it disgusts me that many in the press and academia seem determined to deny him that rightful place in history. He assumed the office of the presidency in 1969, a time of great turmoil, a time when 550,000 of our finest Americans were fighting an unpopular war in Vietnam, a time of unprecedented social unrest at home, a time when our country was struggling through the last throes of integration and desegregation.

But despite it all, and the unrelenting hostility of the national media, President Nixon managed to lead America out of the Vietnam War and bring back our POWs with honor, while establishing fundamentally new relationships with the Soviet Union and China.

It was Nixon who initiated the war on cancer, who proposed far-reaching welfare reform, who established the Environmental Protection Agency, who brought about the end of the draft and approval of the Twenty-sixth Amendment, granting our eighteen-year-olds the right to vote. President Nixon left a legacy beyond Watergate, a legacy of vision that foresaw developing geopolitical trends long before his contemporaries.

Richard Nixon was a fascinating man, a brilliant and complex statesman, and one of the most disciplined individuals I have ever encountered. He was a multifaceted person, and could be a different man under different circumstances—like most of us. Although often described as insecure, President Nixon had the self-confidence to surround himself with intellectual giants—men like George Shultz, Alexander Haig, Henry Kissinger, Arthur Burns, and Pat Moynihan (then ambassador to India and later a Democratic senator from New York). President Nixon sought out superior minds of diverse ideas and disciplines. It seems so unlikely that a man such as Richard Nixon would so badly misjudge and mishandle Watergate, which he viewed as a trivial matter that in no way should have been the undoing of his presidency—an assessment with which I am in total agreement.

I will never forget visiting the president in August 1974, only weeks after his resignation.

When I went to his home, I expected to find a man utterly devastated by what had befallen him. I knew he wasn't well. I knew Pat Nixon was terribly despondent. And when I went to visit, I almost felt as if I was headed to a wake, and wasn't sure I would ever see President Nixon alive again. How much, I wondered, can one man take?

Within moments of my arrival, Richard Nixon and I were tossing a football, first in his living room and then on his back lawn.

We chatted about history, his presidency, and, of course, Watergate. President Nixon told me his main regret, possibly only regret, was that he hadn't seen it coming, that he hadn't nipped it in the bud before it ever became such an overwhelming burden. He was convinced that if he had distanced himself from the burglars immediately and punished those who were directly responsible, the whole mess would have been a footnote, or less, on his presidency.

But President Nixon focused mainly on what his resignation meant for the country and President Ford, and was adamant that his own tragedy not adversely impact either the republic or the presidency.

"We can't allow partisan politics to enter into this," he said as we stepped out onto the back lawn. "Go out for a pass."

I jogged a short distance and turned as a perfectly thrown spiral pass arrived in my gut and knocked me back a step. Remarkable. This physically ill, mentally depressed, middle-aged man who appears so awkward and uncoordinated had just delivered a picture-perfect bullet pass like a star athlete in his prime. A walking contradiction, I thought at the time, a man so complex and unusual that I'm not sure anyone could truly figure him out or really understand what makes him tick, including himself.

I lobbed the football back and he caught it gracefully.

"Republicans and Democrats have to get behind this president and support him," he said.

In the later years, I visited President Nixon on many occasions at his residence in Saddle River, New Jersey, just an hour from my own home. I was always struck by the sharpness of his mind and—believe it or not—his charisma. Despite his image as a stiff and humorless man, I found Richard Nixon fun, charming, enchanting, and witty. Certainly he was shy and, at first, uncomfortable around people. But he was extraordinarily charismatic and, on an intellectual level, perpetually engaging.

President Nixon was truly a citizen of the world, a man who understood history and could discuss the great leaders and great nations with great passion. He remained utterly fascinated by politics and politicians, and to his dying day remained an astute observer of the political universe. Often, he would write or call me, analyzing current affairs in the context of world history, considering the geopolitical implications of a particular policy, or hypothesizing about potential political scenarios.

In 1981, President Nixon called and asked if I would be willing to serve as president of his foundation, which was formed to raise funds for a library. I told him that I'd be more than willing, that I would be honored beyond measure, and immediately began raising funds.

I contributed $1 million myself, and the Olin Foundation donated another $1 million. We called business leaders across the country and appealed for their help. I found them amazingly receptive and supportive, and all told we raised about $26 million to build one of the finest presidential libraries ever erected. Built on the site of the president's birthplace in Yorba Linda, California, the Nixon library was the first presidential library ever constructed *without taxpayer funds*—a fact which gives me, and gave him, great pride and satisfaction. It was a joy to be a part of that effort.

JOHN H. TAYLOR, EXECUTIVE DIRECTOR OF THE NIXON LIBRARY &
BIRTHPLACE FOUNDATION, AUG. 12, 1998

*I was President Nixon's assistant from 1984 to 1990 and worked in
that office as a researcher in the four years beginning in 1980. In 1981,
Mr. Simon agreed to undertake the then Herculean challenge of being
the founding president of the Nixon Library Foundation. This was, I
stress, barely seven years after Watergate. It was an act of extraordinary faith and friendship and resulted in the establishment in 1990 of
the first presidential library ever to operate without taxpayer funds. Bill
Simon has an absolutely relentless desire to achieve his goal.*

*The president has always commanded great loyalty among the peo-
ple who served with him, just because of the kind of man that he was.
But Mr. Simon was among a handful—a large handful, but a handful—whom the president would say was 100 percent rock solid. Bill
Simon offered a kind of loyalty that was not blind, but was fervent,
intellectually rigorous. He was just utterly dependable, always available, always eager to help if the president asked....*

*Obviously, the Nixon administration did not end in an orthodox
manner. But President Nixon was proud as he observed the Ford
administration—that President Ford came to rely so heavily on Secretary Simon's advice during critical debates on how to fight inflation
and boost economic growth. When Richard Nixon looked at that
administration, captained by his second vice president, he was proud
to see his last secretary of the treasury playing a key role, proud as
well to see the man whom he nominated to be chairman of the Council of Economic Advisers, Alan Greenspan, also playing a key role. It
was a source of comfort and pride to the president to see Bill Simon
helping to continue the legacy.*

————

In January 1994, the library added a new "think tank" devoted to
philosophical and strategic analysis of America's world role.

The Nixon Center for Peace and Freedom (now based in Washington) was launched in Yorba Linda on the twenty-fifty anniversary
of President Nixon's first inauguration, and I was honored to serve as

master of ceremonies at an extraordinary reunion of the cabinet. Henry Kissinger spoke of President Nixon's foreign policy legacy. George Shultz discussed his domestic legacy. Bill Rogers talked about his impact on politics.

But President Nixon stole the show with a grateful and graceful speech, combining his unprecedented insight and infectiously optimistic thoughts about the world's future with characteristic humor and wit. President Nixon predicted that in the twenty-first century "freedom, political freedom, will be the rule rather than the exception because the communications revolution has had the effect of making dictatorships unviable. They cannot stand having their closed societies open up."

In reviewing his own career, the president posed a question on everyone's mind: Was it worth it?

"Politics," he said, "is never going to be heaven, and sometimes it's hell. But it was worth the trip."

I remember upon hearing those words thinking how privileged I was to have been along for at least part of this great man's journey. Three months later, Richard Nixon died, and the world lost a true Renaissance man.

Regardless of the way President Nixon is portrayed in the press, I am honored and humbled to have my name associated with his, and strongly believe that when the shock of Watergate and Vietnam subsides, history will deal fairly with the thirty-seventh president. Richard Nixon may well have been the last casualty of Vietnam and the era of cynicism that unpopular war generated. Yet he did not permit the tragedies that befell him to destroy his presidency or himself. Lesser men would have given up the fight.

In the Center
of the Storm

Shortly after taking the oath of office, Gerald Ford prepared to
address the nation for the first time as its new president. I stood
with the entire cabinet, waiting for the moment to make our entrance
before the audience and the television cameras. It was a somber
moment, the likes of which had never before been witnessed in America: a president who had not once been elected nationally accompanied by a cabinet he played no part in selecting.

President Ford spoke for only seven minutes, "just a little straight
talk among friends," in an atmosphere thick with emotion and uncertainty. There were myriad questions: Where is this country heading?
What have we done in ousting our twice-elected leader, Richard
Nixon? And what manner of man is this who takes his place?

Politically and emotionally, the nation was still dealing with
Watergate. Militarily, the war in Vietnam had not ended. Economically, we were struggling with inflation. And while the energy crisis
had abated for the moment, it lingered in the background like a cancer in remission, but uncured.

Gerald Ford, the most unpretentious of men, promised nothing but
honesty, candor, and openness. The new president was humbled but

not intimidated by the challenges ahead. I was immediately impressed and confident that the nation was in good hands. But my role, if any, remained uncertain. I did not, at that moment, know if I would stay or leave—or even if I had any choice in the matter. President Ford had not expressed his wishes to me.

Around the same time, Billy Salomon developed a brain tumor, leaving the future leadership of Salomon Brothers in doubt. Although the tumor later proved to be benign, Billy's fate and the firm's were unclear in the summer of 1974. John Gutfreund, managing partner, came to see me.

"Please come back," John begged. "I am not a managing partner. I'm not good with people. We will be equal partners. You know the success that the two of us can bring to this firm."

———

JOHN GUTFREUND, JUNE 17, 1999

Bill was extremely gregarious, personable, and a member of the fraternity of municipal traders. He got along with people. He is a man of strong opinions but very sociable. He is also a shrewd judge of character and of the markets, and he uses his abilities extremely well.

Bill networked well and I thought he would be wonderful as a great outside representative for us. I could do a reasonable job as an inside person, but I had none of Billy's sociable qualities. I thought he would have been a big positive for Salomon.

Whereas we are different, I have a high regard for Bill. He is a loyal, decent guy. When I had some trouble in my life, he was totally loyal to me. He was willing to stick his neck out for me, which was darned nice of him. But Bill is that way. Bill is a believer in friendship and loyalty. If you are his friend, you are his friend. It is a rare quality.

———

When I went into government, I told my partners at Salomon Brothers that I'd be back in two years. With the change in administrations, I thought it might be an appropriate time to return to private life. The president who had appointed me was gone, and the new president deserved a cabinet of his own design.

A president elevated to the White House through the normal election process has an eleven-week span between election day and inauguration to recruit key personnel. Additionally, having just survived a prolonged campaign process, he is surrounded by a multiskilled and large staff of advisors. Even presidents who rise from the vice presidency, assuming the high office upon the death of the chief executive, have active operations that ease their transition.

Gerald Ford had none of those advantages, and while I was more than happy to help him in any way that I could, I was equally mindful of staying out of the way if that was his preference. Henry Kissinger shared my sentiments and we went in together to hand-deliver our resignations to President Ford.

President Ford quickly glanced at the papers we handed him, saw what they were, and handed them back.

"I will not even consider accepting your resignations," the president said. "You are among the few people I intend to keep. I would like you to pledge that you will stay throughout my administration."

The president had requested my services in his administration; Salomon Brothers would have to wait. It was as simple as that. I immediately got to work on the goals and objectives of the new president.

Only four weeks after his administration began, President Ford made a decision that probably cost him tremendous political capital.

After attending services at St. John's Episcopal Church just across Lafayette Square from the White House on September 8, 1974, the president announced that he was granting a "full, free, and absolute pardon unto Richard Nixon for all offenses" he committed or may have committed while president.

I was on Air Force II flying home from Europe with Federal Reserve Chairman Arthur Burns when we heard the news. I felt a sense of relief, and hoped that, as President Ford had said at his inauguration, the "long national nightmare" was truly at an end.

Gerald Ford simply viewed the pardon as the right thing to do, so he did it, with a full realization of the likely political and historical consequences. By pardoning Nixon, President Ford sacrificed any potential "honeymoon" he may have had with Congress. Additionally, some pundits in the press had convinced themselves that there was some sort of "deal" between Presidents Nixon and Ford—an utterly absurd hypothesis that some know-nothing prognosticators continue to advance.

Regardless, with the congressional elections looming, many Republican politicians were running scared in the wake of Watergate. Compounding their election-year jitters, the economy was in a dither: the longest recession since World War II; unemployment above 6 percent, and projected to rise even higher by November; inflation running at a disastrous 12 percent. More than any other issue, the battle against inflation defined the basic theme of the Ford years vis-à-vis the Nixon administration.

President Nixon, the pragmatist, had accepted as sound, and inevitable, the mixed private and public economic system that had prevailed since the New Deal. Although he thought the system was susceptible to abuse when liberals were in control—as it surely is—Richard Nixon believed firmly that the mixed economy could succeed beautifully under prudent administration.

President Ford, in contrast, was convinced that a mixed economy was inherently predisposed to waves of inflation tempered only by the troughs of recession.

Consequently, the Ford administration proceeded from the assumption that what was needed was not simply responsible management, but a return to the principles—economic as well as social—on which the country was founded.

President Ford, who had considered becoming an economist when he was in college but turned to law, had a firm grasp on the economic and political intricacies of the federal budget, a result no doubt of having served many years on the House Appropriations Committee. He enjoyed fitting together the various pieces of an economic puzzle as much as Henry Kissinger enjoyed calculating international strategy.

In place of President Nixon's economic policy team—which included the secretary of the treasury, the chairman of the Council of Economic Advisers, and the director of the Office of Management and Budget—President Ford established an economic policy board based on a model designed by Bill Seidman, who had been economic adviser to Ford when he was vice president.

The board consisted of all cabinet members (with the exception of the attorney general and secretary of defense) and met about four times annually. The policy-shaping body was an executive committee that included the secretary of the treasury, the director of OMB, the executive director of the Council on International Economic Policy, and Bill Seidman. The committee was eventually expanded to include Henry Kissinger, as secretary of state, and Rogers Morton, as secretary of commerce.

President Ford had, in my opinion, assembled perhaps the best team of economic advisers in history, and certainly one that worked together in harmony. Typical was the relationship between myself and Bill Seidman.

L. William Seidman, a successful businessman from Michigan, was brought in as an assistant to then Vice President Ford in February 1974. Upon Ford's ascension to the presidency, Seidman was named assistant to the president for economic affairs and executive director of the Economic Policy Board. President Ford wanted both of us to be actively involved in establishing economic policy, an idea sure to result in a power struggle if the people involved were inclined to engage in sophomoric turf battles. He assumed, correctly, that neither Bill Seidman nor I could be bothered with such petty internal politics.

Bill suggested that we set up what was the economic policy board, with me as chairman and him as executive director. It was a new and different kind of arrangement and the successor to the economic board which, under President Nixon, had not been very effective. We met almost daily in the Roosevelt Room, which is directly across the hall from the Oval Office, and played an ongoing and critical role in formulating the president's economic policies.

———

L. William Seidman, May 11, 1994

Bill was the opposite of the type of person you normally find in government. He was not only willing to make a decision, he was eager to make a decision—and the faster he could make it, the better. He took a real leadership position and was always ahead of almost everybody . . . No one ever questioned that he was working very hard and that he wanted to do a great job. He was, in my view, probably the most effective secretary of the treasury we've had in modern times. Simon was a very effective spokesman for economic policy.

———

President Ford was under relentless pressure from members of his own party to loosen the money supply and boost federal spending to create jobs—a solution that was obviously a stopgap and irresponsible, and one that would saddle the nation with even greater problems in the future.

The president asked my advice and that of Alan Greenspan, chairman of the Council of Economic Advisers; Jim Lynn, head of the OMB; and Fed chairman Arthur Burns. Unanimously, we implored President Ford to reject the rallying cry. The nation had a bitter pill to swallow for the inflationary policies of the past, and a spoonful of sugar was not going to make it go down any easier.

"Mr. President," I said, "don't try to cure the economy with the very methods that have wrecked it. If we can't finally control inflation, we won't have much of an economy left to argue about."

We reminded the president that while nobody likes the results of inflation, everyone loves what causes it. Americans love the spending, the creation of money and purchasing power. They love government spending programs, but those programs lead to massive deficits—so we create more money to finance even larger deficits. We urged President Ford to put the government on a diet and to

adopt policies to promote savings, investment, and increased productivity. We noted that, in the long run, increased productivity
would mean more goods and services at cheaper prices and, consequently, more jobs.

President Ford, always a true portrait of political courage, listened
intently and made a decision, a sound decision for the nation, if not
so good for the shortsighted interests of politicians. He fully understood that good economics is frequently bad politics, and that there
could be no overnight cure for an economic crisis that had been evolving for decades. Gerald Ford was not about to jeopardize the economic health of the nation to salvage a few congressional seats.

The economy could not, and did not, turn around in time for the
election, and the Democrats swept the 1974 congressional elections,
winning huge "veto proof" majorities comprised partially of abrasive
young liberals. (The "veto proof" majorities were disorganized and
weakly led, thus the new Congress was more of an irritant than a
force; President Ford vetoed sixty-six bills, and fifty-four of his vetoes
stuck.) We lost forty-three members in the House of Representatives,
three senators, and four governors.

Since I was the most vociferous spokesman for the Ford administration's economic policies—and the GOP was eager to shield the
president, who would shortly face the electorate himself, and feared
a reverse coattail effect—I took the blame, gladly, and continued to
advocate controversial but necessary positions. I urged deregulation
of businesses, even those that liked regulations, such as the airline
industry, opposed tax cuts and budget deficits, and battled with the
State Department over international controls of world trade in
commodities.

In the press, I immediately became "the controversial William E.
Simon." In some Washington political establishment circles, I was
sneeringly referred to as "William the Terrible." Columnists said I was
simplistic and inflexible on matters of domestic policy, and that I bun-
gled international affairs while wreaking havoc in the Department of
Treasury. Commentators opined that I possessed a "hydrofoil mind"
that zips along at 90 mph, but barely breaks the surface. There were

perpetual rumors and "news" leaks that I was leaving the cabinet, although I had no intention of doing so.

"If I were the president," I told columnist Tom Braden of the *Washington Post*, "I'd get rid of Bill Simon about next May, because by that time he'll be so bloody that Gerald Ford will get credit for letting him go."

I was amazed at the news interest in me, a cabinet member, and stunned when *Playboy* magazine asked for an interview. A "playboy," I most assuredly am not.

———

PETER J. OGNIBENE, PLAYBOY *MAGAZINE, PUBLISHED* MAY 1975

My first meeting with Simon was late in the afternoon of the day after Christmas. When I walked into his office, I saw him standing behind his desk, staring intently at a paper in his hand. He stood seemingly frozen in that position for almost a minute before he noticed me. Later, when we were talking, he seemed similarly intent when he answered my questions. Discipline and concentration are what make this man tick, and I suspect these qualities have been the keys to this noneconomist's ability to learn and function in this most complex assignment.

Simon is a believer, and his faith in the American system of private enterprise seems almost unlimited. "Government is a menace," he says, asserting that the country would be much better off if businesses were permitted to operate unfettered in the market place . . . Simon seems to relish being "in the center of the storm" and there is no doubt that is where he is. I think he feels a strong sense of loyalty to Ford and neither man would stand to gain if the treasury secretary and the president were to come to a parting of the ways before Congress had acted on the administration's economic proposals. How long Simon will stay—or survive—in office is anybody's guess. I suspect that the key to his tenure will be how well—or, indeed, whether—he can continue to defend, in public, presidential proposals that run so contrary to his own personal philosophy and preferences.

Back in his Wall Street years, Simon swam every day and played an occasional round of golf or set of tennis. Formerly a surfing enthusiast, he once took his wife on a South Pacific odyssey in search of the "perfect wave." But his present thirteen and fourteen hour workdays at Treasury leave him no time for such activities. He's up before dawn and at work until at least 8 p.m.; at the office he is constantly in motion. While others are being seen lunching at the Sans Souci and other Washington bistros, this workaholic is gulping down a sandwich, Coke, and fruit at a desk piled high with papers. Food is of such little importance that he sometimes eats the same kind of sandwich day after day for months at a time. (He recently switched from liverwurst and Swiss to ham salad.)

———

Toward the end of 1974, I publicly characterized the projected deficit in the new Ford budget as "horrendous." We'd had budget deficits for a decade and a half, and the proposed 1975 budget would have raised the federal debt ceiling to $604 billion from $465 billion. I believed strongly that the nation needed to begin immediately following more prudent and responsible fiscal policies, and said so.

There is a finite pool of savings in the United States, and that pool exists not only in the pockets of individuals but in our savings and loan associations, our savings banks, our commercial banks, life insurance companies, pension funds, and so on. From that pool of money businesses large and small get the resources needed to grow, to increase productivity, to spur home building, and to provide the American people with goods and services. However, as the federal government continued to grow, creating agencies and bureaucracies and preempting many of the functions of the free market, its demand on this limited pool of savings grew as well.

Now, when the United States government, which has the highest credit rating in the world, moves into the capital market, it moves in at the head of the line and preempts investment money from all other borrowers. Who gets hurt? At first, it's the housing industry and small businesses. But as the effect of government borrowing works its way down the ladder, it begins to prevent some of the better-rated corporations from raising money.

I was adamant that we needed to reverse that process which had exerted such tremendous and unnatural upward pressure on interest rates. My message was simple: We have to stop this. NOW!

President Ford understood my concerns, and took no offense at my position or outspokenness. But presidential aide Donald Rumsfeld[1] hit the roof and accused me of "betraying" the president, an outrageous allegation. I never would, never could, and never did betray President Ford. Such disloyalty is unthinkable and I was deeply offended.

Immediately after Don and I had it out, the influential *Commercial and Financial Chronicle* reported that my resignation had been accepted and that I would be leaving shortly. When I refused to take a hint, leaks went out to Helen Thomas of United Press International (UPI) and columnist Joseph Kraft, who happily passed along the "good economic news" that "Simon is on his way out." Columns overflowed with conjecture, quoting high level "White House sources," without attribution, claiming that if I didn't resign I would be fired at any moment.

I told the press that rumors of my resignation constituted "the most ridiculous speculation I have ever seen in my life" and reaffirmed my commitment to stay as long as the president wished, but the stories, fueled by leaks, persisted. Obviously, someone was trying to force my hand.

"If they get me, they get me," I told Carol late one night. "But at least I'll know I was right."

The leaking and back biting quickly grew tiresome, and there were days when my secret thoughts drifted back to our quiet and happy times in New Jersey, when I wondered if maybe it wouldn't be best for the Simons to go home. Although my goals were partially unfulfilled, we had accomplished a great deal, and by and large both my family and I had benefited from our time in Washington. There's something to be said, though, for knowing when it's time to move on, and for a brief period I entertained thoughts that my time had come.

However, President Ford boosted my spirits considerably when, on his own initiative, he publicly declared his unwavering support for me.

"Bill Simon," the president announced, "is my secretary of the treasury, and he will stay in that job."

In any case, the rumor mongering stopped abruptly after Charlie Bartlett, a syndicated columnist for a number of Chicago-based newspapers, implicated Don Rumsfeld. While that battle was past, there were other pressing challenges and I channeled my energies toward the problems at hand—both domestic and foreign.

————

CHARLES BARTLETT, SYNDICATED COLUMNIST, AUGUST 1, 1994

I was very concerned when these stories started appearing, mostly in the New York Times, *but also in other papers, saying that Ford was tired of Simon and would like to get rid of him, that he wanted him out. I felt there was something funny going on and I made inquiries among my colleagues in the newspaper business and learned that the rumors were coming out of Don Rumsfeld's office in the White House. We all knew he was restless and looking for a cabinet post. Rumsfeld had two positions he could go for—one was Defense and the other was Treasury. I wrote in my column that Simon was being undermined by Rumsfeld, by his people anyhow, with the purpose of creating an opening in the cabinet for Rumsfeld. I called Rumsfeld—I had known him for a long time—and I said, "Rummy, this does not look good to me." He listened and said, "All right. This will stop immediately. It has gone too far."*

I said, "You've got to do more than that, because you've really undercut Simon. He's got to go next week and sell the tax bill to the Ways and Means Committee, and you've really done a job on him." Then, I called Bill at home, and he was in a low mood. "Carol and I have been talking and maybe it would be smart to go back to New Jersey," he said. I said, "If you wait fifteen minutes, you may change your mind." Sure enough, he did get a call from Rumsfeld very shortly.

As secretary of the treasury, I frequently traveled the globe, often with Carol and the younger children who had yet to go off to college. We had marvelous experiences, ranging from tea with the royal family in Buckingham Palace to touring the Louvre with the French minister of finance, experienced diverse cultures, and met fascinating people. And occasionally, my sense of humor and adventure got the better of me.

Once, in 1974, I was in Egypt with two of my top associates, Jack Bennett and Gerry Parsky, for a meeting with President Sadat (who later presented me with the Order of the Nile award, a high honor). We were on a motor launch in the harbor at Alexandria, with Egyptian soldiers serving as bodyguards. One young soldier confided nervously: "If anything happens to you, I will never see my family again."

"You're kidding!" I said.

The sober expression on his face indicated that he most definitely was not joking.

I leaned over to Jack and Gerry and whispered, "On the count of three, dive."

"One . . .

"Two . . .

"Three!"

Over we went, followed by a phalanx of soldiers, fully clothed, still carrying their guns. Gerry and I popped up laughing, but the guards were not amused. In fact, one of them was so laden down with soaking wet clothes and a rifle that he couldn't keep afloat and I had to rescue him!

———

BRENT HARRIES, FORMER PRESIDENT OF STANDARD & POOR'S, FORMER EXECUTIVE VICE PRESIDENT AT McGRAW-HILL, AUGUST 31, 1994

I was doing some business in Rio de Janeiro, staying at the Sheraton. I went down one Saturday morning to the pool. And there was Bill Simon, sitting there with his briefing books. Just then, the news photographers arrived for a press conference and the media guys started asking about the United States treatment of the Brazilian monetary situation. "Mr. Harries will answer that," Bill said, and

*walked away. I could have said something that would have shaken
the world!*

*Later, Bill and I decided to take a swim in the ocean, and, of
course, his bodyguard and the Brazilian secret service had to tag
along. "Watch this," Bill whispered to me, and dove into the ocean.
Now, Bill can stay underwater forever and when he didn't come up,
the secret service guy from Brazil went berserk, racing all around in
a panic. And up pops Bill, laughing his head off.*

————

In November 1974, Gerald Ford became the first American president
to visit Japan. The trip included a stop in South Korea and a meeting
with communist leader Leonid I. Brezhnev in the Union of Soviet
Socialist Republics, where Henry Kissinger played a pivotal role in
negotiating a tentative agreement on arms control, and where I met
with the Soviet general secretary on economic issues.

Brezhnev was a gregarious and hard-drinking man, and a delightful host. Since I was in Russia at the time of my birthday, Brezhnev
sang "Happy Birthday" to me, presented me with a watch and shot-
gun, and invited me to go boar hunting with him in the Crimea. He
called me "Williamsimon" as if my name were a single word.

After every meeting I had with Secretary Brezhnev, and there were
several, the "psychological group" of the Central Intelligence Agency
would always pump me for information and insight into the character and health of the Soviet leader. After my Russian birthday celebration, they asked if Leonid Brezhnev appeared mentally distracted
in any manner, and seemed eager for my observations.

"Well, he did consume a half bottle of vodka," I dutifully
reported, an observation that seemed to fascinate the CIA. "And I
consumed the other half."

The following April (1975) I was in the Soviet Union again when I
led the U.S. delegation at the fifth annual session of the joint U.S.–USSR
Commercial Commission. Negotiations on East–West trade were affa-
ble and we issued a joint press statement declaring as much.

What the press statement didn't reveal was the luxury accommo-
dations that had been prepared for me and Carol, Gerry Parsky,

Jack Bennett, and the rest of the delegation. In the heart of socialism, we were housed in an artificial cocoon in the Moscow suburb of Lenin Hills, where the czarist aristocrats had once lived. The hypocrisy of the Russian leaders proclaiming economic egalitarianism, and then maintaining mansions for themselves and their friends, made me think of a line from George Orwell's *Animal Farm*: "All animals are created equal, but some are more equal than others."

Negotiating with Secretary Brezhnev for four hours in the Kremlin Gold Room was an extraordinary experience. Even communists, in their heart of hearts, seem to know the folly of their economic theory.

Back in the U.S.A., however, our problems were mounting in early 1975. High inflation sapped confidence and we were in the worst recession since the Depression.

In his 1975 State of the Union address, President Ford reported: "The state of the union is not good." The president proposed a $16 billion tax cut ($12 billion in individual income taxes and $4 billion in business taxes).

Although I am usually a strong proponent of cutting taxes, at that point I felt a general tax cut would fuel the fires of inflation without really putting more spendable income into the hands of consumers. Industry was already operating at full capacity and, therefore, was incapable of producing more goods. Consequently, a tax cut would simply mean too much money chasing too few goods, which would only mean an increase in prices.

I argued strenuously that the $305 billion budget which President Ford inherited from President Nixon should be cut by up to $10 billion, and maintained, against my usual instincts, that a tax cut would be irresponsible at that point.

————

PRESIDENT FORD, OCTOBER 25, 1994

Bill Simon . . . didn't agree with our tax cut proposals. But typically of Bill, when the decision was made, Bill, publicly and otherwise, supported it. That is one thing I really admired and respected Bill for. In a cabinet meeting, he never hesitated to speak his mind. He had a strong agenda, which he felt very strongly about. He didn't like

to compromise because he thought he was right. Bill had strong con-
victions and he stood by them. You can imagine sitting there and hear-
ing Bill talk about economics and Kissinger talking about foreign
policy and its relationship to economics. That was really a great
debate! Bill would fight like hell for whatever his views were in a cab-
inet meeting or an Economic Council meeting, but if he lost he would
join the team and be supportive. That's the sign of, I think, a good
public servant. I think Bill was a bit of fresh air in Washington....

Bill had a problem with the press... They knew he was smart.
They knew he was honest. They knew he had firm convictions. But
the press basically didn't agree with his philosophical views, so instead
of giving him an even-handed treatment, subjectively they wrote in
their own views and in many cases were critical of Bill....

Bill never made any real effort to cozy up to the press. That's not
Bill's nature. The Washington White House press corps, they think
they are God, and the only way you can maybe mitigate their ... out-
right antagonism, is to try to be a friend. That doesn't guarantee you
get a headline or a good story, but at least it may help. To my knowl-
edge, Bill never made any real effort that way, and sometimes that
exacerbates the way they treat you. He got a bad press, and it was too
darned bad, in my opinion.

———

By the spring of 1975, our efforts were beginning to pay off; inflation dropped below 8 percent, still much too high, but incredible
progress nonetheless. Some strangulatory regulations had been
rescinded, although too many remained. The president maintained a
valiant fight with the overwhelmingly Democratic Congress on
spending, and vetoed dozens of bills—including politically expedient
but unwise legislation for housing, education, day care, and labor.

Throughout the summer of 1975, I was perpetually summoned to
Capital Hill to defend my proposals and ideals against increasingly
strident attacks.

Walter Heller once suggested that reporters who cover economic
affairs should be required to take a basic course in economics, and to
pass it. I would suggest a similar requirement for members of Congress.

Congress displayed little interest in rolling back the size of government or making a real effort at tax reform, although the idea of tax breaks was appealing to the politicians, as well as the concept of providing make-work civil service jobs.

President Ford, acutely aware of the political realities, asked Congress to pass a $16 billion tax reduction, which he hoped would stimulate the economy and get people back to work. Congress instead approved a cut of $22.8 billion. Congressman Barber B. Conable, a Republican from rural Alexander, New York, urged President Ford to veto the measure; Arthur Burns, Alan Greenspan, and Jim Lynn were urging him to sign it.

———

ALAN GREENSPAN, CHAIRMAN OF THE FEDERAL RESERVE, JULY 6, 1999

It was Bill who originally asked me to come down to [Washington] to consider replacing Herb Stein [as chairman of the Council of Economic Advisers]. In fact, he called me twice. The first time, I said "No." I did not want to go; I had a thriving private business. Bill asked me to come down and I told him that there were many others who could do the job, and gave him a number of names. He called me back and said that I was the only one they wanted. It was Bill who was actually the strongest proponent of my coming down.

Our general views of how government should function were very similar: free market oriented, less government intervention. That is a view that is prevalent today, but was not back then. Bill was the senior economic spokesman for the administration. I was a consultant, largely to the president, but also as a member of the Economic Policy Board, of which Bill was chairman. He and I almost never disagreed; we were essentially on the same side of all issues.

Bill was a very good secretary of the treasury. He had a very straightforward set of principles, to which he adhered—principles that are very much the same as mine . . . He was very much an activist. He was a very effective public servant, one who came in at a period in which the ideas that he held—which are conventional wisdom today—were not [widely accepted]. . . He was one of the people instrumental in changing the way government works.

———

We in the Ford administration were perpetually advocating positions that were roundly criticized at that time and came into general acceptance only during and after the Reagan presidency.

In an August 1975 speech in Bloomington, Indiana, I described the federal food stamp program as a "well-known haven for chiselers and rip-off artists." The response from the Left was immediate. George McGovern, chairman of the Senate Select Committee on Nutrition and Human Needs, accused me of voicing a "deliberate misstatement" and opined that I could not possibly defend the charges "because they are false."

I had, however, done my homework and promptly offered more than a hundred pages of single-spaced evidence that what had begun as a $14 million experiment in 1962 had ballooned 47,000 percent, to $6.6 billion.

Letters poured in from all over the country, from the forgotten Americans who were fed up with a government that was too big, too powerful, and too expensive. The more I saw of government, the more I recognized the limits of what it can do for people, as opposed to what it can do to them.

Many in the administration, particularly Alan Greenspan, were also advocating positions which, until the failures of the Carter administration and the successes of Ronald Reagan's first term, were just beginning to gain popular acceptance.

In a speech to the Tax Foundation in 1975, I felt that I was speaking for millions of Americans who were disgusted with the tax system and wanted it replaced with one that was understandable and equitable.

I said that we needed to return to the basic principles on which our income tax system was implemented—equity, efficiency, and simplicity.

I proposed "radical simplification," envisioning a system that would abolish deductions, tax credits, and subsidies and substitute a system with a simple progressive income tax for individuals, which would range between 10 and 12 percent on the low end of the income scale to 35 percent or thereabouts for people on the upper end. Very wealthy taxpayers, who could escape taxation by sheltering income, would pay more, but the working men and women would pay less. At the time, tax rates ranged from 14 to 70 percent of adjusted gross income.

Shortly after delivering that speech, I directed assistant secretary Charles M. Walker to prepare a comprehensive report on the tax structure, incorporating my ideas for reform. The result was a remarkable report, "Blueprints for Basic Tax Reform," which, then and now, is the seminal work on tax reform.[2] Written primarily by deputy assistant secretary David F. Bradford, the report presented two specific model tax systems: a plan for broadening the base of the income tax and a plan for a consumption or "cash flow" tax.

The first model, geared toward broadening the tax base, involved integrating corporate and personal income taxes, taxing capital gains at full rates (after an adjustment for inflation), and replacing the complex rate structure (at the time, rates ranged from 14 to 70 percent) with three brackets, ranging from 8 to 38 percent. Companies were, and are, taxed on their earnings and stockholders on their dividends. That, to me, is double taxation. Although it is politically popular to "tax corporations," the simple fact of the matter is that in the end corporations don't pay taxes, people do—in the form of higher unemployment, higher prices for consumers, lower real earnings for workers.

The second model, based on the consumption or cash flow tax, would differ from an income tax in that it would exclude savings (although the withdrawal of savings for consumption of goods and services would be taxed). That plan also called for the three-bracket rate structure, with rates ranging from 10 to 40 percent.

While "Blueprints for Basic Tax Reform" did not result in the total overhaul that I felt was needed, it did change the tenor of the debate and seemed to add academic support to the president's general economic agenda, which was centered around the Tax Reform Act of 1976. There was a heated debate with the economists, several arguing against it, several claiming it wouldn't pass Senate Finance. I was so infuriated I blew my stack.

"You know, the trouble with you goddamned economists?" I said. "You come down here and all of a sudden you become politicians. Now, give us economic advice, like the president asked. He's got political advisors to take care of the political side."

———

PAUL W. MACAVOY, FORMER MEMBER OF THE COUNCIL OF ECONOMIC ADVISERS, JUNE 29, 1994, AND MARCH 16, 2000

Bill Simon was the senior advisor to the president on economic policy, and took that role in hand and made it into a leadership position, something Treasury secretaries don't generally do. The Council of Economic Advisors was headed by Alan Greenspan in that period, another person with strong leadership qualities. These two were the two strongest personalities in domestic policy, and certainly in economic policy. In international policy, there was Henry Kissinger.

One of Ford's early interests was in trying to develop a reform plan for regulation of American industry that would take us out of the set of controls that seemed to be causing the relative decline of American industry compared to elsewhere in the world.

Ford was a president who invited help, who knew he needed help, who was honest and diligent and dedicated and patriotic and nice in every way. But he needed a lot of help by some very terrific brains. And I think those three on the economic policy and international policy side—Simon, Greenspan, Kissinger—really provided what was required.

The big Simon contribution, I believe, was leadership. Kissinger knew no economics, although that didn't stop him from practicing it, and Greenspan was an advisor, but the position of leadership was Simon's. If he hadn't taken that position of leadership in dealing with Congress and the interest groups, regulatory reform never would have occurred. It was truly a turning point in our country's position.

Simon was extremely demanding, but very gracious of praise when things went well. Being a bond trader on the floor of Salomon Brothers required the kind of habitual behavior for which he's notorious: quickness, sharpness, decisiveness, instantaneous redirection of potential, emphasis on saying something that has push, drive, and shove....

I have a theory of Simon and Greenspan. My Simon/Greenspan theory is this: Power is influence. It is the ability to make your case for doing X with a president who is listening, who has built a reliance on your advice because it has worked. The president was, to my mind, a really honest, very straightforward, not terribly complicated person. And if he thought he could rely on you, he would take what you said with an openness that I haven't seen very much in my life.

———

When Gerald Ford ascended to the presidency and suddenly had the burdens of the nation dropped on his shoulders, he faced an additional and unprecedented task: the selection of a vice president. Ford, the first vice president selected under the Twenty-fifth Amendment, would choose his successor. He selected former New York governor Nelson Rockefeller, infuriating the right wing of his party.

Rockefeller, who had spent his entire adult life yearning for the presidency (he sought the Republican nomination in 1960, 1964, and 1968) and settling for multiple terms as governor of New York, was a rough and tumble politician, tough as nails. He lavishly rewarded loyalty and mercilessly destroyed many opponents. On his own turf, Nelson—with a combination of political savvy, a seemingly endless supply of family money, influence, and unmitigated gall—was unbeatable, the ultimate power broker.

Nelson Rockefeller had served as undersecretary of state in 1944 and undersecretary of the Department of Health, Education, and Welfare from 1953–1955. But his power base was undeniably on the Hudson, not the Potomac. Like many New York politicians, Nelson had a grossly inflated view of his importance in national politics. I liked, but did not trust, Nelson Rockefeller, and considered him a classic, duplicitous politician—a crafty, clever manipulator, yet a respected adversary.

In the fall of 1975, Nelson Rockefeller, as vice president, devised a hare-brained plan for a $100 billion federal Energy Independence Authority to develop energy resources, similar to the largely autonomous Urban Development Corporation that he had created in New York. The fact that the UDC came perilously close to financial collapse—and the obvious parallels between UDC and EIA—did not seem to register with the vice president.

In Nelson's dream world, the EIA would dispense $100 billion over ten years in the form of loans, loan guarantees, and stock purchases to encourage development of high-risk energy sources that could not attract capital on their own merits. Under his proposal, Treasury would launch the EIA by purchasing $25 billion in a public corporation's stock. After ten years, the EIA would go out of business, and Treasury would spend the next decade trying to recover the taxpayers' investments.

The proposal was ludicrous.

First of all, not very many government programs go out of existence, and I knew very well that it is a whole lot easier to create a bureaucracy than to dismantle one. Second, the EIA would invariably subsidize some good investments, which would be made anyhow because they were good investments and, therefore, did not need government assistance. Third, EIA would invariably subsidize bad investments, all the while diverting capital from other sectors of the economy. The government can hardly run itself; how in God's name would it run something as complicated as the utility industry? Clearly, Nelson Rockefeller's proposal directly contradicted the economic priorities of the administration.

In the cabinet room one day, I was sitting next to the vice president when he started on about his Energy Independence Authority. We all knew the plan was insane. Alan Greenspan astutely and acutely saw that the EIA had the potential to become a corrupt patronage mill like so many of New York's public authorities. Conservatives opposed it on philosophic grounds. The American Petroleum Institute

expressed concern that Nelson Rockefeller's bureaucratic Franken-
stein would wreak havoc on the industry and the economy. Even liberals like Senator Edward Kennedy opposed the measure.

Exasperated by what I considered a senseless and time-wasting
debate, I turned to President Ford and said: "Mr. President, this man
next to me wants to do to the United States of America what he did
to the state of New York!"

If looks could kill. For a moment, I really did think Nelson was
going to hit me. Shortly thereafter, though, I received a call from the
president that floored me.

"Bill, do me a favor," President Ford said. "Lay off Nelson. I've
got to throw him a bone. I am going to support it."

I was astonished: "Mr. President, you're not!"

"This is a terrible idea, Bill. There is no chance Congress is going
to enact this. Absolutely none. I don't want to get into screaming and
yelling over this. We don't have to fight about things that have no
prayer, and Nelson Rockefeller's idea about utilities has no prayer."

President Ford announced his support for the plan on September 22,
1975 (as fate would have it, the day he was shot at by a woman
named Sara Jane Moore outside the St. Francis Hotel in San Francisco). As the president requested, I made no effort to undermine the
proposal, and directed my staff to neither support nor condemn EIA.

Vice President Rockefeller, however, expected my support, and
when he didn't get it, suggested publicly in October 1974 that I
should resign if I could not stand by the EIA plan. The vice president
seemed to have difficulty remembering that he was not, and would
never be, president, and that I served at the pleasure of Gerald Ford,
not Nelson Rockefeller. In any case, President Ford submitted the proposal to Congress, but never actively pursued it and, as he predicted,
EIA died a quiet death. Nelson never forgave me.

Aside from the folly of the vice president's proposal, energy policy remained a focal point for the administration and the nation. The
president was intent on formulating a sound strategy.

The president had appointed Frank Zarb administrator of the Federal Energy Administration in December 1974, two months after my successor, John Sawhill, left. John was aggressively promoting an increased gasoline tax and mandatory energy conservation measures, which neither I nor the president could support at that point. I had advocated an energy policy that would discourage consumption by allowing prices to rise naturally. Our goal was to remove price controls on domestic oil, impose a tariff on imported oil, and deregulate natural gas prices. John Sawhill opposed decontrol, and President Ford fired him. Frank Zarb, who was then serving as executive director of the newly created Energy Resources Council under the secretary of the interior, was the logical successor. It took a full year of negotiation and compromise before Congress took action.

In December of 1975, Congress finally passed the Energy Policy and Conservation Act of 1975 to phase out, over a forty-month period, government price controls on domestic oil. Alan Greenspan and I knew, as did President Ford, that the bill was inadequate, and we all favored an immediate end of controls. Additionally, since the bill rolled back the price of oil by 12 percent but stipulated that the price could increase gradually, the provision was contrary to our strategy of saving energy by raising prices. Also, it would prevent oil companies from immediately acquiring the funds they needed to expand their search for new sources of energy. While the president's policy advisors wanted him to veto the bill on principle; his political advisers wanted him to sign it out of practicality, since it was probably the best that could be hoped for.

I called the White House shortly before midnight on December 21. The operator told me the president was in his quarters, and that she had not put through any calls in at least an hour.

"Could you ring him?" I asked.

"Mr. Secretary, it's five minutes to twelve."

"Please ring him. Please."

Presently, the president answered the phone.

"Hi, Mr. President," I said. "I'm awfully sorry to bother you this late, but I know you are going to be announcing the decision tomorrow, and I wanted to talk to you about it."

I pleaded with the president for half an hour, articulating all of my reasons why he should not sign the bill. President Ford listened patiently and politely, and told me he had carefully considered all of the issues and had decided to sign the legislation.

It was a letdown, certainly, but at least the president has heard me out. President Ford had an admirably high tolerance for diverse views—so long as they were coupled with loyalty once a decision was made—and appreciated my candor even when he disagreed with my conclusions. And always, once the decision was rendered, I gave it my 100 percent support as a loyal member of the team.

"Thanks a million, Bill, for calling," the president said as he hung up the phone.

It suddenly dawned upon me that I had just called the president of the United States at an ungodly hour, and that the president was not only tolerant, but appreciative of my call. Carol, who was sitting nearby and knew I was disappointed in President Ford's decision, put her hand on my shoulder and said softly, "How can anyone get mad at a man like that?"

I wouldn't know.

Unfortunately, President Ford's core decency would ultimately cost him the 1976 election.

THE FORD PRESIDENCY

For a man who spent his entire life in politics, Gerald Ford had a rare and admirable willingness to place the long-term interests of the country above short-term political considerations. That resolve permeated his administration. The financial collapse of New York City in 1975 is particularly revealing.

The city had lived beyond its means for years, funding one of the largest public university systems in the world, providing an expensive city hospital system, hiring workers it didn't need, and paying them wages they didn't merit. Everyone in the municipal bond business knew that New York was borrowing heavily to finance the promises of its politicians. The practice of borrowing to cover ever-more extensive social programs, borrowing to pay for union-demanded largesse, and borrowing more to pay off debt had worked, but only for a time.

In 1975, the game was over and the piper had to be paid. The city drastically and ominously stepped up its borrowing pace. It went to the market for funds eighteen times and inadvertently alerted the buyers that something was seriously amiss. Understandably, the city's cost of borrowing increased dramatically, as did its need for a transfusion of funds. Suspicious buyers, in response to the increased risk, were demanding a higher return for their investment in New York City notes.

On November 4, 1974, tax-free city notes were going for a whopping 8.34 percent, a record. A month later, the rate was 9.48 percent. The city, desperate for funds, was forced to sell its notes for the highest rate in the country. This was perfectly reasonable given New York City's reckless fiscal practices. The situation was aptly and accurately described by Martin Mayer, author of *The Bankers:* "On the simplest level, the story of New York City's fiscal collapse is the tale of a Ponzi game in municipal paper—the regular and inevitably increasing issuance of notes to be paid off not by future taxes or revenue certified to be available for that purpose, but by the sale of future notes. Like all chain-letter swindles, Ponzi games self-destruct when the seller runs out of suckers, as New York did...."[1]

Mayor Abraham Beame, an accountant and clubhouse Democrat who had campaigned on a promise to preserve the city's free university system at any cost, did not see it that way.

When Beame came to see me in December 1974, he portrayed Gotham as a random victim of some terrible financial plague and argued that the U.S. Treasury should buy New York's notes.

Although not stated anywhere nearly as bluntly, or honestly, as this, the mayor's proposal in essence was: The city of New York would continue to spend above its means to accommodate politicians who promise more-more-more. It would continue to finance debt with debt. It would continue to expand public works programs at the behest of unions and further inflate its already obscene payroll. It would maintain a pattern of ever-escalating social programs without increasing revenue (taxes). And in the end, the federal government would underwrite this game, with no strings attached.

I was astonished. For one thing, I didn't have the authority to do something that stupid. For another, I'm not that stupid.

"Mayor, if we did that, the taxpayers would end up financing the campaign promises of every profligate local politician in the country," I said, stating the obvious. For some reason, an old Texas proverb came to mind: "Now is the time to raise the cow's tail and look the situation squarely in the face."

Abe Beame was, let's say, piqued, by my response. We ended our meeting when I requested the city's balance sheets, so that we could carefully analyze the situation for ourselves and, perhaps, find some reason to assist New York in some way. The city never did provide the records, for reasons that shortly became evident: Apparently by accident, an attorney representing Bankers Trust discovered that the city, which was constitutionally required to balance its budget, lacked the tax receipts required by law to cover the $260 million it sought to borrow. Bankers Trust and Chase Manhattan refused to go through with the underwriting.

On April 14, 1975, when several note issues were to mature, the mayor discovered that it was virtually impossible to market the city's paper. Unable to sell a $550 million issue of short-term obligations, the city had to turn away owners of city paper who were demanding payment. The city was at the precipice of bankruptcy. Politicians and tabloid press were predicting the end of Western civilization should New York go under. I thought that a bit of an exaggeration.

In any case, because of its size relative to the other metropolitan areas of the state, New York City's politicians dominated the state legislature. They were more than eager to raid state coffers to help the city, and authorized a $2.3 billion short-term loan.

Governor Hugh Carey, however, decided enough was enough and courageously used his line-item veto to eliminate funding. Governor Carey, a Democrat, actually impounded some funds to prevent the city from raiding the state treasury. Simultaneously, the New York State Urban Development Corporation defaulted on $104.5 million worth of bond-anticipation notes.

Investors simply refused to buy any more New York paper. And who could blame them? There was genuine fear that one of the greatest cities on earth would default on its loans—an occurrence which, some predicted, would create a nationwide panic. Default, I insisted, would not have a widespread catastrophic impact, nor was it inevitable—assuming the state and city took tough actions.

In a September 16, 1975, letter to the congressional Joint Economic Committee, I indicated that a federal rescue operation would do more harm than allowing the city to collapse fiscally. Even if the city declared bankruptcy, I argued, it would have sufficient cash from tax revenues to maintain essential services and pay holders of long-term bonds. Regardless, New York City and its politicians continued to clamor for federal help.

At a meeting at the White House in late September of 1975, three leading New York bankers—David Rockefeller of Chase Manhattan, Ellmore C. Patterson of the Morgan Bank, and Walter Wriston of the First National City Bank—all urged the president to consider some sort of federal aid or guarantee. They simply wanted to buy time and argued that the city was making a genuine effort to control spending: Some 23,000 city jobs had been eliminated just since January; public works spending had come to a virtual stand-still; schools had been left half built; libraries had cut their hours; the City University of New York had imposed a tuition for the first time; city-operated hospitals had removed thousands of beds; fire houses and police stations had closed. Governor Carey also requested federal help, fearing that default would erode the city's tax base, and further exacerbate its problems by causing an exodus of employers from New York.

Salomon Brothers tried to help with an appropriate free-market proposal. Dale Horowitz, who chaired the committee that was the liaison with the city, committed Salomon to be a manager of the first issue of notes by the Municipal Assistance Corporation, a state entity empowered to collect the sales and stock transfer taxes in the city and to use that stream of revenue to back the issuance of debt instruments.

On June 25, 1975, a syndicate was formed to handle the issue, led by Salomon Brothers on the investment banking side and Morgan Guaranty Trust on the commercial banking side. Salomon Brothers and Morgan Guaranty brought in 363 other financial institutions.

The initial underwriting, a $1 billion issue with maturities running from 1977 to 1990 and interest rates of 6.5 percent to 9.5 percent, was the largest municipal flotation in history. But the bonds were not salable even at a 9 percent yield, triply tax exempt, and Salomon Brothers took a $5 million loss. Its effort to save the city was little more than a finger in the dike. Between December 1, 1975, and

June 30, 1976, the city would need another $3.7 billion to keep it operational. Time was running out.

After several meetings with New York City and state officials, other administration officials and I concluded—reluctantly—that it would be appropriate for the federal government to intervene in the city's problems, but only with tight strings attached.

I told Congress that if it insisted on providing emergency aid to New York City, it should do so in a manner that would not create a new federal bureaucracy, be narrowly restricted, and be so financially stringent that no other city would be tempted to follow the same path. At a Senate hearing on October 1, 1975, I reiterated the advice; I told the senators that if Congress decided to bailout the city, the financial terms should "be made so punitive, the overall experience so painful, that no city, no political subdivision would ever be tempted to go down the same road."

The next morning, the *New York Post* rolled off the presses with a howling headline: "SIMON ON U.S. AID: MAKE CITY SUFFER." An Atlanta paper screeched: "SIMON THROWS N.Y. TO THE WOLVES." Later, *New York* magazine dubbed Federal Reserve Chairman Arthur Burns the city's "lord high executioner." *Newsweek* described economic counselor Bill Seidman as exulting in New York's collapse. And the *New York Daily News,* with one of the most famous headlines of all time, screamed: "FORD TO CITY: DROP DEAD."

In November, President Ford proposed direct aid to New York, on the condition that the city balance its budget, and on the condition that I, as secretary of treasury, approve all loans.

An extensive analysis by the Treasury Department left no doubt as to the source of the problem: New York was spending three times more per capita than any other large American city. A main culprit was the cost of maintaining its municipal work force. New York City had far too many "workers" on its payroll, paid them exorbitant wages, and maintained the extravagant perks—days off for giving blood, extended lunch hours, guaranteed "rest" periods during the day, generous vacation and sick leave privileges, a pension system second to none, and so on.

It was time to end the largesse. The city was essentially put on a fiscal diet with a three-year plan to eliminate its operating deficit, curtail capital spending, and establish an accounting system that would generate credible and comprehensive data susceptible to an independent audit.

With those conditions, Congress in December 1975 enacted, and the president signed, legislation authorizing me to make loans of up to $2.3 billion annually through mid-1978 to help New York City meet its obligations. In return for the loans, the city would be required to make the type of hard financial/policy decisions that its leaders had refused to make in the past. Only after officials from New York City and New York State accepted responsibility for the city's financial plight did real progress take place.

Every one of those loans was repaid on time or ahead of schedule, with interest. Ultimately, New York City dug itself out of its financial hole at no cost to the nation's taxpayers. In fact, the federal government made money on the deal.

Shortly after the New York City crisis, Great Britain faced similar problems. Prior to Margaret Thatcher's election in 1979 as prime minister, Great Britain was perpetually in financial trouble, mainly because of the socialist and neo-socialist policies of the Labour Party. In 1976, Prime Minister James Callaghan came to us pleading for an International Monetary Fund (IMF) loan. He claimed that England, and therefore western Europe, and therefore the civilized world, was in jeopardy if the funding was not approved—and the United States had to do something about it.

Historically, the United States has always been there to assist its (often ungrateful) friends. America, as a nation, has an obligation to share its blessings with the less fortunate, for the same reason that a wealthy individual has a responsibility to uplift the downtrodden. The citizens of this great country are incredibly generous with both their money and their time.

But there is a difference between being a charitable benefactor and host to a parasite. I was not at all opposed to lending a helping hand to England or other allies, but I was adamantly opposed to bankrolling its reckless ways, for precisely the same reasons that I was against bailing out New York City absent stringent financial concessions.

Internationally, there was great pressure to approve a loan for England. Prime Minister Jim Callaghan, West German Chancellor Helmut Schmidt, and French President Valery Giscard d'Estaing were all calling President Ford. They implored him to "lean" on me. Henry Kissinger was on my back as well.

As close friends, Henry and I could disagree without either of us taking offense. We vowed early on that if there was ever a disagreement, we would resolve it ourselves, without involving the president. Our disagreement over aid to Britain marked the one and only time we violated that pact.

We went to visit the president on a Sunday afternoon and found Gerald Ford in a small study outside the Oval Office, working with one eye on a televised football game. The sound on the television was turned off.

"I am quite familiar with what's going on, but go ahead and make your case," the president said.

Henry Kissinger argued that Britain had to be saved financially to protect our international interests—namely, stability in Europe—and to preserve our alliances. I argued from the standpoint of economic responsibility, maintaining that the United States could not subsidize the extravagances of foreign governments. Any aid, I insisted, must be conditioned on economic reform.

"The market works!" I argued. "The market is going to drive the pound down because they won't do what they ought to do."

President Ford listened carefully and made his decision.

Unlike Mayor Beame in New York, the president noted, Prime Minister Callaghan acknowledged at least some of the root causes of his troubles and had in fact already implemented some reforms. Not enough, certainly, but at the very least it was a gesture of good will that was conspicuously absent when New York came begging.

President Ford decided in favor of aid, conditioned on economic reform. Six months later, the pound was stronger than it had been in three years.

PRESIDENT FORD, OCTOBER 25, 1994

When Jim Callaghan was prime minister, Great Britain was facing a serious financial crisis. He had inherited a Labour government from Harold Wilson who, in my opinion, was not a very effective prime minister. Jim Callaghan, again in my judgment, was a very good British prime minister, for a Labour government. In any case, Great Britain was in dire need of an IMF loan, or IMF support. If they didn't get it, it would go through a terrible financial, fiscal crisis.

Jim Callaghan called me and urged that the United States should give its concurrence to IMF support. "The two people you have to convince are Arthur Burns and Bill Simon," Callahan told me.

I talked to Bill Simon. Bill was very adamant that the British government, in order to straighten out their fiscal mess, had to cut down on expenditures. They had too big a pension program, too many social programs, a whole litany of things that a socialist government had pursued for I-don't-know-how-many-years. Bill said unless they cut back, the IMF should not be supportive.

Then I called Arthur Burns. Arthur was more sympathetic than Bill had been. He recognized the Labour government had been much too generous with all their spending, but he said, from an international point of view, it would be catastrophic for Great Britain to go down the drain financially. The end result was Jim Callaghan has promised to take necessary steps and Bill did support IMF aid to Great Britain. . . .

Now, New York in the seventies, under various mayors, had given pay raises too generous, pensions too generous, expenditures that were not covered by adequate taxation. The city was on the verge of bankruptcy. It was similar to the problem England was facing. Many people felt that if the second largest city in the United States went bankrupt, the implications nationwide would be catastrophic. I happen to agree with that.

The problem was that, at the outset, there was no real honest effort by the mayor [Abe Beame] or the governor [Hugh Carey] to clean house. While Callaghan made some tough decisions, New York City and State just wanted money. They expected us to bail them out, without them taking any corrective action. The two key players, from my

*point of view, were Bill Simon, because he was secretary of the trea-
sury, and Vice President Nelson Rockefeller.*

*Nelson wanted to be more lenient, and I can understand that
because he had been governor of New York State. Bill, on the other
hand, tended to be more difficult. Negotiations went back and forth
and finally I made a speech where I laid the law down and told New
York that unless they made some fundamental changes, we were not
going to help them.* The New York Daily News *totally distorted what
I said with that headline: "FORD TO CITY: DROP DEAD."*

*But New York City and the state finally agreed to a plan, which
was primarily the work of Bill Simon. What we did was to loan them
money at the outset of the fiscal year, when they had a cash shortage.
At the end of the fiscal year, their real estate and other taxes came in
and they could pay us back. So, we helped them when they needed
money at the beginning in return for them repaying us at the end of
the fiscal year. We charged interest on the money we loaned them. The
net result was that over the five or six years of the program the federal government made about $40 million. So Uncle Sam came out of
it smelling like a rose. New York City overcame a fiscal crisis and
straightened out some of its outrageous expenditure programs. Bill
Simon was the major architect of that program.*

———

By the fall of 1975, just a few months after President Ford announced
that he would seek election to a full term the following year, the president was forced by circumstances to consider his own political future.
The president was slipping in the polls—wounded, no doubt, by his
decisions to pardon President Nixon and to grant conditional amnesty
in 1974 to Vietnam War draft dodgers and deserters—and undertook
a major restructuring.

President Ford prevailed on Nelson Rockefeller, who had proven
himself to be less than a team player when he publicly broke with the
president over the proposed New York City bailout, to take himself
off the ticket as vice presidential candidate. Nelson's popularity with
the general public was dismal; a September Harris poll showed only

34 percent of the American public wanted him on the ticket. Additionally, the conservative wing of the Republican Party had never forgiven Nelson for opposing Barry Goldwater in 1964. Further, Ronald Reagan was gearing up for a primary challenge and it was thought that having a liberal like Rockefeller on the ticket would split the GOP, and quite possibly swing the right wing to Governor Reagan.

At the same time, the president shook up the cabinet with a series of major changes. In what became dubbed by the press as the "Halloween Massacre," President Ford requested the resignations of Defense Secretary James Schlesinger, a caustic man, and William Colby, the CIA director who had put his foot in his mouth one time too many on Capitol Hill. He replaced Jim Schlesinger with Don Rumsfeld. He recalled George Bush, who at the time was chief of the U.S. liaison office in Beijing, and put him in charge of the CIA. Elliot Richardson was brought home to take over the Department of Commerce, and replaced as ambassador in London by Anne Armstrong. Pat Moynihan resigned as ambassador to the United Nations and was replaced by former Pennsylvania governor William Scranton. Henry Kissinger was asked to relinquish his duties as National Security Advisor (that role would go to Brent Scowcroft) and concentrate solely on his duties as secretary of state. Only after a direct appeal from the president did Henry withdraw his resignation letter.

Nelson Rockefeller's withdrawal from the ticket was announced publicly on Monday, November 3, 1975, sparking immediate speculation as to who would succeed him on the ticket. At the time, President Ford was considering several potential running mates, including: Senator Howard Baker, John Connally, former deputy attorney general William Ruckelshaus, Elliot Richardson, Anne Armstrong, Senator Robert Dole...and me.

It was fascinating and revealing to note how the mention of my name as a possible vice presidential candidate raised the volume of the media megaphone and lowered journalistic standards. Truth was less relevant than ever. With my conservative beliefs widely known, there was a deliberate effort to smear me as some kind of far right weirdo. The media seemed to go out of its way to print the most uncomplimentary photo they could find. In my case, it was a shot of me with slicked back hair and thick glasses, looking like some kind of space alien.

Once, Carol and I were accompanied by a reporter on the way to Andrews Air Force Base. A week later, Carol, who had heard every word of the interview, read his article in the paper.

"This is terrible," she said. "Number one, you never said any of these things. Number two, he never asked you about these things. It's all a lie."

"Toots," I said, "welcome to Washington. If you don't speak to reporters, they will kill you. If you do, they will lie about you. It's just the way it goes."

I fervently believe in freedom of the press and full disclosure of whatever the public needs to know to pass informed judgment on those who inhabit high public office. But every right carries a responsibility. Far too often, journalists embrace the former and ignore the latter.

One occasion in particular caused me to blow my stack. I got wind of a story that was being spread around Washington claiming that I had been engaged in laundering drug money while a senior partner at Salomon Brothers. I was told that this absurd story was being peddled by Mel Elfin, *Newsweek*'s bureau chief, and a reporter named Jim Bishop.

I invited the pair to my office and asked Elfin for an explanation. He offered not a shred of fact (because there was none) to support this vicious rumor. Instead, he said that since I was a leading candidate for vice president, it was his job to smoke out whatever damaging information he could find about me. Floating stories like this, he said, was a way of getting people to come forth with information that journalists might not find through a normal, straightforward inquiry.

"Even if it ruins a person's reputation?" I asked incredulously. Elfin merely repeated his mantra, explaining that he had some sort of cosmic responsibility to investigate everybody and everything. I dared him to print his story. In the end, Elfin declined and the rumor disappeared, but not before he had spread it over a fairly wide field with his inquiries.

The selection of a vice presidential candidate remained an unresolved issue right up until the convention. But then, so did the selection of a presidential candidate. Ronald Reagan, the former governor of California, challenged Gerald Ford at the convention in Kansas City, forcing the president to campaign hard for his share of the delegates. President Ford campaigned on his twenty-seven-year record of public service, his efforts to restore the economy, and his success in putting Watergate in the past. Governor Reagan agreed with much of what President Ford had done, but attacked the administration's policy of détente with our Cold War enemies and negotiations over a new Panama Canal treaty.

Meanwhile, Nelson Rockefeller was taking his sweet time delivering New York's delegates to President Ford. I suspect Rockefeller was hoping for a deadlock between the president and Governor Reagan, figuring that he might emerge as the compromise candidate. Eventually, it would have become clear that was not going to happen, and Rockefeller did, at a late hour, deliver the New York delegation.

Gerald Ford won nomination on the first ballot: 1,187 to 1,070. After winning the nomination the night of Wednesday, August 18, President Ford retired to his suite to make the final decision on a running mate. Some southern delegates were lobbying for Ron Reagan (an effort that Reagan himself discouraged) and actually threatening to nominate him from the floor and foist him upon Ford.

Rockefeller, who had been drinking, was acting bizarrely, even for him. At one point, he yanked a phone out of the wall for no apparent reason. At another, he grabbed me by the lapel and threatened, "You do anything to my brother, David, and you'll be sorry!" David Rockefeller was then chairman of Chase Manhattan Bank, which had grown flabby and less profitable during his tenure. There were some rumors that I would replace him.

"Oh, knock it off, Nelson," I said. "Why would I want to go to a lousy bank like Chase when I can go to Salomon Brothers and be a managing partner? You must be joking. Why would I take a hundred thousand dollars a year to work for a bank that's going to go broke? Get off it."

I was answering his threat with an insult and did not and do not consider Chase a "lousy" bank. I was simply trying to irritate Nelson to the point where he would either hit me, and give me an excuse to flatten him, or, preferably, just go away. He backed off, and went looking for someone else to bully.

Cary Grant, the great actor and a loyal Republican, witnessed the entire incident from the top of the stairs. "That was quite a scene you played, Bill," he said.

"Cary," I said, "it was no act."

President Ford and his political advisers spent the entire night debating the running mate issue. By midmorning on Thursday, George Hinman, one of Rockefeller's operatives, sent word that the southern conservatives would drop their threat to draft Reagan if President Ford selected Senator Robert Dole. The president asked Rockefeller to run Bob Dole's name by two moderate Republican senators, Hugh Scott of Pennsylvania and Jacob Javits of New York. Nelson reported back that while Senators Scott and Javits weren't thrilled with Bob, the Kansas senator was acceptable. President Ford called Senator Dole, and the campaign to retain the White House began in earnest.

I was at most mildly disappointed in not having been chosen. I would have run if President Ford had asked me to join the ticket, but I certainly didn't lose any sleep over his choice of Bob Dole.

———

PRESIDENT FORD, OCTOBER 25, 1994

My decision, ultimately, was very pragmatic. We knew that Carter would carry all or most of the south, which he did. We knew Carter would probably carry New York, Pennsylvania. What we had to do was find somebody who gave us strength . . . It was a very practical decision. It came down to Dole, Howard Baker, and Bill Simon. A lot of people thought Bill was too hardline, too dogmatic to be my vice president. But nobody ever questioned his integrity or dedication.

The Jimmy Carter–Walter Mondale ticket would unquestionably be difficult to beat. The Republican Party carried political baggage because of President Ford's courageous decision to pardon President Nixon. In addition, too many voters had come to see the GOP as a narrowly vested interest, barely distinguishable from big corporations, bankers, and the chambers of commerce—a misconception as potent as it was false. Even our traditional base constituency of skilled workers, farmers, white collar workers, business professionals—the expanded American middle class that covers such a broad social and economic field of our population—was severely shaken by Watergate and our inability to fully match our domestic policy to our political rhetoric. I campaigned mightily and never for an instance lost hope.

During the campaign, I paid a visit to Senator Hubert Humphrey, a liberal Democrat from Minnesota who was dying of cancer in Memorial Sloane Kettering Hospital. Despite our obvious philosophical and political differences, I considered Hubert a principled and decent man, and his fate pained me greatly. At the hospital, they were reluctant to let me in.

"Please," I pleaded, "just give me ten minutes."

"Five."

I walked in and Hubert Humphrey, emaciated and clearly at death's door, but still the ebullient, loquacious man who preached the "politics of joy," hopped out of his bed and gave me a hug and kiss. He lumbered back into his bed and I sat next to him.

"Bill," he said solemnly, "everyone on this floor, every single person, they're gonna die, you know. And I go down and talk to them every afternoon. I walk down the hall and there are patients at the door of every single room. It's like a campaign, people shaking my hand, wishing me well. Except this time, it really is for all the marbles."

That day I accompanied him and he introduced me to the people on the ward.

"This is my friend, Bill Simon, secretary of treasury. It's his job to print money, and mine to spend it!" Hubert told the other patients, his smile characteristically endearing and radiant.

He introduced each person by name and we shook everyone's hands, for forty-five minutes, before strolling back to his room.

Hubert was utterly exhausted, and I put him in his bed and said my last farewell.

"Now, look, I want you to tell Jerry Ford something for me," Hubert Humphrey said, suddenly regaining a spark of energy. "We can't allow Carter to win. He'd be a disaster! Here are ten things he's got to do to prevent Carter from beating him."

Hubert knew a great deal about winning and losing. His advice and perspectives were both fascinating and invaluable. After serving as Lyndon Johnson's vice president, and supporting the president's position on the Vietnam War, Humphrey was narrowly defeated by Richard Nixon in 1968. However, he returned to government a mere two years later when he was elected to the Senate. Twice more, in 1972 and 1976, he sought the presidential nomination, but lost to George McGovern and Jimmy Carter, respectively. I spent three hours discussing politics that day with Hubert Humphrey, and never saw him again.

To win on November 2, President Ford had to carry at least five of the eight biggest states. By October, surveys showed us winning only three: California, Michigan, and Ohio. Polls in late October showed we were behind but closing fast, and confidence soared.

On Election Day, we were surprised but pleased to carry New Jersey and garner its seventeen electoral votes. At midnight, we had a slight lead in New York. But when the precincts from the city reported, it was all over in New York, an ominous sign.

Jimmy Carter won a close race, mainly by sweeping most of the South and winning narrowly in a few major northern industrial states. By the slimmest of margins—2 percent of the popular vote—Gerald Ford became the first president since Herbert Hoover, forty-four years earlier, to be turned out of office by the voters. To this day, I am convinced that momentum was on the side of the president and if the election had been held a week later, he would have won.

I was truly heartbroken for President Ford, a man who richly deserved the support of his countrymen. He presided over the nation during an extraordinary time in our history, and did his best to make decisions that were sound, regardless of the political implications. When courage was called for, he gave more than his measure. When principle was in short supply, he drew a line and stood his ground.

In the brief two years of his presidency, Ford rescued the nation from the depths of political crisis, restored faith in the dependability of our democratic institutions, ended the depreciation of the dollar, reined in federal deficit spending, brought down the inflation rate, faced the leaders of America's adversaries with courage and determination, and stood firm before a political opposition foolishly intent on expanding government, weakening our defenses, crippling our economy, and shrinking our liberties.

I had come to Washington because, as corny as this may seem, I wanted to repay a small amount of what this country had given me.

But when I saw the abuses that Washington had inflicted upon private enterprises and our freedoms, I could only shudder about the world we were building for our children. I believed strongly that we were at a crossroads in our national history.

For more than forty years, the power of central government was increasing in our daily lives. As our freedoms were chipped away, we had lost some of that glow that is particularly distinctive about the American experience. Our boldness and vitality were drained a bit; our ingenuity was being challenged by nations around the world. Some nations had even come to believe they could play us for patsies. Our free enterprise system, the greatest engine for social progress that the world has ever known, had slowed down perceptively, and was chugging along in second gear, far below potential.

I was leaving Washington, as I told the press, a very frightened forty-nine-year-old man with a deep concern for the direction my country was headed, but with an abiding hope that it was not too late to turn back.

––––

JULIE SIMON MUNRO, DAUGHTER, AUGUST 24, 1998

I lived in McClean, Virginia, between the ages of nine and twelve, and those were pretty idyllic years for me because we had a house with a lot of property and a barn. I was truly animal crazy and was able to live out my dream of owning and caring for my pony. I probably spent more time with the horses than at home. We had a dog and kittens and hamsters and bunnies and guinea pigs and fish and birds, and I took care of them all. Often, they'd get loose and run wild throughout the house. My father thought that was a hoot. He loved all the commotion and frivolousness that went with children.

We had twenty-four-hour Secret Service protection at our house and my father used to try to ditch the agents when he'd take us out for ice cream or to McDonalds. I thought it was pretty funny, although I'm not sure the Secret Service agents were amused....

I remember going to Art Buchwald's house for Easter and my father dressed up as the Easter bunny. I remember my parents hosting dinner parties for people who were in the news, like the Fords, the Kissingers, the Schlesingers, and the Bushes.

Although I am sure there were parts of it that were exciting for my mother, especially meeting heads of state and living in Washington during a historic time, she was not a "politician" and I think she felt the stress of being in the public limelight all the time. My father, on the other hand, seemed to thrive on it. He worked constantly and hardly ever seemed to be home. I definitely felt second fiddle to my father's job and tried to capture his attention by writing him notes and leaving them in his sock drawer. I drew pictures of hearts and told him that I loved him and missed him.

———

My family life had suffered during those years, simply because I was so terribly busy. As a family, we lost the nights and weekends where there were no preplanned events. There was no time for those important occasions when a family just stays home and talks or reads or watches television or cleans out the basement. We were constantly on the go, perpetually in the spotlight. Either I was working or we were attending some function or other. I had become a part-time husband and father. Even before the election, Carol and I had pretty much decided to return to New Jersey. My two-year commitment had already been doubled, and four-and-a-half years of fifteen-hour days had taken a toll on me and on Carol.

Government had changed our marriage, as it does many marriages. Serving at the top level of government is a heady experience and it is very easy for an individual to forget that he is not as large as the office he holds, not as impressive as his press releases would indicate. Sycophants fawn over you. Everyone is deferential. You begin to think you are invincible. If you had an ego to begin with—and I guess I did—it inflates in Washington.

For four years, I was a detached husband and father. I had become so absorbed in my position, and myself, that I didn't even realize the strain and tension in our marriage. Carol couldn't wait to leave the Washington establishment behind.

———

Carol Simon, May 16, 1994

I will not tell you that I was unhappy to leave (Washington); I was not. The first three years were wonderful and I loved it. I got a Ph.D. in politics and I experienced a world I didn't know a thing about. I grew a lot as a young woman. I met every head of state. We went on wonderful trips. The red carpet was always rolled out for us. We had the best of everything. But it was a very grueling schedule. There were luncheons, dinners, all the time. We refused a lot, but not enough as far as I was concerned. It gets a little boring for your children and a little disconcerting for you, when they say for the tenth time, "Can you help me with my homework?" and you respond, "No, dear, I have to go the British Embassy tonight." What do they care about the British Embassy or the British ambassador or anything else, except their homework? That gets old after a while.

What I realized about Washington is that everybody was coveting his own little fiefdom, his own political gain. Even Bill was burned out—those are his words, he told me he was "burned out"—with the constant press that was so down on him....

When you think of it and when you look at the percentage of marriages that have survived in Washington, it's pretty frightening. Men, even Bill, get a taste of this power. It's not the money. It's the power. It's an ego thing. And it can get the best of you. Bill got used to a way of life where nobody contradicted him. So I was the only one who

would disagree with him, and it made my position very uncomfort-
able. He was very difficult to live with.

———

I'm not sure where my life would have led had I declined President
Nixon's offer and stayed on the comfortable road I was following on
Wall Street. But by listening to my instincts, taking a risk, and beginning a new journey on an unknown path, I learned more about life,
discovered more about myself, stretched my horizons farther, and
savored experiences far richer than I would otherwise have ever
known. Some people might call it fate. Some might call it luck.

But I would call it God's plan.

A TIME FOR TRUTH

After leaving government, I had so many options available—politically and professionally—that I was reluctant to choose any one
over any other. I didn't want to limit my choices, so I was keeping
everything on the table just as long as I could.

George Shultz offered me a position with Bechtel Group, an international engineering and construction firm where he was president.
That seemed to have potential. Frank Shakespeare, who had been
director of the United States Information Agency (and would later
become Vatican envoy and chairman of the Heritage Foundation, a
conservative think tank), wanted me to join him in a venture to purchase radio stations. That sounded like fun. There were literally scores
of other business offers that I was considering. Additionally, political
power brokers in New Jersey were floating my name for governor. I
thought perhaps a gubernatorial run in 1977 could set the stage for a
presidential run in 1980.

But none of those options really excited me, and for a while I just
bided my time. Carol and I traveled a bit—India, Brazil, various other
destinations—but I was restless and eager to get back to work.

While in Washington, my assets, which were placed in a blind trust (and badly mismanaged), declined sharply and, after four-and-a-half years in the capital, the Simon family "fortune" was half of what it had been and a quarter of what it should have been. It was time to rebuild our nest egg.

My first inclination, of course, was to return to Salomon Brothers, where I had been so very happy and productive. There I had been given the freedom and time to meet my family responsibilities and pursue the extracurricular activities, such as philanthropic endeavors and the Olympic Committee, which rounded out my life. It seemed only natural that I would resume my career with Salomon Brothers, particularly since Billy Salomon was about to pass the baton to a new leader.

Billy had survived his encounter with a benign brain tumor, but the scare had forced him to confront his own mortality. He was planning to retire in 1978, at the age of sixty-four, to spend more time with his lovely wife, Virginia.

There was a question whether John Gutfreund, who had served as managing partner while I was away in Washington, was the logical heir apparent, or whether I, with the prestige of a former cabinet member, was the appropriate successor to Billy Salomon. Billy would not guarantee that I would inherit his mantle the following year. Instead, he offered me a chance to come back as a senior partner, making a quarter of a point less than Johnny Gutfreund.

Returning to Salomon Brothers seemed as appropriate and natural as going home to New Jersey, but Carol and George Shultz convinced me that it would be unwise. Carol observed that the firm would have inevitably changed in my absence and questioned whether it could ever be the professional home I remembered. George suggested that I had changed in Washington, become more worldly and politically sophisticated, and that working at Salomon Brothers would never be the same.

I decided that both Carol and George were right, and in the spring of 1977 advised Billy Salomon that I would not be returning to

Salomon Brothers. He expressed both shock and disappointment at my decision.

———

WILLIAM SALOMON, FEBRUARY 22, 1994, AND JUNE 10, 1999

Bill [Simon] had been gone for four years and John Gutfreund had achieved a certain position. I didn't feel it would be right after a four-year absence to say, "Bill, come back. You can serve in this capacity." But I made a mistake. As I stated at my eightieth birthday party, I should have said, "Bill, I'd like you to come back. If you want to come back, write your own ticket." I think he might have come back, and knowing his fairness, I don't think he would have taken advantage of the situation with John Gutfreund. I think Bill would have fought hard to retain the partnership principles . . . Bill would have stood up to those people who were only interested in the immediate dollar. . . .

If I had hired Bill and told him he was the heir apparent, we'd still be a partnership and we'd be beating everybody's brains out . . . In hindsight, it was dumb on my part. That was my error of judgment.[1]

———

In May of 1977, Carol was diagnosed as having breast cancer. A routine exam had detected a lump in Carol's breast. She was operated on by a dear friend, Dr. Ames Filippone from Morristown. Dr. Filippone gave me the bad news. "Bill," he said, "it's malignant."

His words cut through me like a knife. Carol was adamantly opposed to the only treatment that the doctors thought would give her any chance of winning this battle: chemotherapy. We were warned that without chemotherapy, Carol would likely be gone in a very short period of time. With chemo, the doctors thought there was a reasonable chance that the disease could be forced into remission for a decade or more. To me, the choice was crystal clear. To Carol, however, the prospect of death seemed abstract, even unreal.

"I don't want to do it," she said. "I'll lose my hair."

"What the hell do you care about losing your hair?" I said. "We're talking about losing your life."

We had a long discussion and eventually Carol consented. She underwent a radical mastectomy and endured months of nauseating chemotherapy (but never did lose her hair) with a grin-and-bear it determination and the quiet courage that had always been her hallmark. Carol struggled through, relying on her faith, an inner resolve, God, and on me and our children. She dealt with the cancer with the same elegance and strength with which she handled everything. Carol didn't for a second think that the cancer would defeat her (nor did it, until eighteen years later). Her optimism and strength fortified the entire family.

After several months of treatment, the disease was in remission, and it appeared that we had all dodged the bullet. We gladly resumed our normal lives.

Early in 1977, I joined Blyth Eastman Dillon & Company Inc. as a senior consultant on economic and financial matters, a $200,000-a-year, part-time job. It was a homecoming of sorts since the firm was a successor to Union Securities, where I first began my Wall Street career in 1952. I also joined Booz-Allen & Hamilton, a management, technology, and market research firm, as a $150,000-a-year consultant on global economic trends. Neither position consumed all my time, or even a fraction of my energy. So, over the next few years, I accepted a large number of other positions, serving as a consultant and serving on a number of corporate boards. But by and large, I was bored.

I was having trouble getting back into the groove. I didn't like being a corporate director, and found that activity decidedly unsatisfying. It paid well (the various corporate positions were bringing in about $2 million annually), but wasn't leading to the type of big deals that would interest me. The work was dreadfully dull—lots of meetings, little direct control, no opportunity for the adrenaline rush on which I thrive. During those first few years out of government, I thought I had made a dreadful mistake by not returning to Salomon Brothers. For the first time in my life, I felt professionally unfulfilled.

Much of that was a result of the changes I had undergone in Washington and my growing interest in the power of ideas.

A half century ago, the great Harvard scholar Joseph A. Schumpeter predicted that capitalism, because of its very success in raising the standard of living to unprecedented heights, would weaken the institutions necessary for its survival, giving way to a centralized, socialized bureaucracy of intellectuals which would exploit the productive capacity created by private enterprise.

In his seminal work, *Capitalism, Socialism and Democracy*, the Austrian-American economist and social theorist pessimistically predicted that the leaders of the free market would allow themselves to be converted to a creed hostile to their own existence because they would be unable to articulate a moral basis for free enterprise.

In Washington, I became convinced that Schumpeter was right. America's leading colleges and universities—the training ground for America's leaders—were increasingly pro-socialist, pro-government regulation, and anti-capitalist in their philosophy, direction, and mission.

Although I consider myself an optimist, I was concerned about the state of the nation, and fearful that we were well on the way to losing our traditional freedoms. I was reminded of—and perhaps haunted by—what the historian Gibbon said of Athens. "In the end," he wrote in his epitaph for the ancient Republic, "more than they wanted freedom, they wanted security. They wanted a comfortable life and they lost it all—security, comfort and freedom. When the Athenians finally wanted not to give to society but for society to give to them, when the freedom they wished for most was freedom of responsibility, then Athens ceased to be free."

Was America following the same course? Were our nearsighted political leaders selling us short? What we witnessed in the 1976 election was a severe decline in the confidence of the American people, not only in their government, but in all of the institutions that are so important to our society—church, school, military, government. We were much too ready to doubt ourselves and our political and economic institutions, rather than those who attacked us so self-righteously. There seemed to be a national state of self-flagellation.

Even though the next presidential election was nearly four years away, I felt it was imperative for the Republican Party to begin offering an alternative to Jimmy Carter, an alternative based not on the pragmatism of the past, but on the principles upon which this country was founded.

What the GOP needed, in my opinion, was the courage of its convictions, a renewed belief in the fundamental truths of liberty that the party of Abraham Lincoln embodies, along with the guts and vision to take the truth to the people. We could succeed only if we acted as statesmen, rather than politicians, if we built and expounded a platform of programs instead of platitudes, and offered serious ideas and practical policies based on common sense and common decency.

I argued in every forum available to me. I wrote newspaper columns and delivered radio addresses, traveled the country campaigning on behalf of various conservative candidates. I began speaking regularly to groups across the country, and learned somewhat to my surprise that people were willing to pay to hear me speak (something with which I was never comfortable). And I continued to work on a project I had begun just before leaving government: a book on my observations in Washington—a modern equivalent of Barry Goldwater's famous 1960 manifesto, *The Conscience of a Conservative*. It would be called *A Time for Truth*.

A Time for Truth was suggested in 1976 by *Reader's Digest*, which had published several articles and essays that I had written. Since I had never written a book, *Reader's Digest* hired a writer, Edith Efron, to help me. Edith is an outstanding writer who happens to share my philosophic beliefs. For two years, we worked and reworked the manuscript, eventually completing a thorough examination of my intellectual journey. I recounted the lessons I had learned as energy czar and treasury secretary, the battles over New York City and the federal budget, and warned of the erosion of economic (and therefore individual) freedoms. Two of the greatest economic minds of the century—Milton Friedman and F.A. Hayek—endorsed *A Time for Truth* in a preface and foreword, respectively.

Still, Reader's Digest Press, which published my book as a McGraw-Hill title, predicted the book would sell no more than 5,000 copies, and that I should be satisfied with that since I would reach the few people who were receptive to my message. I always suspected there were a lot more people—to borrow from President Nixon, a "silent majority" of Americans—who understood the principles of freedom.

I was not surprised by the reaction of liberals. I expected them to disagree with me, and anticipated their knee-jerk reaction. Much more unsettling and disappointing was the general reaction of the business community. Perhaps like me before my Washington experience, some business leaders were too preoccupied with their immediate concerns to pay much attention to the intellectual assault on everything that makes their freedom and prosperity possible. Others, however, simply did not have the stomach to fight for it. Many, sadly, had lost their faith and hope in the competitive free-enterprise system. In the face of an enemy assault, they were willing simply to capitulate. They yearned to be accepted as "socially responsible" and feared they would be labeled "insensitive" or "conservative." I was appalled and felt betrayed by those who should have been my philosophical brethren.

Remarkably, though, there emerged an enormous groundswell of support from an aroused citizenry, common folks who saw what was happening to their country. I received mountains of letters from concerned Americans, who understood a great deal more than their alleged leaders, in politics and business, could have ever imagined.

As I traveled the country to appear in bookstores, taking part in numerous television and radio interviews, word of the book began to spread, and sales surged. *A Time for Truth* made the *New York Times* best-sellers list for twenty straight weeks in 1978, and rose as high as seventh on the list during July and August. Supreme Court Justice William Rehnquist (now chief justice) wrote me a wonderful note: "Anyone who can generate a preface by Milton Friedman and a forward by Friedrich Hayek must be worth reading." Golf legend Arnold Palmer wrote suggesting that *A Time for Truth* be sent to "each and every congressman and senator." The book succeeded beyond my wildest expectations, as well as those of the publisher.

———

WILLIAM SCHULZ, EXECUTIVE EDITOR OF READER'S DIGEST, SEPTEMBER 3, 1999

I had written a profile of Bill for Reader's Digest *in 1976 and had a great deal of respect and admiration for him. He was one of the few people in that administration who really stood for anything and I knew he would have a powerful message for the American people once he left office.*

Fortunately, DeWitt Wallace, who founded Reader's Digest, *and Hobart Lewis, then our editor-in-chief, agreed. The result was the* Reader's Digest-*sponsored* A Time for Truth, *a runaway best-seller and one of the most important conservative (indeed, philosophical) books in decades.*

Still, I must admit, as its editor, that before the book came out, I had a best-case and a worst-case scenario. The worst case was that it would sell about 5,000 copies and sink without a trace. The best case was that it would sell enough to be on the bottom of the best-seller list for a couple of weeks. I certainly did not foresee it being the run-away best-seller that it was.

Incredibly, the New York Times *declined to review* A Time for Truth *in either its daily book review or its Sunday Book Review section. That wasn't because of a strike which shut down the* Times *for part of the time . . . It was simply the way the* Times *looks at the world.*

———

Although I was already well known from my Washington years, and in particular for my time as energy "czar," *A Time for Truth* and the resulting interviews, reviews, and requests to speak dramatically increased my public exposure while fortifying my conservative credentials and attesting to my intellectual vitality.

By late 1978, many prominent Republicans and conservatives—
and, most gratifying, a great number of readers who previously knew
next to nothing about my views—encouraged me to run for president.

Around the same time, I was presented with a business deal that
interested me greatly—purchasing the Baltimore Orioles Major
League Baseball team. But it just wasn't meant to be.

In the summer of 1978, I got a call from Commissioner Bowie
Kuhn, who advised me that the Orioles might be for sale.

"If you are interested," Bowie said, "we can lay the Baltimore Orioles at your doorstep."

"I'm more than interested," I said.

The thought of owning a professional sports franchise sounded
like great fun. I've always loved sports, and an opportunity to become
intimately involved in the national pastime was just too exciting the
pass up.

Bowie and I met at my home in East Hampton (he has a home not
far from mine on Long Island) and discussed the purchase of the Orioles. After having some further discussions, Edward Bennett Williams,
one of the nation's most famous trial attorneys and the owner of the
Washington Redskins football franchise, and I began preparing to buy
the team as partners. Williams, who died in 1988, was a fascinating
man whose clients ranged from Frank Sinatra, William F. Buckley, and
John Connally to alleged New York mafia leader Frank Costello and
stock swindler Robert Vesco. He was also the consummate Washington insider, a friend to several presidents, and one of those larger than
life figures.

Ed and I negotiated ad nauseam with the owner, Jerry Hoffberger,
and it seemed we were all precisely on the same page regarding price
($12 million, which I considered an incredibly good deal). But every
time we'd talk, Jerry would come up with some new condition, some
new problem, some new wrinkle. In addition, when word leaked to
the press that I might be involved in a purchase of the Orioles, there
was rampant speculation that if I got my hands on the team I would
move it to Washington, partially because the team's lease in Baltimore

expired after the 1979 season. I must have insisted a thousand times that I had no intention of moving the team anywhere.

Eventually, I'd had enough of Jerry Hoffberger (and told the *Baltimore Sun* that dealing with Hoffberger was like "dealing with the Scarlet Pimpernel") and pulled out. Ed Williams bought the team for a bargain basement price, and kept it in Baltimore.

––––

BOWIE KUHN, FORMER COMMISSIONER OF MAJOR LEAGUE BASEBALL, MARCH 31, 2000

Keeping in mind that Jerry Hoffberger and I did not get along at all, Hoffberger called me and said, "I'm telling you just so you know, we are going to put the Orioles up for sale. But we won't consider any buyer who comes from you. I don't want you having anything to do with this." As soon as he left, I picked up he phone, called Bill Simon, and told him about my conversation with Hoffberger. We met that evening at the club "21" in Manhattan and followed that up later with a lunch meeting at Bill's place in East Hampton.

We took a long walk on the beach, talking it over. Bill said he was definitely interested, but would like to have a partner. I suggested Edward Bennett Williams, and he thought that was a great idea, and they went ahead with it—with my warning to be very careful about leaving my name out of any discussions with Jerry Hoffberger.

Things progressed, but then there were all these leaks to the press and Jerry kept cluttering the deal. When the contract that had been fully negotiated by the end of December still was not signed in February 1979, Bill called me up and said, "Jerry Hoffberger is the most impossible man I've ever dealt with in my life. I can hardly stand to be in a room with him anymore!" That was the end of that.

––––

Meanwhile, President Carter bumbled along and I continued to challenge his policies and philosophies. By 1978, more than two years before the election, conservative momentum was building, as was the budding presidential campaign of Ronald Reagan.

Bill Simon as a toddler, late 1920s.

The Simon family, 1970. Front row: Peter, Mary, Leigh. Back row: Bill Jr., Julie, Bill Sr., Carol, Katie, Aimee.

Bill and Carol's wedding, September 9, 1950, in Spring Lake, N.J.

President Nixon and
Bill discussing energy
policy with the press,
December 1973.

Bill and George Shultz at the conference on energy and oil in Washington, D.C., February 1974.

Moments after what would become President Nixon's final cabinet meeting, Bill told the press that the president said he had no intention of resigning.

Bill meeting with President Nixon, July 1974.

Bill meeting with President Ford, 1974.

Bill and President Reagan in the Roosevelt Room, where Bill was presented with an American flag just prior to the 1984 Olympics.

Bill leading the U.S. Olympic Team at the opening ceremonies of the 1984 Games.

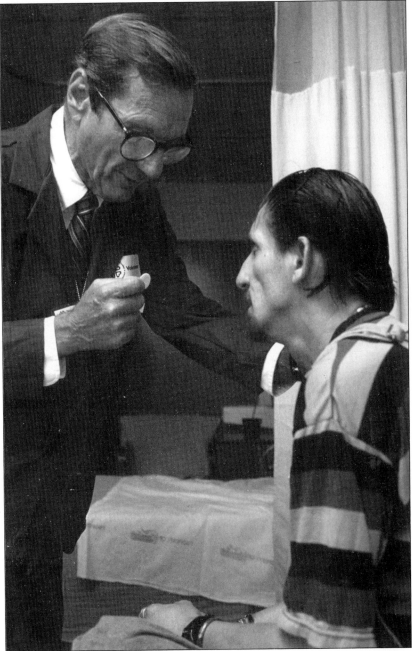

Photo by John Abbott

Bill administering the Holy Eucharist at the Terence Cardinal Cooke Health Care Center in Harlem, N.Y., late 1990s.

Bill with Pope John Paul II, spring 1999.

Despite Governor Reagan's popular and political support, there were a number of power brokers, led by Justin Dart, a self-made California millionaire and former chairman of Dart Industries, who argued that Ron was too old to run for president.

Justin and several other influential conservatives urged me to throw my hat into the ring and pursue politically the issues I had presented philosophically in *A Time for Truth*. In fact, Justin Dart commissioned publications of an abridged version of the book and had tens of thousands of copies printed and distributed.

Reader's Digest was also promoting my candidacy and, in 1979, commissioned a sequel to *A Time for Truth*. My second book, *A Time for Action*, enjoyed substantial success and further enhanced my potential candidacy. Occidental Petroleum alone bought tens of thousands of copies to distribute to employees and shareholders. All told, the two books sold well over four million copies.

My books were best-sellers created as word spread from one little community to another and, eventually, the tide turned in major metropolitan areas. The same trend was occurring all over the political landscape. The people were beginning to seize control of politics once again, and the liberals were absolutely petrified. There was clearly an opportunity for conservatives to seize. The only question was who would seize it.

I was interested in running, but lacked the fire-in-the-belly obsession necessary to pursue the presidency, and never did make a serious effort to win the Republican nomination. By the summer of 1980, Ron Reagan, who had battled with President Ford right to the convention and really never stopped running, had the nomination essentially locked up. (Regardless, Bill Casey, who would become President Reagan's director of the Central Intelligence Agency, showed up at the convention wearing a "Simon for President" button.)

A crucial issue that summer, strategically, centered on who would run on the ticket with Governor Reagan. Four years earlier, when Ron lost the nomination to President Ford, he had declared prior to the convention that he would run with Senator Richard Schweiker, a liberal from Pennsylvania. That declaration undoubtedly lost Reagan conservative support, and he was leery of making another such mistake at the 1980 convention. Several names, including mine, were bandied about as potential vice presidential nominees: Senate Majority Leader Howard Baker, Rep. Jack Kemp, Sen. Richard Luger, George Bush, Don Rumsfeld, Sen. Paul Laxalt, Rep. Guy Vander Jagt, and Anne Armstrong.

Additionally, there was some speculation that Reagan would choose Gerald Ford as the vice presidential candidate. The theory was that the former president would serve as the administration's "foreign policy" liaison—a sort of co-president for international affairs.

I thought it was a terrible idea. Not only was the role demeaning to President Ford, it also opened a constitutional Pandora's box. Additionally, redefining the nature of the vice presidency would inevitably redefine the presidency as well. No one really knew where this adventure would lead. Still, the idea was profoundly appealing to a great many politicians and Republican political tacticians, who viewed a Reagan–Ford ticket as virtually unbeatable.

Both camps appointed advisers to negotiate a deal in which the former president would be guaranteed an "enhanced" role as vice president. President Ford appointed Henry Kissinger, Alan Greenspan, and two longtime aides, John Marsh and Robert Barrett. Governor Reagan tapped adviser (and eventual attorney general) Edwin Meese, (eventual CIA director) Bill Casey, and pollster Richard Wirthlin. It was quickly evident that an appropriate role could not be fashioned for Gerald Ford.

The night before Reagan was to announce his choice for a running mate at the convention in Detroit, the issue still had not been decided. Ron was eager to find some way to get President Ford on the ticket, but was understandably leery of expanding the duties and powers of the vice president. President Ford was extremely reluctant to run for vice president, but still willing to consider the option, assuming a workable relationship could be established. Still, it was all but certain that President Ford would not be joining the ticket, and several other potential running-mates—including George Bush and me—remained under consideration.

PRESIDENT FORD, OCTOBER 25, 1994

I was under pressure in 1980 to run again for president. Betty and I thought about it and thought about it. We had twenty-eight years in Washington and we were happy and settled. I decided in March I would not be a candidate, and I told then Governor Reagan I would not be. I said I'd be glad to campaign if he got the nomination.

Well, the convention was in July, and both Betty and I flew in Sunday night. We were at the hotel, hardly got there, when we got a call from the Reagans. They asked to see us and came down to our suite. They said they wanted to win the election and said the best way was to have me on the ticket as vice president. I was shocked.

I said, "Ron . . . in deference to your request, I'll be glad to consider this. But I am warning that the odds are no."

I had seen vice presidents pushed, pulled, dumped and I wasn't going to do that. So, we agreed that we would each pick three or four people representing us and they would try to put into writing the duties of a vice president, so there would be no misunderstanding. For twenty-four hours, our respective delegates negotiated, but could not agree to a working arrangement, so Governor Reagan and I agreed to terminate the discussion. I promised to wholeheartedly campaign for him, and did.

———

That evening, I went to see Ron in his suite on the sixty-ninth floor of the Detroit Plaza Hotel in Renaissance Center and found the future president perched at a small desk, pondering the selection. Nancy Reagan was sitting nearby on a red sofa, along with advisers Michael Deaver and Ed Meese. Several other aides and intimates were also present.

I told Governor Reagan that I was taking myself out of consideration, that President Ford should not even be a consideration, and that it was time to decisively put an end to the speculation.

"Ron, the press is saying you can't make up your mind, that you are too old to be president, that you are vacillating, that you don't know whom to choose as vice president," I said. "You have got to end this."

EDWARD C. SCHMULTS, JULY 26, 1994, AND JANUARY 24, 2000

I was working on the vice presidential candidate review process for Governor Reagan, along with Bill Casey. Reagan had been negotiating with former President Ford to be his vice president. The polls showed that most vice presidential candidates hurt the presidential candidate. Ford was the only one who actually helped the ticket, according to the polls. So Reagan really wanted Ford to be vice president and there were all these negotiations going on—with Ford represented by Henry Kissinger and Alan Greenspan, Ed Meese and Mike Deaver handling negotiations for Governor Reagan.

We were sitting in Governor Reagan's suite waiting for President Ford to make a decision. The door burst open and Simon walked in, stood in front of Reagan and proceeded to tell him in no uncertain terms that he ought to do what's right, that it didn't make any sense to have the former president serve as vice president. He really let Reagan know what he thought. Reagan just looked at Simon, and Simon spun around and walked out of the room. He marched in, spoke his piece and out he went. And Dick Allen said, "Well, no one ever said Bill Simon doesn't have balls."[2]

———

At precisely 11:42 p.m., Governor Reagan called George Bush and offered him the opportunity to run for vice president. Although I was not going to be on the ticket, I was eager to play a major role in the campaign. In particular, I was interested in formulating and articulating a conservative agenda that would clearly distinguish the Republican Party from the Democratic Party, and was honored to address the delegates at the convention in Detroit.

"The American people must now decide whether they will sell the liberty that is the envy of the world for the empty promise of the welfare state, or whether they will restrict government to its proper functions: defense of the nation, protection of the helpless from the avaricious, and the creation of an environment for sustained economic growth through sensible fiscal, monetary, tax, and regulatory policies," I told the delegates. "Let us never forget personal and political freedoms are inseparable from economic freedom."

I urged the party to adopt five guidelines as the core of the next administration. First, Washington had to stop living beyond its means. Second, the money supply had to be brought into relation with the real growth levels of the economy. Third, we had to cut taxes to encourage capital investment and productivity. Fourth, we had to limit the army of regulators who were strangling industry. And fifth, we had to regain control over our energy destiny.

My role in the campaign was manifold. I served as chairman of the campaign's executive advisory committee, a brain trust that had been advising Ronald Reagan for several years. Additionally, I was part of his economic advisory council, along with George Shultz, Arthur Laffer, Milton Friedman, Alan Greenspan, Arthur Burns, James Lynn, Charls Walker, Herbert Stein, and others. I was also a member of the Reagan "truth squad," a group of prominent conservatives, led by Bill Casey, who traveled the country to make appearances in the same cities where Carter was campaigning.

The "truth squad" very effectively documented President Carter's failings. We pointed out that: President Carter has promised an inflation rate of 4 percent, and that inflation had risen as high as 18.2 percent; the incumbent had pledged to reduce unemployment to 4.5 percent, but it stood at 7.8 percent; Carter had promised a balanced budget but increased the deficit to nearly $61 billion; President Carter had pledged not to raise taxes, only to increase taxes by 75.6 percent. No president in American history had increased taxes so much.

Ron Reagan campaigned hard and effectively, using *A Time for Truth* as his prescription for change and presenting the most principled and philosophic political agenda in a generation. It was an agenda the American people were ready to embrace. On November 4, 1980, Ronald Reagan defeated President Carter by a landslide.

Governor Reagan carried the baton of Barry Goldwater, whose unsuccessful 1964 campaign against Lyndon Johnson made it acceptable to question the efficacy of an all-powerful federal government.

Although Goldwater was denounced as an "extremist," his ideas and ideals were ready for mainstream America after the debacle of the Carter years, as evidenced by Reagan's landslide victory. I viewed Reagan's 1980 win as a belated victory for Goldwater and, more directly, Gerald Ford. It seemed that by delivering a ringing declaration of no confidence and transferring their loyalties to Ronald Reagan, the voters were saying to President Ford: "We're sorry, old friend. We made a mistake in 1976. You were the better man. We voted for the wrong man. Now, we're trying to correct that mistake."

Immediately, I was under consideration for a wide variety of positions in the new administration. There was some talk that I would take over as president of the World Bank, which did not interest me. There was also a lot of talk that I would serve in the cabinet, which did interest me.

One week after the election, Richard Viguerie and Howard Phillips, two of the leading conservative voices, prepared a memorandum for the new administration listing their choices for key cabinet positions. I was their first choice for secretary of defense, secretary of treasury, and director of the Office of Management and Budget, and their second choice (after John Connally) for secretary of state.

Meanwhile, the president-elect asked George Shultz and me to formulate an economic policy, and the role of the Department of Treasury to implement that policy. We produced a document that called for a very strong secretary of the treasury, one who would "be the chief coordinator and spokesman on economic policy, domestic and international." When Ed Meese saw the proposal, he hit the roof.

"If you think you are going to come in and run economic policy the way that paper presents it, you are crazy," Meese told me. "Economic policy is going to be run out of the White House."

I said, "Ed, I was asked by the chairman of the committee, George Shultz, to write a paper on the administration of economic policy. That paper was approved unanimously by the committee.[3] You're the crazy one. You can't run economic policy out of the White House. That's why you have a Treasury Department."

"The decisions will be made in the White House," Ed insisted.

At that point, I had serious reservations about whether I wanted to serve in the Reagan administration at all. Still, Justin Dart was strenuously promoting my candidacy for secretary of the treasury, and in fact told Reagan that no one else should be considered. And I was excited about the possibility of serving as secretary of the treasury under three different presidents.

However, I took myself out of the running on November 26, 1980, because of family considerations. Carol was dead set against returning to Washington. She'd had her fill of politics and yearned to maintain a more normal lifestyle for us and the children. My daughter Julie contacted me in Saudi Arabia, where I was traveling on business, and told me that Carol, after reading a typically sneering article suggesting I would be in the Reagan cabinet, had become profoundly depressed. Julie told me that it was contrary to the best interests of the family for me to return to Washington. That was all I needed to hear.

———

Julie Simon Munro, daughter, August 24, 1998

My mother raised the seven children and supported my father's various passions—the Olympic Committee, business, government, charitable organizations, traveling, sailing the world, etc., etc., etc. My father has a BIG personality, which isn't always easy to live with. I think my mother got tired and burned out with all that running around. During this time, my father was working hard and traveling a lot. I think my parents' relationship was under a lot of strain as my father became disconnected from the family, and especially my mother.

I was really afraid that he would accept Reagan's request and that the well-being of our family would be in jeopardy. I didn't think my mother could take going back to Washington. Even though she was very patriotic, she felt we had done our duty already.

I remember placing a late night phone call to the Middle East, where my father was doing business. I had a very frank discussion with him. Although I was only fourteen at the time, he really listened

to what I said, took it to heart, and promised me that he wouldn't
accept the job.

————

When I announced that I would not be joining the Reagan administration, the response from my friends and supporters was nothing less
than heartwarming. I received dozens of letters, most of them expressing both regret and puzzlement as to why I was not returning to
Washington and urging me to remain involved. Although I refrained
from accepting an official position in the administration, I did serve
the president in various capacities and continued to use whatever
soapbox I had to advocate the principles of freedom. And even
though I was away from government, my celebrity continued.
Throughout the Reagan years, I continued to comment on, and occasionally criticize, the policies and practices of the administration.

————

EDWIN J. FEULNER, PRESIDENT, THE HERITAGE FOUNDATION,
FEBRUARY 4, 2000

I first met Bill Simon in the Nixon administration when he was
energy czar, and he impressed me as a bright young go-getter who was
given a tough and thankless job of seeing us through a very difficult
time. The first time I really got to know him was at the 1976 IMF and
World Bank meetings in Manila. I was a congressional staffer, execu-
tive director of the Republican Study Committee in the House, and
member of the U.S. delegation that he led. He and Arthur Burns and
Bill Seidman were in the delegation, and Bill Simon was the leader....

There I saw Simon in action with his counterparts—finance minis-
ters, senior bankers from Japan and western Europe and the rest of the
world—and I saw a guy who was absolutely comfortable with private
sector leaders, with the chief movers in money circles around the
world, people who were making governments rise and fall. From see-
ing him working with his peers and working to pull our team together,
I saw a guy who could inspire leadership. He got us all thinking
together and working together on issues that were critical ... I was

convinced that Simon could be a candidate for national office. It seemed so logical....

About the first thing he did after leaving government was to become president of the Olin Foundation, and in April 1977, I went to The Heritage Foundation, where I had been a trustee since it was incorporated in 1972. Anything that would visibly and vocally support the ideas of free enterprise and more rigorous academic intellectual activity, I was very strongly in support of. I understood the importance of the battle for ideas....

I remember thinking when Bill's book came out, "What a breath of fresh air!" and how exciting it was that someone who had been in the real world of business and down in Washington articulated the principles of freedom. I wanted Bill Simon to serve on our board. I knew it would be a real signal that Heritage was going to be a significant, longtime player if the author of A Time for Truth, *former member of the cabinet, and successful businessman on Wall Street would lend his name to this fledgling organization. He agreed, and the rest, as they say, is history....*

One of the seminal influences that Bill Simon had ... was [the] Mandate for Leadership [Project], which Ronald Reagan said set the course for his administration in January 1981 but also made Heritage a serious player in the Washington policy community. We were there ready with a policy handbook when this radically different administration came in. It was the Simon idea that set the whole pattern for Heritage and took us from the bush leagues to the major leagues in one giant step.

———

Ronald Reagan inherited the leadership of a nation in crisis. America had spent the last half of the 1970s in retreat—economically, militarily, morally, and spiritually. We were forsaking our values, and running from danger into the arms of defeat. The specter of economic decline with prices skyrocketing, growth collapsing, and markets in a free fall demonstrated all too vividly what happens when our leaders turn their backs on the core principles that gave America the strongest economy and undisputed leadership of the free world.

Like Gerald Ford, Ronald Reagan knew what to do to make America strong and healthy again. His first term was extraordinarily successful. In addition to adhering to the correct philosophy, President Reagan was an extraordinarily adept at communicating his ideas and ideals in a way that struck home with middle America.

Under President Reagan, economic expansion reached all segments of our society. African Americans made record gains under Ronald Reagan. Per capita income for blacks was on the rise. Black teenage unemployment had fallen by a third while the black middle class had grown by 33 percent. For the first time in American history, the black middle class was larger than the black poor.

It is ironic and revealing that the Reagan administration achieved the alleged goals of the liberals by employing policies that contradicted those advocated by the same liberals for so many years.

JIMMY CARTER'S
OLYMPIC BOYCOTT

I can think of only one major issue on which I supported President Carter—the boycott of the 1980 Olympics—and I regret it to this day.

On December 27, 1979, the Red Army crossed the Russian border into Afghanistan to quell an uprising of Muslim rebels. The invasion provoked justifiable outrage in the West and on January 4, 1980, President Carter condemned the "callous violation of international law and the United Nations Charter" and suggested that unless the Soviets withdraw from Afghanistan, we might withdraw from the July Olympics in Moscow.

I was utterly stunned. I agreed with President Carter's characterization of the invasion of Afghanistan, but thought he was bluffing about a boycott. At the time, the president was viewed as vulnerable, both here and abroad. Iranian thugs had just taken over our embassy and the president, preparing to run for reelection, was under attack by members of his own party, including Senator Edward Kennedy. I thought—and hoped—that perhaps President Carter, mauled by his own economic policies and humiliated by his own foreign policies, was merely sabre-rattling.

During those first few weeks of 1980, those of us in the Olympic movement (I was then treasurer of the United States Olympic Committee and would become president in less than a year) were torn over the president's comments. We were unsure how seriously to take his threat, and even less sure of what our stance should be if the president announced a boycott. We continued to hope and pray that the crisis in Afghanistan would be resolved quickly, but found little cause for hope that winter.

On January 20, 1980, Don Miller, executive director of the USOC, met at the White House with Secretary of State Cyrus Vance and presidential counsel Lloyd Cutler. Vance and Cutler stressed that the president was deadly serious about a boycott. Their admonition was proven just two days later when Jimmy Carter sent a message to the International Olympic Committee indicating that unless the Soviets withdrew from Afghanistan within a month, the IOC should move the games to another site. Congress responded with resolutions from both Houses strongly supporting President Carter. The administration then attempted to rally the support of the athletes.

On January 26, Lloyd Cutler asked the USOC to support a change in venue or a postponement of the games. Viewing a move or a delay as far preferable to a boycott, the USOC board (which included seventeen athlete representatives and twenty former Olympians) voted 68-0 to petition the IOC as requested by the Carter administration. The IOC, however, turned us down flat, so on February 2, Jimmy Carter sent Cutler to visit the president of the IOC, Lord Michael Killanin, at his home in Dublin. The meeting, by all accounts, did not go well.

Lord Killanin had little regard for President Carter, largely because when the contract between the IOC and the city of Los Angeles for the 1984 games was signed at the White House, the president refused to make an appearance, even though he was in the next room. Apparently, First Lady Rosalynn Carter had a photo-op that day and Jimmy Carter didn't want to upstage her. So, Lord Killanin was hardly in an accommodating mood when Cutler demanded that the IOC either postpone or cancel the 1980 games. Lord Killanin's refusal to so much as consider President Carter's request apparently resulted in an unseemly tit-for-tat from the administration.

Less than two weeks after Lloyd Cutler's meeting with Lord Killanin, President Carter declined to attend the opening ceremonies of the 1980 Winter Games in Lake Placid, New York. Instead, he sent Secretary of State Vance to open the games. Cyrus Vance delivered an overtly political speech, which the administration spoon-fed to the world press beforehand, for political impact. The IOC was infuriated at being exploited for political gain. The Carter administration, however, kept up the pressure.

At Lake Placid, Vice President Walter Mondale lobbied Robert J. Kane, a wonderful man who was serving his last year as president of the United States Olympic Committee, and Don Miller. The vice president indicated that President Carter was leaning toward a boycott, and asked for the USOC's support. Bob and Don refused to guarantee the administration that the USOC would support a boycott. Public opinion polls, however, were heavily supportive of the president.

Over the next few months, President Carter and his aides exerted tremendous pressure on the committee, threatening to revoke its tax-exempt status and to deny athletes visas. Lloyd Cutler had implied that if we supported the president, Jimmy Carter would push for $16 million in federal funds for the 1984 Olympic Games in Los Angeles—an obvious attempt to buy us off. The White House was even attempting to undermine our fund-raising efforts; after a meeting with presidential aide Anne Wexler, Sears, Roebuck and Co. suddenly withheld a $25,000 contribution to the USOC. Fifteen other companies subsequently held back $175,000 in donations. In my opinion, the president was needlessly putting the entire U.S. Olympic movement in jeopardy, and undermining the credibility of the USOC just as we were on the cusp of making great strides.

———

COLONEL F. DON MILLER, APRIL 19, 1994

We concluded that the reason they were doing this was due to a complete lack of foreign policy. If there was a foreign policy, why, of all things, would you choose the Olympic movement, which stood for good throughout the world, which built international amity and good will? [Baron Pierre de Coubertin, founder of the modern Olympics] once said: "The Olympic movement tends to bring together in a radiant union all the qualities which guide mankind to perfection." We fought it [the boycott] and fought it and fought it ... in the interests of the youth of our country, who had spent so many years training in preparation for these games. How do you compensate an individual for something like that? Then the pan began to get hotter, both public-wise and threat-wise.

Almost overwhelmingly, the public was against us going to the 1980 Summer Games in Moscow. The House voted unanimously not to participate, and the Senate vote was nearly unanimous, with only three senators voting against a boycott ... We have to depend on the American public and American corporations for their support of the Olympic movement. We saw fund-raising beginning to dry up. We were threatened with everything from A to Z, including loss of our tax deduction status and refusal to issue passports to our people. Up to and through the Winter Games at Lake Placid in 1980, [White House counsel] Lloyd Cutler and his assistant were playing the game of good cop/bad cop—with Cutler trying to be the smoothie and his assistant looking for a punch in the nose by being threatening and overbearing. The situation came to a head in Lake Placid when Cutler's assistant threatened: "We will put you out of business and we'll put the International Olympic Committee out of business...."

[For many weeks], no progress was made. We were standing fast. In April, Jesse Owens passed away[1] and we went to the funeral. After the services, we were walking up the aisle and [a reporter] shoved a microphone in my face, right in the church. He asked what I thought about the White House calling our corporate sponsors and telling them to withhold their [donations]. I turned around and snapped, "It was blatant blackmail" ... The next day, I received phone calls from a couple of corporations saying they had calls from the White House. Our fund raising all but stopped and there was very little money coming in.

Carter [called later and said] we should not go to the 1980 Summer

*Games in Moscow. He said that it would do too much harm. He used
the excuse of jeopardizing our national security, among other reasons... Then I said, "By the way, Mr. President, I was very disappointed
to see one of your staff members calling corporations, and you telling
them... that they should stop or withhold their contributions to the U.S.
Olympic Committee." There was a long pause on the other end of the
phone. Then Carter said, "I don't know anything about that...."*

*After all was said and done, the president did invite the sponsors
to the White House, gave them a talking to, and told them to honor
their commitments. But still, we didn't get to go to the Olympics, and
it broke so many hearts, was such a tragic experience for those young
athletes. That was something that really hurt Bill Simon.*

————

As an organization, the USOC was at a critical juncture. For nearly
all of its existence, the organization had played a limited role; its only
real duty was to serve as a conduit for our participation in the Summer, Winter, and Pan American Games. However, the role of the
USOC was greatly changed and greatly expanded with the passage of
the Amateur Sports Act of 1978.

After our disappointing performance at the 1972 Olympics, Congress was deluged with letters from Americans demanding that something be done about it. Unfortunately, Watergate broke out then and
amateur athletics, like a lot of important issues, was quickly forgotten. It wasn't until an outstanding amateur athlete himself, Gerald
Ford, assumed the presidency that a commission was established to
study the Olympics and amateur sports in general. The commission,
which included prominent athletes like Donna de Varona,[2] reported:
"There are three basic modes of sports organizations employed by
successful sporting nations. In one, government is in control. In
another, a nongovernmental sports authority is in control. In the
third, no one is in control." Only the U.S. used the third method.

For years, our athletes had been complaining, with good reason,
about the lack of funding for training and competition and the endless infighting among various governing organizations (particularly

the National Collegiate Athletic Association and the Amateur Athletic Union). Simultaneously, our athletes had virtually no voice in the administration of amateur sports. While recognizing the need for a central sports authority, the various organizations could not agree on which should emerge as that authority. Typical political gridlock kept the administration of amateur athletics mired in the status quo.

———

COLONEL MICKI KING, OLYMPIC GOLD MEDALIST (1972, SPRINGBOARD DIVING), CHARTER CHAIRPERSON OF THE ATHLETES' ADVISORY COUNCIL, JULY 6, 1999

The Athletes' Advisory Council was comprised of one athlete from every Olympic and Pan American sport. And, believe me, plenty of frustration was built up in all of us on that first committee. Now, for the first time, through the AAC, the athletes had a mandatory voice in every phase of the Olympic Committee. The AAC was a crack in the door that we planned to open real wide. This group of athletes was not a bunch of kids rebelling. We were people who were professionals. We had lawyers. We had teachers. We had broadcasters. We had authors. But those early years were still very difficult for us. We needed help from people who would be listened to, people who were not necessarily in the sports arena. We needed someone who could get people's attention. We needed someone to champion our cause. We needed Bill Simon.

Bill was such an important figure, because of the credibility he brought to the table. He was very supportive of the athletes' movement, and when he spoke, everybody listened. He was not just "another jock."

You know what Bill meant to me more than anything? He was unbiased. He didn't have a hidden or personal agenda. His only agenda was to be right and correct, and fair. Bill brought balance and fairness and wisdom from the business world that transcended sports and really helped to make issues clear. Bill Simon played an important role at a very volatile time in the athletes' rights movement.

The USOC is essentially an organization of organizations. The member organizations under its umbrella include the national governing bodies for each Olympic sport. As the organization was evolving, it was crucial to select national governing bodies that best represented the interests of the athletes and the movement. The Amateur Sports Act of 1978 designated the USOC as the central coordinating body for the sports on the Olympic/Pan American Games programs, and provided athletes with 20 percent representation. I fully supported that effort and did everything I could to foster the establishment of national governing bodies that would be accountable for the various sports.

Around the same time, the USOC moved its headquarters from New York City to Colorado Springs, a controversial but wise move to consolidate all the national governing bodies at one site. I felt we needed a new beginning, and a new home where we could offer our athletes a first-rate training facility.

———

WILLIAM TUTT, FORMER VICE PRESIDENT OF THE UNITED STATES OLYMPIC COMMITTEE, SEPTEMBER 10, 1999

We were headquartered in New York City, Bill's backyard, but the facility we had was small, basically a three-story walk-up with files on the floors. As an organization we were broke, but the facility in New York was probably worth a million dollars.

Bill had the vision to understand, that we were a very small fish in a very large pond in New York City, and that we didn't necessarily have to be headquartered there. New York tried desperately to keep us. Governor Carey threatened to declare the Olympic house a "state monument," to block us from selling it and moving—a little sabre-rattling more than anything else. Coincidentally, my uncle, Russell Tutt, and Hugh Carey went to school together at Princeton, and they had some conversations. I think Governor Carey came to the realization that he was not going to stop the USOC from moving to Colorado Springs. . . .

Don Miller and I were working together to find the right location for the USOC and we went out there [to a closed Air Force base] and it was all locked up and dilapidated. We managed to find a hole in the fence and crawled through it and climbed through a couple of abandoned buildings with dead cats and dust and dirt. Don walked through the place and said, "This is absolutely perfect!"

Bill was treasurer of the USOC at the time we made our move to Colorado Springs. Bill was one of the key guys who had the vision to say we need our own identity, we need our own profile, we need to be in an area where we are a big fish in a growing pond, an all-American type of environment. He was one of the spearheads that really pushed and supported our move to Colorado Springs. Bill is one of the icons, and probably the major reason the USOC is the dominant Olympic committee in the world today.

———

It was just at the time that the USOC was beginning to emerge as the respected authority it is today that we were confronted with the awful problem of President Carter's threatened boycott. It was an incredibly tense and stressful time within the USOC. Public opinion clearly favored a boycott, while most of the athletes abhorred, understandably, the very idea of giving up the chance of a lifetime for a political statement. I myself had mixed thoughts and could see both sides.

On April 2, 1980, Senator Robert C. Byrd of West Virginia sent me a letter making a strong and persuasive case for a boycott. "The Olympics should be a celebration of peace, and of peaceful human achievement regardless of nationality or political persuasion," Senator Byrd wrote. "No nation has ever served as host for the Olympic Games while that nation was in the process of invading and subjugating another independent nation."

The letter was co-signed by Senators Daniel K. Inouye, John C. Stennis, Alan Cranston, Jacob Javits, Robert Packwood, Frank Church, Edmund Muskie, and Howard W. Cannon—decent, honorable men—and I had no doubt of their sincerity.

On the other side of the equation were a great many athletes, whose opinion I respected greatly. "Three weeks ago my life was, by most estimations, unremarkable," Anita DeFrantz, captain of the U.S. Women's Rowing Team told the Senate Committee on Foreign Relations. She went on to say:

> No one other than my rowing partner was particularly interested in how I utilized my spare time. Suddenly, my desire to compete in the Olympic Games, which is unquestionably the primary motivation to train, became an unpatriotic act. I was stunned, shocked and, quite frankly, I felt betrayed.
>
> My experience as a black woman in this country has taught me that there are many things that defy rational explanation. These last few days I have tried to understand why it is that the Olympic Games should be used to punish Russia. If the president, the House, and, I submit, this committee, and the American people, truly believe that the games are so important to the Russians that the United States could effectuate a withdrawal of Russian troops from Afghanistan by refusing to participate in those games, then why weren't the games used to prevent the invasion of that country and prevent the subjugation of that people?
>
> I don't understand why the games, if they had to be used, could not have been used to prevent bloodshed, instead of trying to punish those who have participated in bloodshed.

How could one argue with that? My natural inclination, of course, was to resist government/political interference in the Olympics. I didn't see how a boycott could possibly do anything other than harm the Olympic movement. I was also offended at the Carter administration's politicization of the games and worried about the precedent it would set. Four years later, the games would be held on U.S. soil. How would other nations respond if we boycotted Moscow? On the other hand, I firmly believe an American citizen has an obligation to support his president in matters of foreign policy. Foreign governments, both friend and foe, should be reminded that Americans will stick with their president through thick and thin, and that the people will not be turned against their leader.

So, I was of a mixed mind. But I couldn't stay on the fence and neither could the USOC. We had to take a formal position, knowing full well that to do so would cut deep and lasting lesions into an organization that we had worked so hard to unify.

The USOC House of Delegates convened April 12, 1980, in Colorado Springs to take a vote. We were in a no-win situation. If we supported a boycott, we would dash the dreams of hundreds of American athletes who had trained so hard and so long for the privilege of competing in the Olympics, and violate our own constitution.[3] If we rejected a boycott, we would stand in stark opposition to the president of the United States and, even worse, perceived as supporting the Russians.

In speech after speech, there were several reasonable arguments advanced for participating in the games despite the president's position: our reluctance to be used, and to allow the Olympic Games to be used, for political purposes; the fact that our athletes had worked so hard for an opportunity—a once in a lifetime opportunity for many—to compete; legitimate skepticism over whether a boycott would have any impact at all; and finally, and most importantly, the fact that we are a free nation and as free men and women we had not only a right but a responsibility to exercise that right.

On the other side of the coin, however, the Olympics were being held in an economically, politically, socially, and morally bankrupt regime that had engaged in unparalleled aggression as it pursued its stated goal of destroying the last great bastion of freedom—the United States of America. In terms of raw power, the Soviet Union had long surpassed us in conventional armed forced, and was quickly gaining parity in strategic weaponry. Since the fall of Saigon, seven different nations had fallen to Marxism: South Vietnam, Cambodia, Afghanistan, South Yemen, Ethiopia, Angola, and Nicaragua. But more important than the sheer number of nations entombed in the communist web was their location: South Yemen, Ethiopia, and Afghanistan gave the Soviets easy reach of major choke points for the passage of oil to the West; Soviet strongholds in Southeast Asia placed them in solid reach of the Straits of Malacca, a major choke point for oil tankers steaming toward Japan.

Vice President Mondale addressed the delegates, comparing the situation with that of 1936 prior to the Olympic Games in Berlin. He noted that, notwithstanding the triumphs of Jesse Owens, Hitler had scored a major propaganda victory. "I am convinced that the American people do not want their athletes cast as pawns in that tawdry propaganda charade, and I urge you to respect that undeniable consensus," he pleaded.

The entire night before the meeting, I drafted and redrafted my thoughts on a yellow legal pad, well aware that I was about to give what could be the most important speech of my life, and well aware that my credibility with the athletes was on the line. I worried about the implications if our president was unable to obtain public support and loyalty to resist aggression and preserve world peace. I wondered about the hypocrisy of holding a festival of friendship, goodwill, and peace in the capital of communism. But I was terribly concerned that the future of the Olympic movement would be irreparably damaged if the Moscow games were undermined by a boycott.

By sunrise, I had two speeches written, one supporting a boycott, the other denouncing a boycott, but still did not know with absolute certainty which one I would deliver. As I approached the podium and looked out over the audience of athletes and others who loved both their country and the Olympic Games, the proper course became clear. I pleaded with the U.S. Olympic Committee, and the athletes it represented, to make the greatest sacrifice they could, and to declare themselves Americans first, and Olympians second. As much as I deplored the use of the Olympics as a foreign policy tool, I felt all Americans should stand behind the president, and expressed that sentiment as strongly as I could.

"We are all Americans," I told the athletes. "Whether you agree with the president or not, when you are asked by your country to do something in the name of national security, you do it, regardless of what you think of Jimmy Carter . . . We must demonstrate to the

Russian people and its leaders and the rest of the world that we, the USOC, are capable of moral outrage and are willing to make whatever sacrifice is asked by our president as proof of it."

Don Miller collected ballots in an empty water pitcher. The final weighted vote: 1,604 to 797 in favor of a boycott.

———

MICHAEL LENARD, OLYMPIAN (TEAM HANDBALL, 1984) ATHLETE REPRESENTATIVE AT THE APRIL 12, 1980, MEETING OF THE HOUSE OF DELEGATES, JUNE 3, 1999

Bill gave one of the great speeches of all time . . . Its thrust was: I'm not the kind of person who agrees with the Democratic president, Jimmy Carter. I don't believe what he is doing is correct. I don't agree with his foreign policy. But the office of the President of the United States demands respect and, as Americans, we have to honor the office. As soon as Bill gave his speech, I said "uh-oh." I was going to vote "no" and nothing was going to change my mind, but if anyone was on the fence, Bill's speech changed their mind. Bill's speech was very, very, very effective.

———

Sixty-one nations joined the American-led boycott,[4] leaving Moscow with the lowest number of participating nations, eighty-one, since the Helsinki Games of 1952. The Soviet Union's attempt to use the event as a showcase for communism failed miserably. The 1980 Games were pockmarked by scandal: Hometown officials opened stadium gates during the Soviet javelin thrower's performance, allowing a favorable breeze and ensuring a gold medal. An obviously legal triple jump by an Australian was disallowed. A Cuban was cheated out of a medal in the discus when Russian judges marked his throw a meter short. By hook or by crook, the USSR won more medals in Moscow, 195, than any country in seventy-six years, but the world knew that it had been a fiasco.

Still, I came to view the boycott as a dreadful mistake. It marred the Olympic Movement, domestically and internationally. Athletes who lost their only chance to compete in an Olympics were understandably bitter. The boycott further chilled relations between the USOC and the IOC, and even led to some talk that the International Olympic Committee would rescind its decision to hold the 1984 games in Los Angeles. It resulted in a severe reduction in contributions to the USOC. And, most importantly, it had no effect on Soviet aggression in Afghanistan. It was in the aftermath of the boycott that I, on January 31, 1981, became the seventeenth president of the U.S. Olympic Committee.

My four-year term in office that would span the 1983 Pan American Games in Caracas, the 1984 Winter Games in Sarajevo, and, of course, the Summer Games in Los Angeles. After my election at the Broadmoor Hotel in Colorado Springs, I urged the committee to put aside any divisiveness and pettiness that had at times handicapped our efforts in the past, and to remember that our focus must be on the athletes. We had finished the most difficult and tumultuous four years in our Olympic history, culminating in the supreme sacrifice by the athletes not to go to Moscow. We would be forced to address such difficult issues as amateurism and drug testing. The future of the modern games, not even a century old, was contingent on our success.

And it would all happen on my watch.

USOC PRESIDENT

The premier showcase for the Olympics is the Summer Games. For the first time in fifty-two years they would be held on U.S. soil, during my term as president of the United States Olympic Committee. I was determined to make the 1984 Games the best ever, but knew I was facing an uphill task.

Los Angeles had been selected largely by default and many of its citizens felt more imposed upon than honored to have an opportunity to host the games. We would have to win over Californians as well as Americans in general. In addition, there were lingering concerns that the Soviet Union would boycott the games in retaliation for our boycott of the 1980 Games in Moscow. I was unsure that we could do anything to prevent that from occurring and how we would proceed if it did.

After the brutal terrorist murders at Munich, the financial debacle of Montreal, and the boycott of Moscow, there was not a great deal of interest in hosting the 1984 games. Tehran, Iran, submitted a half-hearted bid, but later withdrew it. Other cities in other countries considered bidding, but opted out. Only Los Angeles, represented by a Justin Dart-led group called the Los Angeles Olympic Organizing Committee (LAOOC) that included such tenacious stalwarts as

John Argue and Paul Ziffren, maintained interest. The USOC endorsed its bid.

However, rather than celebrating the acceptance of the LAOOC bid, many Angelinos and Americans were skeptical and suspicious. The usual naysayers in the press were extremely pessimistic, predicting that an Olympiad in Los Angeles would be a disaster plagued by traffic jams, smog, heat, terrorism, and general chaos. They continually harped on the financial disaster of the 1976 Montreal Games, and took every opportunity to drive that point home to the taxpayers of Los Angeles. Just a month after winning the bid in October 1978, the citizens of Los Angeles passed a city charter amendment that prohibited the use of public funds for the games.

That suited me just fine. I did not consider government involvement necessary, or even desirable; government money inevitably brings government control. The vote by the citizens of Los Angeles offered us an incredible opportunity to produce the first-ever private enterprise games—quite a reversal from the state-sponsored Moscow Games that had become such a symbol of communist corruption and inefficiency. I understood fully that the 1984 Olympics could be a showcase for American ingenuity and enterprise. I also understood that the prospect of failure had significant ramifications for both the future of the games and the cause of freedom. What a fortuitous vote!

However, piggybacking that vote was a decision by the city not to indemnify the International Olympic Committee, as is customary, for any losses. I felt that if Los Angeles wouldn't indemnify, the USOC should. I thought that doing so would demonstrate in a very public way that we had every confidence that the Los Angeles Games would succeed marvelously.

———

WILLIAM TUTT, SEPTEMBER 10, 1999

Part of the Olympic charter says that the host must indemnify the International Olympic Committee from any loss. Los Angeles knew that if it sent a referendum to the citizenry, it would get voted down, so it reneged on that part of the agreement and refused to indemnify.

Bill said, "We have to take some risk here. We are going to sit down with Los Angeles and their organizing committee and put together a program where we, the USOC, will indemnify." We put together a structure with the Los Angeles Olympic Organizing Committee, and that couldn't have happened without Bill's vision and willingness to take a risk . . . He's got guts, but he also has vision. Bill could see potential where others couldn't.

————

The LAOOC had considered several candidates to lead the effort—including Al Haig, Chrysler chairman Lee Iacocca, National Football League commissioner Pete Rozelle, and sports announcer Curt Gowdy—but Justin Dart lobbied very strenuously for Peter Ueberroth. Justin thought that Peter Ueberroth, who had built from scratch the second largest travel enterprise in North America (First Travel Corp.), was a dynamic go-getter, just the type of person needed to serve as chairman of the LAOOC. With Justin's strong support, and my concurrence, Peter Ueberroth was hired. We hit the ground running.

Instead of building new facilities, existing ones were used, such as the Los Angeles Coliseum, which had initially been constructed for the 1932 Games. Tens of thousands of volunteers were recruited (even Peter Ueberroth, who had sold First Travel for $104 million, foreswore his $104,000 Olympic salary to become a volunteer). Millions of dollars were raised from corporate sponsors, a domestic TV contract, and the Olympic coin programs.

Everything seemed to be progressing smoothly, but there were lingering concerns, as early as 1981, that the Soviet Union would boycott the L.A. Games. This had the IOC in a dither, but there were many other bridges to cross before that one. Acting as the chief representative of the Olympic movement in the United States cast me in the eye of numerous storms, not the least of which was the debate over amateurism, which had been simmering within the Olympic movement at least since the Jim Thorpe fiasco in 1913.

Jim Thorpe, the first Native-American to participate in the Olympic Games, was one of the greatest athletes that this, or any other country, ever produced. At Carlisle Indian School, a vocational school in Pennsylvania, Thorpe earned All-American honors in 1911 and 1912 as a halfback, and varsity letters in eleven different sports. In 1912, he led the Carlisle football team to the national championship, scoring twenty-five touchdowns and 198 points. The same year, he was chosen to represent the American Olympic team in several events.

Jim Thorpe won the pentathlon and decathlon, finished fourth in the high jump, and seventh in the long jump. In addition to the gold medals, Tzar Nicholas of Russia gave Thorpe a jewel-encrusted chalice for winning the pentathlon; King Gustav V of Sweden awarded Thorpe a bronze bust for the decathlon.

"Sir, you are the greatest athlete in the world," the king declared.

"Thanks, King," Thorpe humbly replied.

Unfortunately, prior to competing in the Stockholm Games, Thorpe had accepted about two dollars a day to play "bush-league" baseball during his summer vacations in 1909 and 1910, a very common practice for college athletes. He didn't know any better, and certainly didn't mean to violate the Olympic code.

"I did not play for the money . . . but because I like to play ball," Thorpe wrote in a letter of contrition and explanation to James E. Sullivan, the American commissioner of the 1912 Olympics. "I was not wise to the ways of the world and did not realize this was wrong and that it would make me a professional in track sports."

Regardless, in 1913, Jim Thorpe's Olympic medals were revoked and his name was stricken from the record books. The gold medals that Jim Thorpe rightly earned—he was indeed, as King Gustav observed, the greatest athlete on the planet—were given to the second place finishers in the decathlon, reluctant recipients who were threatened with penalties if they didn't accept them.[1] Jim Thorpe went on to play professional football and major league baseball. But he never got over losing his Olympic medals.[2] I had always considered the loss an injustice and tragedy.

When I became president of the USOC, I finally had an opportunity to do something about it. Jim Thorpe's family was pressing hard to have his medals returned and amateur status restored. However, that matter was under the jurisdiction of the International Olympic Committee, not the USOC, and the IOC had responded to the Thorpe family appeals with indifference. As president of the USOC, I lacked authority to take any official action.

However, an opportunity presented itself in 1982, and I took advantage of it. One day, I received a call from IOC President Juan Antonio Samaranch. Samaranch, a former diplomat who had been Spain's ambassador to the Soviet Union and the People's Republic of China, had taken over as president of the IOC just two years earlier.

"Bill, I need a favor from you," Samaranch said.

"Fine, Juan Antonio. Anything you need from me, you've got," I said. "Within reason."

Samaranch told me what he needed (and, frankly, I can't remember what it was).

"I will take care of it, gladly," I responded, "but I'll have to spend a lot of chips doing it, and I want a favor in return. I want Jim Thorpe's medals returned."

Juan Antonio Samaranch promised me only a chance to present the case to the International Olympic Committee, which I did as forcefully and passionately as I could. The committee, to my delight, voted to restore Jim Thorpe's medals. The original medals, long lost, were replaced with replicas, and presented to Thorpe's daughter, Grace, and I was made an honorary Indian. (Odds are that I am the world's only Irish-French-Catholic-Indian with a Jewish-sounding surname. Talk about a melting pot!)

It had taken seventy years to rectify the injustice, and I thought it was high time for the IOC to rethink and redraft its rules on eligibility. The concept of "amateurism" is shaky; in ancient Greece, athletes were supported by the government and richly rewarded if they won. Amateurism, as an Olympic embrace, arose from Victorian England, not out of any sense of athletic purity but because the leisured rich did not want to compete against, or associate with, working-class athletes whose muscles were toned and developed by manual labor.

By the 1950s, the vaunted "amateurism" of the Olympic Games was a sham, and everyone knew it. Eastern bloc nations, eager to prove the "superiority" of communism, funneled enormous resources into athletic training programs and put their athletes on state payrolls while calling them soldiers, teachers, and commissars. Meanwhile, to remain competitive, Western athletes began accepting under-the-table appearance money, university "grants in training," and other benefits. It was a farce.

Jack Kelly,[3] the president of the Amateur Athletic Union in 1970 and 1971, noted sadly, "As many as two-thirds of the athletes signing the Olympic oath are committing perjury (in a moral, if not legal, sense). Instead of teaching the great lessons of our sport—honesty, integrity, and fair play—our code sanctions the worst." Jack was right on the money.

Under Rule 26 of the IOC Charter, an amateur is someone who has not signed a professional contract. I proposed changing that regulation to allow in Olympic and other "amateur" competitions athletes who had signed a professional contract, but had not yet accepted payment nor performed under the contract. Additionally, I proposed allowing athletes to compete as a professional in one sport and an amateur in others, and allowing athletes to accept commercial endorsements—royalties, appearance fees, and the like—so long as they were not paid for an actual athletic performance.

There was, however, long-standing resistance to reform, and the flawed code of amateurism would ultimately have to fall of its own weight. Avery Brundage, president of the IOC from 1952 to 1972 and an athlete who had competed in the 1912 pentathlon, refused to even consider altering the rules. "The Olympic movement today is a revolt against the twentieth century—a devotion to the cause and not the reward," he said at his inaugural. "If the games become contests between the hired gladiators of various nations with the idea of building national prestige or proving that one system of government or another is better than another, they will lose all purpose."

The IOC hemmed and hawed for years and simply refused to face the uncomfortable truth about its code of amateurism, claiming it wasn't the right time. The amateurism issue reemerged at the 1984 Winter Games at Sarajevo, Yugoslavia, the first Olympic competition

held since I had become president of the USOC. Eventually, I proposed that if there was no eligibility standard which all 151 nations
involved could abide by, the games should be open. It had become
downright silly; as long as a track star Carl Lewis funneled his income
through The Athletic Congress (TAC) trust, he remained eligible, but
Ingemar Stenmark, the great Swedish skier, was banned for taking
cash openly.

If we couldn't have honest amateurism and simple rules that all
nations could adhere to, I argued, we might as well open it up and let
the best athletes in the world compete.[4] I often felt like the little boy
in *The Emperor's New Clothes*—telling a truth that no one wanted to
acknowledge. Despite its high-minded ideal of shielding the Olympic
Games from the corruptive influences of money, the IOC has often
found the allure of wealth difficult to ignore. Consider the scandals
of 1998 and 1999, when it was revealed that Salt Lake City officials
had essentially bribed members of the IOC for the right to host the
2002 Winter Games. Or consider an incident with which I became
involved almost immediately after assuming the presidency of the
USOC.

Horst Dassler, heir to the Adidas shoe empire, had for quite some
time been promoting a plan to market the games. Dassler's plan was
to establish a marketing agency that would act as the IOC's agent,
taking a 15 percent commission on every dollar raised. The glitch,
however, was that Dassler needed to convince some 150 national
Olympic committees to surrender their license to the five rings in
return for a cut of the revenues.

Shortly after I became president, Horst Dassler paid a visit to my
New Jersey home, where he met with Don Miller and me over coffee.
Dassler explained his plans for his marketing agency, International
Sports and Leisure (ISL). But Don and I were not interested. Dassler's
"share the wealth" plan would, we thought, result in a windfall for
the smaller national committees, at the expense of the larger, better
organized committees, like the USOC. Besides, neither of us thought
it wise to cede control of U.S. Olympic Committee finances to an
international organization. Under federal law, the USOC had exclusive

rights to market the Olympic name and symbols in the U.S. Why would we give up that right?

Dassler then played his trump card: If Don and I could get the USOC to join ISL, he would kick back to us 5 percent of the proceeds. A quick calculation indicated that he was talking about providing each of us with somewhere between $5 million and $10 million! It was quite an offer. It was also, in our minds, a bribe.

"That's the most dishonest thing I ever heard of," I said with disgust. I asked Mr. Dassler to leave.[5]

Shortly thereafter, Don Miller heard from David McKenzie, Australia's representative on the IOC. McKenzie was profoundly disturbed by the IOC's relationship with ISL, and was eager to meet with Don and me in August 1981 to discuss what he viewed as a very unholy alliance. But McKenzie never made it to our scheduled meeting in Colorado Springs. While vacationing in Hawaii, David McKenzie was found dead at a sauna in Waikiki, an ice pick thrust in his throat. There were suspicions, never officially confirmed, that McKenzie was set up (by whom was never clear) because he was planning to blow the whistle on ISL. I was, and remain, curious about David McKenzie's death, but at the time I was too busy planning the 1983 Pan American Games and 1984 Olympic Games to spend much time on cloak-and-dagger theories.

I was also too busy to make a real effort to succeed Bowie Kuhn as commissioner of baseball, although I did seriously consider it for a while. In 1983, I was among four candidates under discussion to succeed Bowie. The others were Peter Ueberroth, Yale University president A. Bartlett Giamatti, and Jack Valenti, president of the Academy of Motion Picture Arts and Sciences. I knew I had the support of many of the owners, as well as Bowie, and it would have been a thrill to serve as commissioner of Major League Baseball. However, I felt the positions would have placed too many restrictions on my professional and personal lives (and, after the 1978 discussions to purchase the Orioles fell through, I still harbored a dream of someday owning a major league franchise, which I obviously would not be able to do if

I became commissioner), and withdrew from consideration. (Peter Ueberroth became commissioner after the 1984 Games.)

Meanwhile, I was dealing with other issues of Olympian proportions.

The year 1983 began with controversy when the coach of the American basketball team, Bobby Knight, caused a stir with a speech in Gary, Indiana. Bobby is one of the greatest collegiate basketball coaches of all time, and a good friend. However, he does have a temper (once, while coaching at Indiana University, where he has coached since 1971, winning three national championships, Bobby Knight stuffed a boorish spectator in a garbage pail!) and a propensity to display it at inopportune moments.

At the Pan American Games in 1979, Bobby was involved in an altercation with a police officer in Puerto Rico. Although U.S. players, assistant coaches, and team officials who witnessed the incident all insisted that the policeman was at fault, Bobby was charged with aggravated assault and, after he fled the commonwealth, was convicted in absentia and sentenced to six months in prison.

I reviewed the matter extensively and concluded, without any doubt, that Bobby Knight had been railroaded. As far as I was concerned, it was over and done with. However, Bobby managed to resurrect the issue in 1983 when he chose to disclose to an audience in Gary, Indiana, that when he fled Puerto Rico in 1979, he had dropped his pants in the window of the plane "because that's the last thing I wanted those people to see of me."

Immediately, there was uproar with the governor of Puerto Rico and many American citizens insisting that Bobby be fired. I stood by Bobby, although his remark was rather impolitic, and in time that storm blew over. However, there were other crises on the horizon.

———

BOBBY KNIGHT, BASKETBALL COACH, MAY 15, 2000

I was getting a lot of crap because I got into that horseshit situation in Puerto Rico in 1979 when I coached the Pan American team.

The Hispanic caucus in Congress started to raise hell and bitch about me coaching the Olympic team, but Tip O'Neill [then speaker of the U.S. House of Representatives] called them in and shut them up. Then, at a meeting in Indianapolis with Olympic Committee members from all across the country, there was going to be some trouble.

But Bill was the Rock of Gibraltar. He got up to address the committee and said, "Before we get started, just let me say how pleased I am that Bob Knight is going to be our basketball coach." There wasn't going to be any question and there wasn't going to be any debate. He simply eliminated any opposition. There is nobody who admires or respects Bill Simon more than I do.

If Bill Simon was on my basketball team, he'd be my captain because of his leadership qualities, because of his determination, because of how responsive he would be to my dictates to him as a player on the floor. I can tell you without reservation that Bill Simon, on my team, is the captain. He is one tough son-of-a-bitch. I understand that other people might use the same phrase—"tough-son-of-a-bitch"—to describe Bill Simon. But I am one guy who really understands what the total dimensions of that phrase imply.

———

In August 1983, the U.S. Olympic Committee and American athletes were forced to seriously consider the issue of drug testing for the first time. Illegal use of performance-enhancing drugs had been an issue for some time, but testing was haphazard and unreliable. That changed at the IX Pan American Games in Caracas, Venezuela, when more sensitive testing protocols resulted in the most heavily publicized drug scandal ever to hit amateur sports. Fifteen athletes, including two Americans, were stripped of their gold medals after testing positive for banned substances. The incident sent shock waves through the athletic community, and required an immediate response from the USOC.

In September, we officially launched the U.S. Olympic Committee Task Force on Drug Control. Its mission was to immediately establish and implement the IOC's doping control program, enhance research and educational activities, and deter the use of banned substances.

Although our intent was to declare war on drugs, not athletes, we instituted mandatory, random doping tests at domestic competitions. It was crucial to deal with the problem quickly and decisively with the Olympic year quickly approaching.

The year began with the Winter Games at Sarajevo, where a controversy arose over whether Radio Free Europe and Radio Liberty could cover the games in the Eastern bloc.

The Soviets had denied press credentials to eleven journalists, arguing that the CIA had once covertly funded the stations. The president of the stations, former Olympic yachtsman Julian Roosevelt, the American representative on the nine-member executive board of the IOC and descendant of President Theodore Roosevelt, caved in entirely and opposed granting press credentials to Radio Free Europe and Radio Liberty reporters. Granted, the stations' purpose was propaganda, but that is also the purpose of all media in the unfree world. In April, the USOC executive board voted to remove Julian Roosevelt from the USOC administrative committee for not representing its interests with the IOC. He was replaced by Anita DeFrantz.

Meanwhile, the IOC was terribly strapped, largely because a prime source of funding, American television networks, which paid hefty sums to broadcast the Olympic Games, had partially dried up. NBC had canceled its broadcast of the 1980 Moscow Games and ABC was demanding an enormous rebate if a boycott or other glitch diminished interest in the upcoming Olympics in Los Angeles.

Concurrently, the Soviets were complaining about everything— heat and smog, private financing, security preparations—and seemed to be searching for an excuse to boycott. When the leaders of the Eastern bloc sports organizations met in North Korea in September 1983, Tass, the Soviet propaganda agency, reported their opposition to "professionalism and commercialization of sports" and cited concerns over "reliable guarantees of security" and "problems of accommodation and transport."

It was an ominous sign, but we remained optimistic that the Soviets would ultimately agree to come, and continued to push ahead with all plans and preparations, including those for an ambitious torch relay. The idea behind the torch relay and Olympic flame originated with Theodore Lewald of Germany in 1928, who proposed to the IOC, of which he was a member, to light a flame in Olympia, Greece, and transport it by relay to the host country. Four years later the proposal literally came to light. A flame was lit at the Amsterdam Games and again four years later in Los Angeles. The first Olympic torch relay was organized by Carl Diem, founder of the Graduate School of Sports in Cologne, Germany, for the 1936 Berlin Games. A torch was lit in Olympia and carried through Europe to Berlin for the opening ceremonies. Torch relays have been a part of the games ever since.

The relay to L.A. was a particularly enterprising effort, requiring a torch flown from Greece to New York, where it would be hand carried across the country. The relay would begin on Tuesday, May 8, 1984, and traverse the country on a 9,000-mile journey to Los Angeles. Any individual, organization, or business that wanted to donate $3,000 could designate a torchbearer to run a kilometer.

The first morning of the torch run, I met at the United Nations Plaza Hotel with Peter Ueberroth, New York Mayor Ed Koch, Los Angeles Mayor Tom Bradley, AT&T[6] Chairman Charles Brown, Olympian Rafer Johnson, Julian Roosevelt of the IOC, and the first two torchbearers—Gina Hemphill, granddaughter of the great Jesse Owens, and Bill Thorpe, Jim Thorpe's grandson. We were all as excited as children on Christmas, despite the steady downpour outside.

At 8:40 a.m., Peter plunged the torch into the flaming caldron and the torch was ignited. He handed the torch to Gina and Bill. They took off up First Avenue, beginning a procession that would continue for another eighty-one days. It was while the flame was making its way through Manhattan, held by the second runner, ninety-one-year-old Abel Kiviat who had won a silver medal in the 1,500-meter event at the 1912 Stockholm Games, that we learned that the Soviet Union was boycotting.

Although the news was not exactly a total surprise, it was devastating and immediately stole the attention from the torch relay. Media from all over the world were seeking comment and explanation. So I cancelled plans to join a relay commencement ceremony at the United Nations Building and instead went over to the Olin Foundation offices on Madison Avenue, where I made myself available for hour upon hour to an endless stream of reporters. I told the press that I was disappointed, but not disillusioned, and hopeful, but not optimistic, that the Soviets would change their minds.

Meanwhile, the big question was the broader impact of the boycott on the L.A. Games and the Olympic movement. Bulgaria and East Germany promptly joined the boycott. By Saturday, Vietnam, Mongolia, Laos, and Czechoslovakia announced that they would not come to Los Angeles. But China announced that it would send an Olympic delegation for the first time in thirty-six years—a gutsy decision. Later, Hungary and Poland joined the boycott. That made ten.

We had until June 2, the official deadline for announcing participation, to convince the Soviets to change their position. Juan Antonio Samaranch traveled to Moscow with Mario Vasquez Rana of Mexico, president of the Association of National Olympic Committees. Jesse Jackson, who was then seeking the Democratic presidential nomination, met with Soviet Ambassador Anatoly F. Dobrynin, but got nowhere. Our hopes were fading.

On Monday, May 14, Marat Gramov, head of the National Olympic Committee of the USSR, said at a Moscow news conference, "We have faced subversive elements and provocations guided by the United States, but never before has the anti-Soviet campaign been so extensive. It threatens not just the tranquility and health of our nations but their very lives." Gramov specifically referred to private anti-Soviet groups in the L.A. area, which had publicly declared their eagerness to help Russian athletes defect. But there was no question that the Soviets were retaliating for 1980 and, despite claims to the contrary, trying to build momentum for a mass boycott.

Simultaneously, Olympic committees in other nations were being threatened by mail. For instance, China, Singapore, Nigeria, Zimbabwe, Sri Lanka, and South Korea all received similar letters, all postmarked from the Washington, D.C., area and purporting to be from the Ku Klux Klan. (An investigation by the State Department and FBI found no proof that the KKK had anything to do with the threats; rather, it strongly indicated that the letters were part of a Soviet disinformation plot.)

On May 16, Peter Ueberroth traveled to Washington and met with Secretary of State George Shultz, FBI Director William Webster, and Mike Deaver of the White House, but there was little that could be done from Washington.

The IOC called an emergency meeting for Friday, May 18, 1984, in Lausanne. I flew out on Thursday for what would be the first face-to-face meeting of Olympic officials from the U.S. and the Soviet Union since the Kremlin announced its boycott. The day before, Ueberroth met with Gramov, but reported no progress whatsoever. Don Miller and I met with Peter Ueberroth and the LAOOC delegation at the Lausanne Palace Hotel. I recommended sanctions against boycotting countries and a bilateral U.S.–Soviet agreement banning future boycotts. Additionally, I suggested that the IOC consider establishing five permanent Olympic sites, and asking the member nations to commit themselves to participate regardless of future political considerations.

Apparently, this was all too much for Lord Killanin to take. Killanin, the former IOC president, attending in an advisory capacity, rebuked me, reminding me of America's role in the 1980 boycott. He failed to see the distinctions between the 1980 boycott on principle and the 1984 boycott for retribution. Lord Killanin was a jolly Irishman, big-hearted but somewhat slow-witted and ponderous. Once, in an op-ed piece for the *Sunday New York Times,* I described him as follows. "Explaining something sensible to Lord Killanin is akin to explaining something to a cauliflower. The advantage of the cauliflower is that if all else fails, you can always cover it with melted cheese and eat it."[7]

The meeting, however, was fruitless. Immediately after its conclusion, Gramov announced, "The decision is final." The IOC denounced the Soviet's decision, saying it "causes grave damage to the members of the Olympic movement." The Soviet boycott, the third major boycott in the third straight Olympiad,[8] represented a grave threat to the Olympic movement. It was crucial to limit our losses and prevent further erosion of the Olympic movement. The Soviets were trying to convince nations to boycott and we were pleading with them to attend.

On June 4, we were able to announce that 142 nations would attend the L.A. Olympics, a new record. We not only beat the record (the previous record, 122, was set in Munich), we shattered it. The boycott had been contained to a just fourteen countries. We had the funding, the facilities, the staff, and the volunteers to succeed. The torch was on its way to L.A.

The torch relay was a huge success, even though the first day festivities had been dampened by the announcement of the Soviet boycott. It was also a wonderful tool for building enthusiasm step-by-step across this great nation. Cheers of "Go USA" and "to hell with the Russians" greeted torchbearers as they zigzagged across the country. My turn came in Los Angeles, on the final day. When I carried the torch, I was filled with pride and had chills up my spine. I handed it off to Vicki Ueberroth, Peter's daughter.

Afterward, I headed over to the Coliseum for the opening ceremonies, a marvelous display designed by David Wolper. Wolper, a man of inestimable talent who had produced dozens of documentaries and films (including such classics as *Roots* and *The Thorn Birds)*, could have named his price—whatever he charged would have been a bargain. But like so many others, Wolper donated his skills. The results were fantastic. After Wolper's breathtaking production, President Reagan declared the Summer Games open, the first U.S. president to do so. Ten Olympians[9] and Bill Thorpe, Jr. carried the Olympic flag into the Coliseum.

Suddenly, Gina Hemphill sprinted out of the tunnel, holding the torch high, and ran exuberantly around the track before handing off to Rafer Johnson, the 1960 decathlon champion and silver medalist at the Melbourne Games. Rafer carried the torch around the Coliseum track and, with the torch held high, climbed a hydraulic staircase to light the torch the cauldron that would burn throughout the games. The torch relay raised $10.9 million, which was distributed to Girls Clubs, Boys Clubs, YMCAs, and the Special Olympics.

Fueled by the energy pent up over eight long years since the U.S. had participated in the Olympics, and inspired by a hometown crowd, America shined for sixteen days as a record 140 countries sent 7,800 athletes to compete in the L.A. Games. Edwin Moses won his ninetieth straight 440-meter hurdle. Carl Lewis's four gold-medal performance in track and field matched Jesse Owens' feat in Berlin forty-eight years earlier. Mary Lou Retton came away with five medals in gymnastics, including the first individual gold medal ever won by an American woman. Michael Jordan and Patrick Ewing led the last of America's all-amateur basketball teams to an easy gold medal. Valerie Brisco-Hooks became the first woman to win the 200 and 400 meter sprints; Greg Louganis, quite possibly the greatest diver in history, was the first person in fifty-six years to win both diving events (a feat he repeated four years later). Joan Benoit won the first woman's marathon. And wrestler Jeff Blatnick, perhaps more than any other athlete, symbolized the Olympic spirit. Jeff overcame cancer, as well as his opponents, and became only the second American ever to win a gold medal in Greco-Roman wrestling. In all, the U.S. came away with 174 medals, 83 of them gold. Seventy-one Olympic records were set. Despite the boycott, the Olympic movement came out of the games stronger than ever.

———

BILL HYBL, PRESIDENT OF THE USOC, SEPTEMBER 2, 1999

There would not be the Olympic Games today without the games in Los Angeles in 1984, when Bill Simon was president. The Olympic movement worldwide was bankrupt. In 1980, the U.S. boycotted the Olympic Games in Moscow. Tehran was to host the games in 1984, and backed away. Los Angeles stepped up with a guarantee from the United States Olympic Committee, on Bill's watch. The games were a commercial success, and a tremendous boost for the two hundred nations that competed in a spirit of fair play, international competition, and good sportsmanship. Los Angeles was the turning point for the Olympic Movement worldwide.

There is one particular episode that truly demonstrates to me the passion Bill has for the Olympic Committee and the Olympic movement. The USOC has always had a flag-raising ceremony for the team in the Olympic Village. And in 1984 in Sarajevo, Yugoslavia, we went out and there was nobody there. Bill personally rounded up athletes, rustling them around the flagpole—and then led them in singing the "Star Spangled Banner." He isn't exactly Pavarotti, but it was terrific, and one of those small but very significant moments.

Also in Sarajevo, Bill worked very hard so the Voice of America could cover the games. The Eastern bloc countries were trying to exclude any coverage by members of the Voice of America staff. Bill took a very hard freedom-of-the-press stance, and he won. . . .

We have been through some tumultuous times together, whether it was the Tonya Harding[10] case, or what has gone on recently between Salt Lake City and the IOC.[11] He understands and is willing to speak out. He is forthright and his commitment to the U.S. Olympic Committee is unshakable.

——

The 1984 Olympic Games, the most elaborate and extensive in all of history, posed an almost unbelievable challenge. That challenge was spectacularly met and it was achieved without tax dollars. We were blessed with good weather, little smog, and freeway traffic that was much lighter than anticipated. But mostly, we were blessed with good old-fashioned Yankee ingenuity and pride.

Thanks to prudent management, corporate sponsorships, and television rights, the L.A. Games realized a profit of $225 million, most of which was shared with various national and international sports organizations. It marked the first profitable Games since 1932, the last time the Summer Olympics had been held in the United States. The USOC, which for so long had been a hand-to-mouth organization, emerged from the 1984 Olympics with a $110 million nest egg. The money went into a number of investments—domestic stocks, foreign stocks, securities, real estate—and each year a percentage of profits are shared with member organizations.

The Olympics that nobody else wanted, the first Olympics run by a nongovernmental organization, were a stunning success. In 1985, the USOC established a foundation—the U.S. Olympic Foundation—with me as chairman and Don Miller as president, to invest the assets.

———

WILLIAM TUTT, SEPTEMBER 10, 1999

Bill is also the godfather of the U.S. Olympic Foundation. As we saw the bonanza that was going to result [from the Los Angeles games], Bill said, "We have to protect this asset, and ensure that we provide for the future of our Olympic athletes." He was concerned that the administration would rapidly spend the money and have nothing to show for it once we got to the next Olympics, so we put together a structure which is the U.S. Olympic Foundation. It was really all Bill's doing. It worked, and it still works today.

Bill has a brilliant financial mind and a sixth sense that enables him to be in the right place at the right time. But he creates the right time just by the way he can see around corners. We would have no endowment in the Olympic movement, we would have no foundation, we would not be in the position we are in today, without the vision and the fortitude and the leadership and guidance of Bill Simon.

———

In January 1998, I started the William E. Simon Olympic Trust for the Support of Athletes. The purpose of the $1 million trust is, as stated in its mission statement, to provide "with a minimum of bureaucracy and maximum flexibility, a source of funds for the support of athletes needing assistance." Grants are not limited to athletes expected to qualify for the Olympics. I wanted to recognize and support the many personal benefits of athletic training and competition, even for those who lack the talent to compete at the very highest level.

My Olympics experiences rate among the most rewarding of my life, and the awards I received—Samaranch bestowed on me the Silver

Olympic Order (the most prestigious honor bestowed by the IOC); I was inducted into the Hall of Fame in 1991 and received the General Douglas MacArthur Award in 1999—are among my most cherished.[12]

In an era when so many of our institutions are under attack, the majesty of the Olympic movement, and its ability to transcend political chaos and carry on, is a great comfort and inspiration.

———

DONNA DE VARONA, OLYMPIC GOLD MEDALIST, REMARKS AT THE UNITED STATES OLYMPIC COMMITTEE DOUGLAS MACARTHUR AWARD[13] LUNCHEON, SEPTEMBER 14, 1999

Bill, at a time that it was very important to us, lent his credibility to a movement being reshaped by many forces . . . When we needed a peacemaker and a leader and one that was visible, it was Bill Simon who said, "I will step up."

I loved watching the combination of Bill Simon and the late Colonel Don Miller as they battled to bring the American Olympic team and the committee to prominence. They shared vision, they shared power, and there was no secret agenda. Because the agenda was to make our athletes the best in the world and to make our committee the most respected, we have what we have today: the best athletes, the best system, the best program.

Bill lead this movement through difficult times—near bankruptcy, boycotts, restructuring, athlete's rights battles, leadership battles—but of all the things he has given me as a person, the most important is his personal time. Of all the things I have earned through the Olympics, it's not the gold medals I treasure most, it's the friendships . . . Thank you for your leadership, your credibility, your time—and for lighting the way for me in my life.

LEVERAGED BUYOUTS

When I became president of the United States Olympic Committee, it was obvious that my labor of love would consume a great deal of my time, passion, and energy for the next four years, as it surely did.

My professional life was in a state of transition. I had ruled out returning to Salomon Brothers or government and really wasn't quite sure where my path would lead. Early in 1981, I had the great fortune to meet a dynamic young businessman named Raymond G. Chambers, and my business life took on a new dimension—one that yielded more wealth and more fun than I ever imagined.

At the time, I was trading heavily in the stock market on the theory that equities were a bargain because interest rates had risen to outrageously high, and ultimately unsustainable, levels. I borrowed large sums to take large positions, essentially betting that interest rates would fall, stock values would rise, and I would be able to use gains in the stock market to pay off the loans, while taking a reasonable profit.

The risk was substantial; at one point, I was $13 million in debt, a figure that far, far exceeded my assets. But I was pretty confident that I was right and that the payoff would more than cover the cost of leverage. Of course, if I were wrong....

Ray Chambers was operating on a similar theory, although from a somewhat different perspective. Ray, fifteen years my junior, is an easy-going man who happens to be one of the most insightful businessmen of our times, although you'd never have guessed that from his background.

Ray sang and played piano for a rock band until the mid-1960s when he decided to put his Rutgers University accounting degree to use as a tax accountant at Price Waterhouse. Three years later, he left Price Waterhouse along with an auditor named Frank Walsh to run a nursing home business. Ray served as chairman and president of what was then called Metrocare Enterprises, while Frank was executive vice president. In 1969, Ray and Frank took the company public at a considerable profit.

When Ray left Metrocare in 1975, he was all of thirty-two years old, and wealthy enough to retire, if not in luxury then certainly in comfort. But Ray was hardly ready to retire. It had occurred to Ray, as it had occurred to me, that equities were a bargain. However, he had taken that theory a step farther, reasoning that if equities were cheap, then the companies themselves might be undervalued and might make a good investment if they could be acquired. The question was how to acquire them.

Ray and Frank had used their Metrocare proceeds to buy a few small, undervalued companies, tapping the assets of the company they were buying as security for the loans they needed for the purchase. That way, they could put up a relatively small amount of their own money to acquire the company in which—because it was undervalued—the sum of the parts was worth more than the whole.

In a sense, what Ray and Frank were doing was similar to the way most folks buy a house. Since few people have the assets available to buy a house outright, most borrow against the value of the property. The lender's interest, then, is secured by the value of the property being purchased.

By using a similar strategy to acquire undervalued companies, Ray and Frank largely started, on a very small scale, the business strategy that would come to be known as the "leveraged buyout." The term "leveraged buyout" refers to the purchase of a company using borrowed money—often money borrowed from the seller or a third party—for a substantial part of the purchase price. The remainder of the purchase price usually comes from the new management and outside investors, such as venture capitalists like me. Ray and Frank would purchase an undervalued company and then sell off assets to reduce the debt. Because the assets were worth more than the purchase price—again, the sum of the parts was greater than the whole—they were able to cover the cost of the loan and make an extraordinary profit.

I was introduced to Ray by a mutual friend from the Morris County Golf Club, an insurance agent named Ted Godfrey. Ted knew me and he knew Ray and he thought the combination of our respective talents had incredible potential.

"With you and Ray," Ted said, "one and one makes six."

Ray explained what he and Frank had been doing and I was immediately intrigued by the potential. But I suspected their leveraged buyouts could be successful on a much larger scale. At the time, there was a fundamental restructuring of American business going on, creating an extraordinary opportunity for investors with the vision and the nerve to take a sizable risk. In short, structurally sound subsidiaries were selling for 40 to 60 percent of their book value because they had become more trouble than they were worth to the parent company.

In the first half of this century, many leading companies were owned by the family dynasties or the entrepreneurs who created them. When they needed money, they would simply turn to their banks for a loan or issue stock to a relatively small circle of investors. By and large, they tended to nurture and manage their companies carefully. But after World War II, the dynamic changed drastically. The post-war economy was so expansive that companies could not possibly raise on short notice the millions upon millions of dollars needed to sustain growth. So they resorted to selling their stock shares to the public at large. Consequently, the ownership of major American companies broadened. In the past, maybe a dozen investors owned three-fourths to four-fifths of a company, and several hundred jointly controlled the remaining 20 to 25 percent. After World War II, the ratio flip-flopped. Eventually, the big-money investors controlled a quarter or less of the stock, and the thousands of small investors held the bulk.

For many companies, particularly the relatively small ones, this was an unhealthy development since it largely separated control of companies from the people who ran them. Chief executives, no longer accountable to a small and intensely interested group of shareholders, embarked on empire-building crusades. Some companies became cumbersome conglomerates—sumo wrestlers attempting to compete in figure skating. Unrelated, disparate businesses are difficult to manage, and oddball subsidiaries—even good ones—can be hard to explain to shareholders.

Additionally, the cheap dollar and high interest rates of the 1970s had contributed to that trend. Expansion-minded companies with the option of building new facilities or buying out the depressed stocks of other firms came down strongly on the buy side. The economy had created a market for mergers and acquisitions; companies merged and acquired like there was no tomorrow.

When Ray and I came along, companies were eager to "deconglomeratize" by divesting themselves of those subsidiaries that had little to do with the main business. The key was to acquire these companies, often financially sound but mismanaged, and to turn them around. The vehicle through which to do this was debt.

Ray and I saw leverage as the means through which investors like us could acquire undervalued businesses. Through borrowing against undervalued assets, we could acquire companies by putting up relatively little capital and leveraging almost the entire purchase price. A successful LBO depends largely on three factors: the ability to borrow against the company's assets—in other words, to "leverage" the assets; the ability to retain or attract a strong management team; and the potential for each participant's stake in the deal, including management's, to substantially increase in value.

By the early 1980s, the economy was perfect for leveraged buyouts. With inflation rampant, the replacement value of the leveraged assets increases every day. With interest rates rising, today's debt will be paid off with cheaper dollars tomorrow. With economic uncertainty, companies look to spin-off units, not acquire new businesses.

Ray had been fairly content to utilize his company, Hampshire Capital, to make large profits on small ventures. I thought we could get bigger gains, and we agreed to talk about undertaking some joint ventures. The formula would be quite simple: Buy established companies in mature industries, commit capital (but as little as possible), quickly recover the initial investment through fees charged to the acquired company, finance the purchase with the undervalued assets of the acquisition, sell off surplus assets.

I could see the big picture and Ray was extraordinarily adept at tending to details. We decided to give it a go and began looking for companies with good balance sheets and a strong management team that we could retain and rely upon.

———

RAYMOND G. CHAMBERS, JUNE 1, 1999, AND MARCH 31, 2000

Bill thought it was a good time to invest in undervalued corporations and Frank Walsh and I represented a vehicle for doing that. At our first meeting, Frank and I were awestruck. Bill had been secretary of the treasury and was famous in the investment industry. To us, he was kind of like a rock star, and we were a little intimidated. But Bill was intrigued by what we were doing, immediately sensed that it was a timely business and suggested at that first meeting that he would be willing to invest the capital we needed and to help open some doors.

Bill brought, from my perspective, a tremendous amount of energy, enthusiasm, and confidence. Having Bill by your side, you felt you could accomplish anything. No acquisition was too daunting or beyond our reach. He also has perhaps the best instincts of anybody in business that I have encountered....

———

We started off with a few relatively modest acquisitions: the mobile communications division of RCA (Tactec Systems), an oyster farm on

Long Island that supplied restaurants coast to coast (Long Island Oyster Farm Inc.), a firm that rented musical instruments to grammar school and high school students (Mobile Music Man Inc.), and a few others.

Long Island Oyster Farm was kind of a fun deal, largely because of the lender's insistence that we obtain some kind—any kind—of insurance. Now, I wasn't all that confident that we could find someone to insure oysters submerged in the Atlantic Ocean, but Frank Walsh assured us he could take care of that little detail, and by golly he did. At the closing, Frank dutifully handed over the insurance policy, which the lender smugly inserted into a file without bothering to read it.

As we were leaving, I said, "By the way, Frank, just what is it our underwater oysters are insured against?"

Frank grinned. "Fire."

Ray and I formalized our relationship in September 1981 with the establishment of the "Wesray" partnership (a name derived from my initials and Ray's first name) as an acquisition vehicle.

———

FRANK E. WALSH, JR., JULY 8, 1999

Bill brought to the partnership his credibility, his visibility, his contacts, his business judgment, and the guts to make a fast decision when necessary and take a risk. Ray brought to the party his technical ability, his interpersonal skills—which are considerable—and the experience he had in analyzing and buying companies....

We were able to do a lot of things that companies that have to work in a more bureaucratic fashion would not be able to do. We could share ideas, make a judgment, and move quickly....

All people are complex, but Bill is particularly so. The way he operates is probably symptomatic of his training in the bond business, where instantaneous decisions are a necessary way of life. There is no gray in the bond business; it's yes/no, buy/sell, in/out. Bill's impatience, or what is interpreted as impatience, may stem from that. In the bond business, you have a decision before you, you deal with it and move on to the next decision. You don't debate it or talk about it. I think that has carried over to the way Bill approaches a lot of other things. That is a characteristic you will see with a lot of people who have spent their life in the bond business—short, quick, let's do it . . . good-bye.

———

We were humming along quite nicely from the start, making relatively small acquisitions and earning healthy profits, but nothing of historic proportions. And then came Gibson Greeting Cards, which became the textbook example of how to do an LBO and began the leveraged buyout frenzy of the mid and late 1980s.

Gibson Greetings Cards of Cincinnati was brought to our attention in the spring of 1981 by Julius Koppelman, who was head of RCA's communications division. Julius had been impressed with the way we had handled the Tactec Systems deal (and particularly by the fact that we were interested only in "friendly" leveraged buyouts and had no interest whatsoever in a so-called "hostile" takeover) and mentioned that RCA was looking to sell a greeting card company.

RCA had acquired Gibson Greeting Cards from CIT Financial Corp. during the conglomeritization era and was having trouble making it succeed. Greeting cards didn't fit with RCA's corporate product-line strategy, and the company was eager to sell. Despite Gibson's healthy earnings, RCA had been unable to find a buyer.

We flew out to Cincinnati, took a look, and were impressed with what we saw. Gibson had some $200 million in sales and was the third-largest manufacturer of greeting cards in the United States (after Hallmark at $1 billion and American Greetings at $624 million). It held the marketing rights to Garfield the Cat, valuable assets, and excellent prospects—if properly managed. We decided to make a bid.

As soon as Ray and I expressed an interest, Kohlberg Kravis Roberts & Co. (KKR), an investment firm that would later become synonymous with hostile takeovers, floated its own offer, which raised the price. After a fair amount of back-and-forth bidding and counterbidding, KKR concluded that the company was not leverageable and dropped out. History would prove Henry Kravis and his investment firm wrong in a big, big way.[1]

With KKR out of the picture, Ray and I were left alone to pursue Gibson Greeting Cards and immediately began putting together a financing plan. The idea was to put up as little of our own capital as possible, and borrow as much as we could against the assets of the company. We were negotiating with two principal lenders: Citicorp, which ultimately decided it didn't want to be involved, and GE Credit, which agreed to grant us a $100 million line of credit, secured by Gibson's inventories.

The night before the deal was scheduled to close in January 1982, Ray and I were sitting around my small New York City office celebrating, when we were visited by representatives of GE Credit. They informed us, at that late hour, that unless we handed over 25 percent of our equity in Gibson Greeting Cards, they would withdraw their loan. I was incredulous.

"I beg your pardon," I said. "You had a deal with us. We are closing tomorrow and you are trying to blackmail us."

"Blackmail? Well, we wouldn't put it that way, but you can put it any way you want. Besides, don't blame us, we only work for the company."

"Don't give me that bullshit. If you tried a stunt like that when I was at Salomon Brothers somebody, probably I, would have thrown you right out this god-damned window! That's the rottenest thing I've ever heard in my life."

Ray was getting nervous, understandably concerned that I was going to lose my temper and throw the GE representatives out of my office, if not out the window, and convinced me to give in. Even with GE's shenanigans we were able to acquire an $80 million company for $1 million in equity. Ray and I each put up $330,000 while Frank Walsh and the other partners contributed the remainder of the $1 million. Our management fees more than covered the initial investment, so essentially we charged the company we bought for the sum we paid for the purchase, and then some.

In less than a year, Gibson made a turnaround of historic proportions, and I was thrilled with the profits that Ray and I were getting, and equally pleased that the employees with whom we shared equity were reaping the fruits of their labors.

————

RAY CHAMBERS, APRIL 6, 2000

When you are a third-tier subsidiary of a major corporation and you don't own any equity and you have to report up to a vice president who reports up to another vice president, you just don't have that entrepreneurial fire in the belly. If there's one hallmark of the Wesray era it was giving these people, who had been stuck in a bureaucracy, the chance to break out and fulfill their life dream of becoming entrepreneurs.

We specifically looked for managers who would flourish as entrepreneurs and quickly came to the conclusion that we would be better off with a marginal company that had great managers than a great company that had marginal management....

Everybody in Wesray was involved in profit sharing and that created a family bond. Some of our secretaries, who stuck around until the mid to later 1980s, had hundreds of thousands of dollars in their profit sharing plan and were able to retire quite comfortably.

————

That first year, I realized a profit of $12 million—after taxes—on an investment of $330,000. Gibson was succeeding beyond our wildest dreams. Little did I know we were still only at the tip of the iceberg.

In mid-1983, I was approached by Bill Kearns, a senior partner at Lehman Brothers Kuhn Loeb, with an intriguing proposal. Bill is one of my oldest friends, as well as my investment banker. We grew up on Wall Street together in the 1950s and remained close. Bill's got a tremendous sense of humor, but as a businessman he is as serious and shrewd as they come. I enjoyed his company immensely and valued his judgment immeasurably.

"What would you say if I said I could go public with Gibson Greeting Cards?" Bill asked.

"I'd say you were kidding," I replied. "Do you really think the market is ready for something like that?"

Bill started jotting some figures down on a piece of paper and I quickly saw where he was heading. Taking Gibson public was certainly no joke, and the market was certainly ready. In May 1983, we went public at $27.50 per share, for a total valuation of $290 million. That brought us a per-partner profit of about $70 million—we made $200 for every $1 invested over a period of less than eighteen months. From that time on, I relied on Bill Kearns as my investment banker. By the time I left the leveraged buyout business a few years later, Bill had handled over thirty transactions for us, including most of our legendary successes.

For 1983, Gibson Greeting Cards earned $22.4 million, or $2.16 per share on revenue of $241.5 million. At the end of the year, Gibson was carrying $23.2 million in short-term debt and $8.79 million in long-term debt. Just a year earlier, the short-term debt was $46.5 million and the long-term figure was $9.17 million.

Business school professors to this day analyze, and in most cases grossly overanalyze, the Gibson deal. It really is pretty simple to explain, if not so simple to replicate. When we bought Gibson, all the market conditions were wrong—and that is precisely what made it right. Interest rates were too high. Inflation was too high. But that's when a bargain exists. When you can buy companies at 40 to 60 percent of book value and finance it at a time of declining interest rates, you almost can't help but do well. Were we able to forecast the future and know for certain that interest rates would drop, that the stock market would soar? Of course not. But we were willing to take the risk, and that's always the linchpin.

Between 1981 and 1984, we made fourteen acquisitions, mostly of little known companies, and realized incredible profits. Heekin Can, a manufacturer of containers for food and beer, was an $82.9 million company we bought by putting up $1 million in December 1982. Heekin Can was owned by Diamond International, a firm which British businessman Sir James Goldsmith had recently acquired through a hostile takeover. Sir James was reputed to be quite the ladies man and while waiting for him to attend a dinner meeting at my home, Ray and I had a bet over whether he would come with his English wife or his French mistress. We both lost; Sir James came accompanied by an attractive and charming woman from Connecticut. We reached a deal and bought Heekin Can. Three years later, we sold the company at a profit of $28 million.

We put up $1 million to buy Simplicity Manufacturing in March 1983 for $31.4 million, and realized a $48 million profit when we sold the company to an Employee Stock Ownership Plan (ESOP)2 in October 1985. In June of 1983, we bought Anchor Glass Container, a producer of glass bottles, for $169.8 million, and put up only $1 million. Three years later, an initial public offering (or "IPO") of stock, handled once again by my friend Bill Kearns, brought in $21 million. That was a gain of 10,689 percent!

Wilson Sporting Goods was a dandy. Chicago-based Wilson was founded in 1914 as a subsidiary of a meatpacking firm, during an era when animal innards were used to string tennis racquets. By the end of World War II, Wilson was the largest sporting goods manufacturer in the nation. The success continued into the 1960s; then, Wilson was owned by the predecessor to LTV Corporation in Dallas. But after its 1970 acquisition by PepsiCo, the company drifted.

Wilson held one of the best trademarks in sports, but it was ill suited to the mass marketing style of PepsiCo. PepsiCo's main product line consisted of impulse products that were inexpensive and frequently purchased; Wilson manufactured items that are more expensive, durable, and purchased less often. You simply don't sell golf clubs the way you sell soda pop. Additionally, PepsiCo had been using Wilson as something of a training ground for managers, so the best and the brightest were perpetually promoted out of the sporting goods subsidiary.

Wilson Sporting Goods hit bottom with 1984 operating losses of $81 million on sales of $247.6 million—and along we came. I looked at Wilson Sporting Goods for a number of reasons. One, I thought that if we streamlined the business and established a better management system, the company could probably break even, or maybe even make us some money. Two, as a sports nut I thought it'd be great fun to own one of the world's great sporting goods companies. Wilson's logo is on the football used in the Super Bowl, the baseball gloves worn by the likes of Ted Williams and Ernie Banks, and the tennis balls used at the U.S. Open. Its advisory staff included the soon-to-be-legendary basketball star Michael Jordan.

Bill Kearns once again worked his magic and we were able to buy Wilson Sporting Goods, largely through a $45 million subordinated note Bill arranged for the underwriting of the acquisition. Then, we lured out of retirement John P. Murray, a crackerjack businessman who had been president of Prince Tennis Racquets, to run the company.

The leveraged buyout and Jack Murray's leadership helped lift Wilson and its employees to prosperity. By 1988, revenues had grown to $424 million and pre-tax profits recovered to $8.8 million. In just three years, we had doubled the company; leverage had put a very promising company in capable hands.

LBOs were eventually excoriated as unproductive paper shuffling that shifted a lot of money around and left behind only a raped corporate carcass. That is not, however, the history or legacy of Wesray. As I noted earlier, Ray and I never orchestrated a "hostile" takeover. Our deals tended to make companies (and their employees) more productive and profitable. Yes, we made incredible profits. Our average return on equity, compounded semiannually from 1981 through 1988, exceeded 740 percent per year. We also did a lot of good for a lot of other people. In fact, for every transaction completed in 1985 we later donated 10 percent of the profits to charity.

When we took over a company, profits almost always increased, jobs were created, and the community where the firm was based benefited. Far from being hostile invaders, we were often viewed as emancipators, and that was the key to our success.

In 1984, for example, the board of Atlas Van Lines sought us out as a possible "white knight" to stave off a hostile takeover by Edward Bland, former president of Atlas, and a group of Canadian investors. We bought the company for $71.6 million, discouraged the hostile takeover by taking it private, and sold it a few years later at a significant profit.

In 1986, Wesray Transportation, an affiliate of Wesray Corp., teamed with about fifty Avis managers to acquire the number two rental car firm from KKR's Beatrice unit, which had bought Avis from Esmark in 1983. Total price: $1.6 billion, including $265 million in cash and $1.34 billion in debt assumption. The joint ownership deal was a good fit for both partners. Avis needed our credibility in the financial community, and we needed the Avis management to assure commercial viability. The management held 24 percent of the company. We paid off the acquisition debt ($240 million) by selling off the leasing business and a majority of the international division, and promptly refocused the firm by selling non-car rental assets, such as domestic and light-truck leasing operations and some European operations. Less than two years later, we sold the company to an ESOP for $1.75 billion, which included $750 million in cash and assumption of $1.75 million in debt—and came away with a 300 percent profit.

We also succeeded in turning around Proctor-Silex, a New Jersey manufacturer of home appliances. When we bought Proctor-Silex in 1983 for $62 million in cash and $3 million in notes, it was an ailing company—reeling from the effects of a recession in 1981–1982 and struggling to maintain market share against companies like Magic Chef, Sunbeam, and General Electric. We merged Proctor-Silex with Wear-Ever, known for its SilverStone cookware, which we had purchased earlier. After spending $10 million to retool its assembly lines and undergoing a major restructuring, productivity increased dramatically and Proctor's sales increased 10 percent during the first eighteen months after the Wesray LBO. Ultimately, Wesray sold Wear-Ever and Proctor-Silex to the public for a profit of about $90 million (after collecting $2.9 million in management fees and $812,000 in brokerage fees).

Anchor Glass Container Corporation was on the brink of ruin in 1983 when we partnered with Vince Naimoli to buy it from Anchor Hocking. We spun off the company's valuable real estate, moved the corporate headquarters, and transformed Anchor from a barely surviving entity to an extremely successful firm. Taking Anchor public in 1986 infused $28 million in equity into the firm and made nice profits for us as well. On an initial investment of $310,000, I received $37 million in cash and stocks from the offering; Vince turned his $118,000 investment into $14 million. By 1987, Anchor was the number one glassmaker in the nation and number three on *Forbes Magazine*'s ranking of most profitable companies.

————

MERYL STREEP, ACADEMY AWARD–WINNING ACTRESS (AND MY DAUGH-TER'S SISTER-IN-LAW), JULY 2, 1999

Like most indelible personalities, you can't imagine another pair of feet in those shoes. Bill is so completely, idiosyncratically, himself. I can't imagine anybody else playing the role of Bill Simon. He is larger than life....

He taught me something interesting. He was giving us some investment advice and he was saying that you can have a good instinct about something, where to invest, but the most important thing is the second step, the follow-through, to take responsibility, to pay attention. I can't tell you how many times I have used that wisdom in all kinds of different ways—in relationships, in my work, in parenting. I really think there is something quite true in it... Whenever he would give me investment advice, it was life advice.

————

By the mid-1980s, it seemed everyone and his brother was getting into the LBO game—with bigger and bigger offers, and I was getting leery. The game was getting crowded, and any good trader knows that the crowd is almost always wrong. Huge takeover operations, like KKR, were gobbling up firms in a mindless feeding frenzy, failing to pay attention to fundamental values and attempting to leverage firms that weren't leverageable. There was simply too much money chasing too few deals. Takeover "artists" were assuming mammoth, and unreasonable, debts, paying 150 to 200 percent of book value. All they were doing was borrowing to obtain the funds to pay more than the companies were worth. It made no sense.

"The bloom is off the rose," I told Ray. "I think the leveraged buy-out business is over, for the time being. The prices that are being paid today are just ludicrous." I was eager to move into another arena, namely financial services, because I thought midsized bank and thrifts could be bought cheap, and was particularly intrigued by the potential in California and the Pacific Rim. Ray, however, was not interested.

We continued to do some deals together while I began exploring other pastures. By early 1986, I had resigned from the boards of Gibson Greetings and Heekin Can, relinquished all my national directorships, and divested myself of all Gibson stock.

Later that year, I was visited in New York City by Paul W. MacAvoy, a brilliant free market economist and then dean at the University of Rochester, and David Kearns, the chairman of Xerox and a member of the university's board of trustees. They said they wanted to name a business school after me.

"That's very flattering, but I'm really not in the business of buying 'B'-schools," I said, assuming that what they were mainly looking for was a sizable donation in exchange for naming a school in my honor.

"No," Dr. MacAvoy said, "you misunderstand. We want to have the school named after an entrepreneur, a successful business and government leader, who has done all the things you have done. That is an inspiration. We would ask you to do one thing. We need to raise $30 million and the university is willing to pitch in $15 million, so that leaves $15 million to raise. We're not asking you to give anything. We're just asking you to help us raise it. Would you do that?"

"Well, that sounds like a fair deal," I said, turning to Dave Kearns. "David, why don't you start us off by pledging $5 million from Xerox?"

"You're a bastard!" David joked. Xerox came through with the donation.

Within six weeks, we had the $15 million, and the William E. Simon Graduate School of Business Administration was born. The school, of which I am very proud, is distinctive in that it focuses on the incentives and rewards of a free market economy, and how those incentives and rewards influence the sphere of economics. It is consistently ranked among the best business programs in the nation.

Rochester is one of the few business schools, and perhaps the only one, that understands the importance of entrepreneurship—and of course that is exactly what our leveraged buyouts were all about.

———

PAUL W. MacAVOY, JUNE 29, 1994, AND MARCH 16, 2000
The school had been called the Graduate School of Management. It had an excellent faculty, highly expert in two areas—finance and accounting—and pretty good in marketing and production. The faculty was probably uniformly the most conservative of the business school faculties. Quite a number of them had degrees from Chicago's business school, and they had remained relatively pure in their dedication to market economics. But the school was small, and virtually unknown in the business community.

I sat down with the president of the university and some of the trustees and we tried to think of a way to find leadership in the business community that would support us, help us develop a trademark or brand name or to establish a presence. We knew what Bill Simon had done and thought he could be a role model for our students, that a connection with him would identify the school with a business leader—if only we could put his name on the place. We had a need for Simon's name more than we had a need for money, and we approached it that way.

David Kearns and I went to see him in the Olin Foundation office. I said, "Bill, the name of the school is really a problem." He said, "Take off 'management' and put in 'school of business administration.' It's more direct, and it's what you really do."

I said, "That's half of it. The other half is that it needs to be the William E. Simon Graduate School of Business Administration."

Total silence. Bill was really shocked. I think he was expecting us to hit him hard for a major gift, so by catching him off-guard I think we got the opening for him to really consider it.

The renaming took a school that was probably ranked fiftieth in the country and, by itself, without any change in student body or faculty, put it in the top twenty. In polls that rank business schools,

Rochester was never mentioned before it became the Simon School. In the first Business Week poll with a ranking after the renaming, it made the top twenty, and it has stayed there. There was just an immediate and positive impact. Our enrollment of good students more than doubled. Immediately, it was recognized that this place existed and was in the major leagues.

Bill has continued to help change the place internally as well. He goes there to interact with every class. He talks to the students individually. He walks the corridors. He goes to classes and often gives a major talk. He really promoted the Simon School image as entrepreneurial, venturesome, courageous, and free-market oriented....

———

My LBO profits made me an extraordinarily wealthy man and provided the opportunity for a previously unimaginable luxury: my very own yacht. Growing up on the Jersey shore, both Carol and I had a lifelong love of the ocean, and the idea of owning our own boat was enormously appealing. I built Freedom—a boat and a philosophy—after leaving Washington with a fresh and profound appreciation for liberty that I, like most Americans, had essentially taken for granted.

While serving as secretary of the treasury, I had been in the Soviet Union as the leader of the U.S. delegation negotiating a bilateral trade agreement in 1975. It was not until the moment Air Force Two lifted off Soviet soil and the entire American contingent burst into spontaneous elation, that I realized that freedom is not a presence, but an absence—an absence of constraint, an absence of arbitrary restraint, an absence of the governmental chains that had so cruelly bound much of mankind for much of history.

Freedom, a 125-foot sailing yacht custom-built in Italy to my specifications, took three years to build and cost about $4 million. We launched her in 1986 and spent glorious months diving the South Pacific and exploring the world well below the surface. *Freedom* symbolized that ephemeral quality and served as a visible reminder of the lessons I had learned and the appreciations I had gained during my visit inside the grim, stifling communist cocoon.

On *Freedom*, I was an indefatigable seaman and diver, exploring both the surface and depths of the South Pacific and adventuring through Australia and Indonesia, the Solomon Islands, New Guinea, New Zealand, and other exciting and exotic venues. Diving consumed me during those years and provided some of the happiest and most memorable times of my life. One particularly intriguing adventure occurred when Carol and I sailed to Wakaya, a Fijian island.

It seems that a century and a half ago there was a king and queen of Wakaya, and an entire royal family, who presided over the island. But there was trouble in paradise when cannibals invaded the island in the mid-1800s and, quite literally, intended to have the king and queen for dinner. The royal family, or so the legend goes, jumped from a high cliff, committing suicide—which, given the alternative, was probably a prudent decision. For several generations the natives of Wakaya had awaited a new king, one who would, according to local lore, arrive gloriously on a beautiful boat.

When I sailed in on *Freedom*, they assumed I was sent by the gods to preside over their dominion. I was named the king of Wakaya in a coronation ceremony that featured an endless supply of "kava," a potent and highly intoxicating potion made from the dried root of the pepper plant and used for generations by South Pacific islanders on special occasions. We sipped kava throughout the day as the entire village came out to celebrate the coronation. I was presented with a whale's tooth, as a sign of my kingship, and had the option of remaining on the island and living out my days as a monarch.

That was enticing, but there were more enticing fish to fry, and so I set sail for other waters.

California, Here I Come!

In his best-selling novel, *Noble House*, James Clavell recounts the adventures of a Scottish conglomerate struggling to prosper amid the unbridled and unfettered capitalism of Hong Kong in the 1960s. The fictional merchant-banking house in Noble House, modeled after the real-life powerhouse of Jardine Matheson, seeks to become the "taipan," or supreme and undisputed leader of an ocean-spanning trading firm.

I was mesmerized by that novel and intrigued almost to the point of obsession with the Pacific Basin, that vast expanse of people, capital, and entrepreneurial energy stretching from Australia and the Orient all the way to California. Once there were "four tigers" of Asia—Taiwan, Hong Kong, Singapore, and South Korea—now there were suddenly seven on the horizon—with Malaysia, Indonesia, and Thailand joining the ranks of rapidly growing economies. It was a perfect time to pursue my Pacific Basin dream.

I envisioned Hong Kong as a financial hub, with spokes running throughout Asia, particularly Indonesia and Thailand. I imagined a bridge of capital spanning the Pacific Basin and drawing on the enormous assets in Asia while channeling foreign investment into the

United States. Since the keystone of that bridge would be financial institutions, I was looking to acquire commercial banks and savings and loan institutions, also called "thrifts."

At the time, savings institutions had a terrible reputation in the investment community. Since the bulk of their assets were tied up in fixed-rate mortgages, the inflationary times of the late 1970s and early 1980s had wreaked havoc on savings institutions. Accordingly, they were a bargain. I reasoned that if the thrifts could be nurtured back to health, they could be sold at a nice profit to commercial banks. The rejuvenated S&Ls would become a crucial source of venture capital, strategically positioning us to take advantage of the boom I foresaw in Pacific Rim countries.

Gerry Parsky, one of my assistants at Treasury, had become a partner with a large Los Angeles law firm, Gibson, Dunn & Crutcher, specializing in international, corporate, and tax law. I knew Parsky was ambitious, and he told me he had relationships on the west coast where I was eager to establish a toehold. We discussed our thoughts and dreams in some detail and, in 1986, formed a partnership called WSGP, a name culled from our respective initials.

WSGP was created as a merchant banking[1] firm concentrating on the Pacific Rim, financing both investment and trade in a region that offered tremendous potential. The key, not unlike leveraged buyouts, was to identify and acquire undervalued assets. The government was offering an incentive, and our strategy was to take the government up on its offer and essentially do the same thing with the S&Ls that I had done through leveraged buyouts: namely, purchase undervalued assets (undervalued in part because of the government's accounting method), streamline and improve operations, and sell at a profit. We were looking for institutions with large, troubled commercial real estate holdings, which we could market in a very conservative manner.

We knew what we wanted to do, and we knew how to do it, so there was no sense wasting time. In the spring of 1986, we hit the ground running. Parsky promptly brought in two L.A. businessmen,

Larry Thrall, a lawyer and a partner in a Los Angeles real estate management and development company, and Roy Doumani, chairman of
the World Trade Bank in L.A. Larry and Roy had been involved with
Parsky in prior business deals, and he vouched for them. I recruited
Preston Martin, an old friend and an expert in banking who had
resigned that March from his position as vice chairman of the Federal
Reserve. Pres knows banking better than just about anyone, and his
insider perspective on the Washington political and bureaucratic cultures was invaluable. Fortunately, Pres was eager for a change in 1986,
just as we were getting started, and was thrilled to join our enterprise.

With at least a skeletal team in place, we set about to build a
mosaic of financial institutions along the Pacific Rim—strategic part-
nerships in key parts of the world linking trade in the Orient with
financial services in the West.

The long-term plan was to create a healthy investment vehicle that
would fund venture capital initiatives, finance leveraged buyouts,
invest in major real estate developments, and offer other financial services. Ultimately, we wanted to build a two-way bridge of capital that
spanned the Pacific Basin, investing in opportunities in Asia while
channeling foreign investments into the United States.

We were not looking for the quick buck and we were not jumping
blindly into a troubled industry. Every one of our acquisitions would
come only after careful analysis. The acquisition strategy was straightforward and fairly simple: Whether the S&L was healthy or in need
of capital, we would determine the value of the institution's loan portfolio and real estate assets, impose strict controls on the ones we
acquired, and, in cases where the institution as a whole was not particularly attractive, offer to acquire only the best real estate assets. We
established a holding company, H.F. Holdings, in June 1986 to
acquire institutions.

————

LARRY THRALL, FORMER BUSINESS PARTNER, DECEMBER 4, 1993[2]

*I was extremely intrigued by the notion of getting involved in some
way with Bill Simon. He now was a legend—not just because of his*

government experience, but in the leveraged buyout business, which clearly was the hot thing happening in the mid-80s. Always wanting to be in the middle of the action, I was tremendously drawn to that idea....

I immediately realized that Bill is a decision maker. He's relentless when gathering information. He cannot stand for a question to be left unanswered. Bill sees the world in a very broad way and shoots at big targets. His secret is that he sees where the main opportunities are, and goes after them intensely. Everyone else sits around and says, "Gosh, that looks great." They recognize an opportunity but are paralyzed by their own ... inability to act. This guy was totally awesome. He saw where the opportunity was and immediately made it happen. If you didn't want to play the game, if you couldn't stand the amount of voltage Bill put you through, you'd better do something else, because there is no room for inaction....

———

Our effort began in earnest in September 1986 when we agreed to acquire Honolulu Savings & Loan (later renamed HonFed Savings), the largest thrift in Hawaii. HonFed had assets of $1.8 billion, and a negative net worth of $40 million. The thrift was virtually praying for salvation and viewed us as the answer to its prayers.

We put up $57.7 million ($17.7 million in cash, plus the issuance of $40 million in subordinated debt, or "junk bonds," with Salomon Brothers assisting with the financing). Government regulators allowed HonFed to record $107 million in "goodwill," with twenty-five years to write it off. We sold off non-core assets, like foreclosed real estate, and hired a top-flight thrift administrator named Gerald Czarnecki to whip the thrift into shape and to polish what would become the initial jewel in our Pacific Rim investment portfolio. Within two years, assets grew to $3.1 billion, "goodwill" had been trimmed to less than $80 million, and the initiative seemed to be working perfectly—for us, for the investors, for the depositors, and for the federal government.

The HonFed deal was quickly followed by our successful bid for the ailing $1.3 billion Southern California Savings & Loan of Beverly

Hills and, later, the sound Western Federal Savings & Loan. Those purchases formed the initial stitches of our financial mosaic.

Southern California Savings & Loan was a ward of FSLIC (having been declared insolvent by government regulators in mid-1985), and Uncle Sam was desperate for a "white knight" to return the institution to the private sector. We were quite willing to assume that role, and the government was quite eager to have us assume it.

In 1986, I established, along with Parsky and Bruce R. Judge, a New Zealand entrepreneur, International Merchant Banking Services, a new enterprise to oversee investments and allow the various banks and thrifts to "cross-pollinate." Bruce Judge already had a commercial presence in Hong Kong with his Ariadne Australia, a trans-Pacific holding conglomerate in Brisbane. But I thought Ariadne was an underachiever, a huge fish in a small pond, and encouraged Bruce to invest in the United States.

"Why go for the broccoli and potatoes when you can have steak and creamed spinach?" I asked.

Bruce got the point, and agreed to invest $200 million[3] with us, to be split between real estate and financial institutions, the twin prongs of our Pacific Rim initiative.

The Ariadne seed capital contributed to a number of thrifts—including SoCal. We put $5 million into SoCal in April 1987 (other investors, mainly Ariadne, put up a total of $35 million) and the Federal Savings & Loan Insurance Corporation injected $217.5 million. SoCal claimed $60 million in "goodwill" capital, but it had $1 billion in assets. Just like the leveraged buyouts, the whole was greater than the sum of the parts, and we launched two initiatives in the mid- to late-1980s to take advantage of the opportunity: a merchant bank created to acquire financial institutions and real property; and a real estate development company.

At the time, Southern California real estate was booming, both in the commercial and residential markets. For several years, we built a large real estate portfolio and was quite profitable. However, the California real estate market collapsed—partially because of a general economic downturn, partially because the real estate market was overbuilt, and partially because the California S&Ls had financed construction that should not have been financed. We took our fair share of losses in a very difficult economy.

———

Jon Pugh, senior vice president WSGP Realty, December 2, 1993, and February 12, 2000

Gerry, Roy, and Larry knew a ton of people in Southern California. Roy . . . had helped form First Los Angeles Bank. He had made a substantial private fortune himself, was well-to-do and donated to the arts. Larry had been an attorney and had become involved in real estate. He has a really good sense of real estate, is an incredible salesman, and is able to raise money. I headed up the commercial real estate group. Southern California real estate was really booming at the time, at its absolute peak, and we had a really nice commercial real estate portfolio. We were also acquiring residential properties, because they generated cash very quickly. And we had close to $50 million of equity in commercial real estate, most of it in small industrial parks, incubator parks, and the like. . . .

Eventually, the bottom fell out of the real estate market, and everybody suddenly was expected to pay his or her share of the credit lines. I didn't know anybody, except Bill, who could pay his part . . . The Simons were very generous. They didn't break anybody, which they easily could have done to anybody who was involved, ruined them financially if they had chosen to. Most of the developers were allowed out of the project and the Simons picked up the financial responsibilities. None of [the developers] got rich, but none went bankrupt, as so many developers have, because the Simons stuck with them. They were extremely kind to people like me. They could have just said, "Okay, pay up, pal," and they didn't do it. It was awfully decent of them. . . .

———

Early in 1988, my sons, Billy and Pete, paid me the greatest of compliments when they asked to come and work with me. I loved the idea of working with my sons, and the thought of creating a family "dynasty" that would draw on the strengths and contributions of the three of us was indeed appealing.

At the time, Billy was an assistant United States attorney under federal prosecutor (and later the greatest mayor in the history of New York City) Rudolph Giuliani. With the trained mind of a litigator, Billy has the rare ability to surgically deconstruct huge amounts of data and then meticulously reconstruct the information in a way that leaves him intimately familiar with every detail and every nuance. Pete was a partner at Kidder Peabody on Wall Street, a quick-on-his-feet convertible bonds specialist, and a natural trader, a chip off the old block in that regard. Pete's got a real sense of markets and an innate ability to understand the implications myriad factors may have on those markets.

I was immensely pleased and flattered that my sons were willing to forego their own promising careers to work with me. For me, the three Simon men together amounted to a "dream team"—what father does not dream of working with his sons? Carol, however, had a decidedly different perspective. She was vehemently opposed to bringing the boys into the business and expressed her opinion in no uncertain terms.

"You'll ruin the wonderful relationship you have with your children!" she predicted to me.

"You can't work with that tyrant!" she told them.

Despite the entreaties of their mother, Billy and Pete subjected themselves to my baptism by fire. I did not pamper my sons. I worked them hard, came down harshly when they erred through carelessness, and praised them when they succeeded. They took their lumps, just like everyone else. Billy and Pete passed the test with flying colors. We formed a partnership, William E. Simon & Sons, a merchant bank that eventually focused on five core activities: money management, municipal bonds, real estate investment and management, and direct corporate investments.[4]

In the fall of 1988, we purchased Western Federal Savings & Loan, a healthy Marina del Ray S&L, and Bell Savings and Loan Association, an institution in San Mateo with a negative net worth of

$454 million. Those acquisitions would complete the framework for our mosaic, but to acquire those institutions would require considerable financial assistance from FSLIC. We put up $207.5 million in equity capital for 75 percent ownership (and considerable tax benefits); FSLIC contributed $565 million for 25 percent ownership. The new merged institution had assets of $4.3 billion.

Under the initial deal, the government approved our acquisition of Western Savings on the condition that we also take the failed Bell Savings off its hands. In return, the government promised to absorb up to 80 percent of any losses we incurred liquidating problem assets, and granted Western Fed capital forbearance until it could grow out of its troubles. It seemed like a reasonable deal, a rational trade of value for value to the mutual benefit of both parties.

Things seemed to be going well, and I was spending more and more time in homes in California and Hawaii, sailing the Pacific on *Freedom* for months at a time, scuba diving, and surfing. We were well on our way, or so I thought. What we had neglected to foresee, or imagine, was that Congress, which had created the S&L mess, would make it worse, an uncanny skill which our representatives in Washington have mastered to perfection.

In 1988, FSLIC was desperate. And a desperate bureaucracy is the loosest of loose cannons. Losses at federally insured thrifts were running out of control. Neither Congress nor the Reagan White House was willing, in the midst of an election campaign, to do much of anything. And M. Danny Wall, who oversaw FSLIC, was facing a daunting deadline: On December 31, a generous tax benefit that could attract investors would expire. So, he mounted a closeout sale.

In four months, the agency unloaded 114 insolvent thrifts. The government put together some 97 packages hurriedly thrown together in 1988 to shore up collapsing thrifts, mainly in the Southwest. Many of the investors were simply gold-diggers, eager to make a (seemingly) quick and easy fortune, and unwilling to do the kind of research and market analysis we did before every single acquisition. Predictably, many of them failed miserably. Investors lost billions of dollars as a result of mismanagement and, in some instances, outright fraud. Ultimately, the taxpayers were left with the tab.

The resulting outrage on Capitol Hill spurred all manner of so-called "reform" proposals, virtually all of which were destined to make a bad situation far worse. Pres Martin made repeated trips to Washington in 1989 and lobbied strenuously against the thickheaded legislative proposals. He met with lawmakers, their staffs, and regulators. Pres even appealed personally to President Bush, Secretary of the Treasury Nicholas Brady, and budget director Richard Darman, hoping they could and would prevail on Congress. But he couldn't stop a runaway train. Although it should have known better, Congress passed the Federal Insurance Reform & Recovery Enforcement Act (FIRREA) of 1989, a legislative disaster if ever there was one.

FIRREA abolished FSLIC, created a new thrift deposit insurance fund under the FDIC, replaced FSLIC Bank Board with the Office of Thrift Supervision, established the Resolution Trust Corporation to dispose of closed thrifts, and—most importantly from our standpoint—*retroactively* eliminated the use of "goodwill" to meet capital requirements. In midstream, the government changed the rules of the game and required thrifts to "maintain core capital in an amount not less than 3 percent of the savings association's total assets"—and specifically excluded from its new definition of core capital "unidentifiable intangible assets"[5] (read: "goodwill").

FIRREA was supposed to make thrifts more solvent, but had the opposite effect. Overnight, institutions that had been solvent and in full compliance with government regulations were suddenly insolvent, or on the brink of insolvency, and in violation of government regulations.

Consequently, at the end of 1989, HonFed was $65 million short of meeting the government's minimum requirements for capital. We ultimately met the requirement in mid-1990 when the Kamehameha School/Bernice Pauahi Bishop Estate, a private educational trust funded by descendants of Hawaiian royalty, invested $50 million for 23 percent of the bank's equity.

The Bishop Estate, the largest landowner in Hawaii, had previously invested with us in a very successful transaction,[6] and was eager to invest in HonFed. WSGP had to dilute its stake in the thrift, but the infusion of cash from Bishop, plus the sale of some real estate holdings, put us into compliance. At the same time, however, the sweeping real estate recession that had begun on the east coast and worked its way across the continent was wreaking even more havoc on the California market.

By 1990, it appeared market conditions were again ripening for leveraged buyouts, and with my encouragement Parsky began putting together a plan to reenter the LBO market, and we courted Tokio Marine & Fire Insurance, the world's largest property and casualty insurer. Tokio Marine, a Japanese company, agreed to invest $100 million for all of our investment projects except those involving savings and loans (at the time, we had interests in five thrifts and two commercial banks). In turn, the new partnership, WSGP Partners, hoped to raise another $300 million from a small group of institutional investors. The fund would be used for friendly takeovers of medium-sized companies, including some overseas. WSGP closed with Tokio Marine on July 12, 1990, putting up $10 million to Tokio's $100 million and promising the Japanese company participation in all future WSGP deals outside the financial services industry.

Over the previous year, though, I was warned on a number of occasions by a wide variety of people—partners, advisors, lawyers, and family—of Parsky's increasingly troubling behavior. For example, during the first part of 1990 I was told that Parsky was undertaking various side deals that left us in the dark, and potentially exposed us to legal liability.

Ultimately, I chose not to go forward with the new fund because I had lost trust and confidence in Parsky for a number of reasons I do not wish to belabor here. Instead, I decided to focus on WSGP's existing investments and commitments, which I believed were headed into stormy seas, and work through William E. Simon & Sons with respect to future activities.

Meanwhile, we still had joint ownership of several S&Ls. With the Bishop Estate investment, we were able to salvage HonFed and turn a more than respectable profit.[7] But some of our other holdings, particularly Western Federal Savings & Loan, were too far under water after the government changed the accounting rules retroactively. We had acquired Western Federal on the promise that the government would live up to its word to recognize "goodwill" as an asset. However, with the passage of FIRREA, the government reneged. Our risk-based capital stood at about 5 percent, and the government was suddenly demanding 9 percent, and our core capital, which needed to be 4.4 percent, was at 2.14 percent. To meet capital requirements, we would have had to have raised $150 million.

We looked everywhere, even Hong Kong, for help, but investors felt it was just too much of a risk. We asked the government to provide assistance, since it had both created and then exacerbated the S&L problem, but it refused. Unlike businessmen, for whom the bottom line is the bottom line, the bureaucrats were concerned only with covering their own bottom, even if it did not make economic sense.

When the government threatened to seize Western Fed, they said the institution needed an infusion of $150 million because the rules had changed. I suggested the government put up the money for a simple reason: If the government infused the funds, there was a reasonable chance we could turn things around, and the government would get its money back. On the other hand, if the government shut down the institution, it would cost taxpayers $750 million. So, the government regulators had a choice—to come out even or ahead, or almost certainly lose three-quarters of a billion dollars. By picking the guaranteed loss, the government wrote another chapter in a book filled with irrational, arbitrary conduct.

On June 4, 1993, federal regulators seized the profitable Western Federal Savings & Loan, placed the S&L in receivership, and turned it over to the Resolution Trust Corporation, a federal agency. I instantly lost $40 million because the government reneged on its promise.

We were ultimately vindicated on July 1, 1996, when the U.S. Supreme Court held in *U.S. v. Winstar Corp.*[8] that the government had breached its contractual obligations. By a 7-2 margin, the high court held that when the government enters into agreements with individuals or businesses, it must abide by the terms of those agreements or pay damages. It ruled that the government was wrong to change accounting rules retroactively at a time when our thrifts were operating at a profit within the contractual arrangements made at the time of the purchase. Although we had been legally vindicated, the costly and time-consuming nightmare we endured at the hands of a group of overzealous regulators had wiped out our investment in the thrifts.[9]

——

JOAN MANNING, FORMER CHIEF FINANCIAL OFFICER OF WSGP,
FEBRUARY 12, 2000

At the end of 1988, regulators were trying very hard to make deals with investors to acquire troubled thrifts. The year-end flurry of activity was so great, that potential investors could almost negotiate a deal in just a few short meetings and walk away with a troubled thrift. However, not all deals closed in 1988 were done in such a hasty manner. The Simon Group investors closed the acquisitions of Western Federal and troubled Bell Savings in 1988 (merged together as Western Federal), but only after spending millions of dollars on a due diligence process and negotiations with regulators spanning over a year. The closing and funding of the joint transaction was done only after investors were satisfied that they understood and documented the contract and forbearances negotiated with the government.

The Simon Group brought over $350 million of new capital to the thrift industry (over $220 million to Western Federal). Applying FIR-REA to the Simon Group thrifts made no sense. Not only was a significant investment made, but it was done so after spending significant due diligence time and money to analyze the institutions and prepare business plans acceptable to regulators that would take truly disastrous problems—like Bell Savings—off the government's hands. The Simon Group had real dollar solid investments and turn-around business plans to go forward, but once FIRREA passed, there was almost no point. When dealing with small-minded people with power, such as the thrift regulators under FIRREA, it was impossible to adhere to a business plan, because the rules continually changed. There was no logic—the regulators didn't grasp rational business concepts, but would impose subjective restrictions. There was no way to know what the rules or restrictions really were or when they would change *again. The process was so distasteful to me that I will never again work in a regulated environment—especially not in a thrift.*

After FIRREA passed, I decided to leave the thrift industry and go into consulting; the day after I left the Simon Group, I found out that I had breast cancer. I remember coming home from the doctor, crying, and as I walked in the door the phone was ringing. It was Bill Simon. He said, "Whatever medical help you need, I'm there for you. I know you have just left our group to start your own consulting practice, but I want you to continue working for us and stay on our payroll. I want to make sure you have insurance. I want to make sure you are taken care of until this is behind you and you are well enough to start your own business."

Bill made a commitment to me, and he didn't need to do that. He called me when I was in the hospital and they were telling me I was going to die. He sent me flowers. He made sure I was employed with insurance, rather than trying to start up a business while dealing with surgery, chemo, and radiation. He even brought me holy water from Lourdes, which I still have today. Bill Simon, very quietly and privately, came through for me in a big, big way. He made a significant difference in my life at a time when I really needed it. There is no way to adequately describe the difference his actions made on my recovery. It is an understatement, but I am forever grateful.

———

Although my experience in California was not entirely negative, I did make some poor and costly decisions. My own regrettable errors in judgment were compounded by the unquestioned trust I placed in someone I thought was my friend, and my rather naive reliance on the integrity and good faith of the government. In retrospect, perhaps I should have viewed *Noble House*—in which avarice and the quest to become *taipan* leads to everything from double-dealing to kidnapping and murder—as prophetic.

CONQUERING THE
NORTHWEST PASSAGE

During a diving expedition in the spring of 1987, I feared that I had lost something more precious than my own life. My sons, Billy and Pete, are both strong. I brought them with me in the spring of 1987 to dive the Great Barrier Reef and to explore the coral islands, reefs, and shoals off the eastern coast of Queensland. The Great Barrier offers magnificent sights—vibrantly colored sea life clearly visible in crystalline waters, more than 350 species of coral, summits of a drowned coastal mountain range—and I was eager to experience its splendid beauty with my sons.

However, they were novice divers who had just recently been certified, and I foolishly led them way over their heads. We were down about eighty feet when a swirling funnel, powerful as a fire hose, blind-sided us, nearly ripping the tank off my back and sending me tumbling and spinning out of control. I grabbed for Pete, but couldn't reach him as he was dragged below. Billy was nowhere to be seen and I didn't even know what direction to begin looking for him. Groping in the dark, living any parent's worst nightmare, and fearing that I had lost a son—or two—I searched frantically for Billy and Pete, all the while fighting the funnel. They weren't in front of me. They weren't behind me. They weren't to my left. They weren't to my right. I couldn't see them below and I couldn't find them above. Gradually, I worked my way up, praying, but not really expecting, that they had somehow found their way to the surface. They were not in sight.

I was about to descend again when, all of a sudden, Pete popped up, a big grin on his face. Together we found Billy, who was also safe and sound. Once again, God had blessed Bill Simon.

One might think that would be plenty of adventure and excitement for a mature gentleman. But I had gradually become fascinated with the Northwest Passage, the elusive and dangerous water route over the top of the Earth from Europe to the riches, real and imagined, of the Orient.

Explorers began searching for such a route as early as the fifteenth century and four hundred years of their best efforts had proven unsuccessful. A great many brave adventurers succumbed to the elements— fierce, gale-force winds, sudden and unpredictable changes in weather that can rip and crush sturdy ships. Not until September 1906, when Norwegian explorer Roald Amundsen's historic three-year effort culminated victoriously, was the passage conquered. Since Amundsen, there had been only fifty-five successful traverses of the passage in all manner of vessel, ranging from submarines to sailing ships. No one had ever taken a yacht through the more difficult west-to-east route in a single season.

I wanted to be the first. I had become mesmerized by the mysteries of the Arctic with its fragile ecosystem, polychromatic topography, and such exotic wildlife as polar bears, whales, caribou, snowy owls, and musk oxen. I wanted to see this unique region of our planet before my time on earth expired. My dream of continuing the pursuit of Cabot, Hudson, Frobisher, Davis, Cooke, Franklin, and Amundsen—trailblazing pioneers whom I admired greatly as much for their spirit and effort and sense-of-life as their particular achievement—became an obsession.

Where would the world be without such adventurers, men who could see not only the danger, but the potential glory and reward?

Where would America be had it not been for the vision of the industrialists, the fortitude of innovators, the foresight of investors, the courage of risk-takers in every line of endeavor? They were people who dared to be different, who pushed the edges of the envelope, pioneers whom I hoped to emulate in some small way. I wanted to follow in their footsteps as a kindred soul. Voyaging into the "Arctic Grail" and conquering the Northwest Passage remained a dream that longed to be chased.

My dream was neither a lark nor the foolish fantasy of a middle-aged businessman. The Northwest Passage was another challenge and adventure, not wholly unlike the financial challenges and adventures of trading bonds, the political and logistical challenges and adventures that presented themselves in Washington, or the moral and theological challenges and adventures presented through Catholicism and my service as a Eucharistic minister.

The Northwest Passage holds a certain fascination for every sailor, every explorer, and every dreamer. For centuries, there was serious and legitimate doubt whether it was even possible to sail over the top of the world, through the Arctic wasteland between the Atlantic and Pacific—the vast region between the Bering and Davis straits—to the suspected wealth of Cathay.

There was, of course, an alternate route via Cape Horn, the southernmost point of South America, and Drake Passage, one of the stormiest and most dangerous passages in the world. The 500-mile strait between Cape Horn and the Antarctic Peninsula—sometimes as seductive as a mistress, other times as murderous as a psychopath—was often a fatal attraction for bold sailors. Westerly winds, sweeping over the ocean, engulf ships in thick mist and fog that bewitches, enchants, and confounds even the best navigators.

I experienced firsthand the wrath of Drake Passage in January 1995. Thirty-six hours out of Chile, sailing due north from a journey to the Antarctic and heading for the passage, we were hit with a sudden storm at 3:00 a.m., when I was peacefully asleep in my cabin. Awakened by an explosive BANG! on our port side, I was catapulted like a rag doll, flung a good ten feet into the bulkhead. Crumpled on the floor in shock, confusion, and disbelief, I gathered my wits just in time to experience a second pounding on the starboard side, and then another on port. I crawled to the wheelhouse where my captain was bravely but futilely struggling against a furious storm striking us from three or four different directions at once. For a day and a half, we were at the mercy of the seventy-five-foot waves and seventy-knot winds, bobbing and tossing us like a cork. One wave would hurl us skyward, and then suddenly the bottom would quite literally fall out and we'd come crashing back to the surface, where another torrent would take its best shot. Unlike many of our forebears, we survived that storm, but came away with renewed respect for the power of nature.

The quest for a northwest route was thrilling. Arctic history, adorned by myth and lore, only added to the allure. Sir John Franklin's journey in 1845 convinced many sailors that the Northwest Passage existed, even though it claimed Franklin's life and vessels. It was over a half century after Franklin's expedition that the Northwest Passage was finally conquered. Amundsen of Norway set out from what is now Oslo in June of 1903 in the *Gjoa,* a forty-seven-ton, seventy-foot former herring sloop, a workboat. Amundsen crossed the North Atlantic, hugging the coast of Greenland, and headed into Lancaster Sound, where he encountered the thick ice that had doomed previous efforts. The violent winds, ice floes, and fog were a constant threat, but Amundsen and his crew found relatively safe harbor at King William Island, northwest of Hudson Bay. For two years, the Amundsen expedition remained at a port they named Gjoahavn (today Gjoa Haven), building observatories and conducting scientific experiments, before resuming the westerly course. After several months, including a protracted period stuck in the ice, Amundsen spied a whaling ship from San Francisco and realized he had reached Alaska, and conquered the Northwest Passage.

The explorers who would follow in his wake were a hardy few. Typically, sailors would travel as far as they could during the brief summer, winter-over on the ice, and resume the journey the following year. To complete the entire Northwest Passage in a single season would require perseverance, persistence, planning, and a measure of both daring, good fortune, and just plain luck. I understood, appreciated, and respected both the rigors and rewards of my quest and knew the physical, mental, and spiritual preparation that would be required.

Naysayers declared it impossible for a yacht to complete a west-to-east traverse in one season, and questioned whether it could be achieved at all. But I was eager to give it a go. If I failed, I would at least know that I had pursued my dream, that I had tried my best, and that, more than likely, I had had a heck of a lot of fun in my pursuit.

Since 1986, I had discussed the ambitious goal with my skipper, a jolly, fun-loving New Zealander named Allan Jouning who shared my fascination with the Arctic Archipelago north of Canada. Captain Jouning, an expert sailor who had been with me for a decade,[1] read everything we could find about the passage, and everything we found was more foreboding than what we had read before. I can't remember talking to anyone who thought I could conquer the Northwest Passage, but the skepticism only bolstered my determination. I hate to be told that I can't do something, and I love to prove the defeatists wrong. Friends were quite convinced that I had taken leave of my senses, but those who knew me best knew I could not possibly be talked out of my plan. While *Freedom*, with its sleek Sparkman & Stephens design, lacked speed and strength, I was certain she had the heart to persevere in the crushing ice of the Arctic. I knew that Captain Jouning would bring out her best, and I was perfectly willing to accept the risk.

At the same time, however, Bill Langan, a champion sailor and internationally renowned boat builder who had been the principal designer of *Freedom*, happened on a more appropriate ship: a 175-foot, 920-ton Dutch-built vessel launched in 1961 and converted into a motor-yacht in 1980. While I loved my *Freedom* and felt somewhat like a traitor deserting her for a "stinkpot"—a motor ship—I liked the yacht, named *Itasca* (Latin for "true beginning," a quite appropriate name given the circumstances), so I bought her. Under the knowing eye of Captain Jouning, *Itasca* was upgraded for its coming challenge. Part of the bow was shielded with a thin steel veneer to give her a fighting chance against the pounding, ripping ice. Hot-water plumbing was added to saltwater intakes to prevent freezing.

State-of-the-art communications and navigational equipment was installed to provide a link between my boat and the inhabited world.

While work on the *Itasca* proceeded, I went about assembling a team of fellow adventurers, people who understood the risks involved and were willing to accept them. I quickly enlisted two of my closest friends, George Gowen and Ettore "Barb" Barbatelli, men who I knew could and would respond under pressure. Arctic historian and archeologist John Bockstoce, an extraordinary character who had twice traversed the Northwest Passage (and had undertaken part of the voyage in a walrus-hide Eskimo canoe!), also agreed to join us. Also signing on were: Bill Langan, renowned naturalist photographer Robert Glenn Ketchum, and marine biologists John Loret and Rita Matthews, who were president and vice president, respectively, of the Explorers Club. John and Rita would pursue a scientific inquiry, as well as an adventure, conducting important research on the west-to-east migration of the food chain. Dr. Robert Leach, an orthopedic surgeon and chief physician of the U.S. Olympic Committee in 1980 and 1984, came along as a fellow explorer as well as the expedition's doctor.

I knew I might never get another chance to attempt the Northwest Passage, and told my guests that I had no intention of turning back. "Look," I said, "I am mentally prepared for the worst, and can't imagine any circumstances that would force me to turn back. I want you folks to know, that if you want to join me, wonderful. But when the tough times come—and they are going to come—we are going ahead. If you aren't willing to accept that, please withdraw now." No one withdrew.

Itasca was ready for her August of 1994 rendezvous with history, and so were we. Yet the blunt admonition of the Canadian Arctic pilot was a constant reminder of the dangers of the Arctic: "Life jackets are of minimal use in Arctic conditions. If a man goes in the water, a life jacket will keep him afloat but after only a very few minutes this will be a matter of academic interest only, since he will be dead." We were immediately reminded that the warning was not to be taken lightly.

Barb Barbatelli had arrived at Nome, Alaska, a day before the rest of us and talked Captain Jouning into bringing him out to *Itasca*, despite extremely hazardous conditions. They boarded a sixteen-foot Zodiac boat and began maneuvering through the narrow Nome channel for what, in calm conditions, would have been a pleasant, quick one-mile jaunt. However, conditions were anything but calm and the trip was anything but pleasant. A storm struck and the Zodiac was bombarded by twelve- to sixteen-foot waves. Several times, the little boat nearly flipped, and if it had that would have been the end for Captain Allan Jouning and Ettore Barbatelli. Miraculously, the Zodiac remained upright, and Allan and Barb arrived safely. But the adventure getting to *Itasca* was only a precursor of what lay ahead.

Captain Jouning planned to pick us up at Nome the following day, August 1, but a ferocious Arctic storm choked the passage between the shore and the yacht and forced a change in plans. There was no way to safely board. Given Allan and Barb's experience the day before, we agreed it would be better for *Itasca* to head north and for us to meet her at Port Clarence, seventy-two miles up the Tundra Road. Throughout the day and well into the night, Captain Jouning and his crew fought the vicious seas as he guided *Itasca* toward Port Clarence. At one point, a forty-foot wave broke over *Itasca*'s stern with such force that the entire frame of a six-foot window was punched in and Barb—a man of six-foot-two and two hundred pounds—was flung like a toy and hurled into a television set. Thankfully, he was not injured. When we finally boarded the following day, we found Barb, a powerful, courageous man, shaken but unharmed by an unnerving confrontation with the forces of nature.

The incident was certainly a reminder of the dangers ahead, but in no way undermined my confidence or resolve. As Dr. Leach wrote in one of his journal entries: "After dinner, we talked about getting through the Northwest Passage. Some were a bit cautious about our chances. Bill Simon is not. He says that all the signs are right...Barb feels in his bones that we'll make it. I agree. This will be a first. We'll go for it and make it."

We set sail from Port Clarence on August 3, proudly flying the Explorers Club and United Nations flags that we were so privileged to display; we were the first to be honored with the right to fly both flags. *Itasca* nosed her way into the Bering Strait for whatever might lie ahead. I was sixty-six years old and eager to begin the adventure of an adventurous life.

The passage affords its visitors only a narrow window of opportunity to thread their way through the maze of some 18,000 islands. It was only a matter of time before we would encounter thick ice. We encountered our first ice about 500 miles into our journey, at Point Barrow, the northernmost point of Alaska. For several days, we finessed through areas of heavy ice, making steady but slow progress as we threaded our way along the Boothia Peninsula. We forced our way through James Ross Strait and into Larsen Sound, the crushing force of ice grinding and scraping *Itasca*'s hull. I warned the guests that we were going to have some tough calls going north, and explained how winter had set in behind us, so we couldn't go back even if we wanted to.

The clockwise rotation of ice packs in the Beaufort Sea tends to push ice into the narrow corridor of Larsen Sound. It was near there that Sir John Franklin was defeated. The 129-man Franklin Expedition, sent in search of the Northwest Passage beginning on May 19, 1845, disappeared along with two ships, *Erebus* and *Terror.* For twelve years, various expeditions sought to locate the explorers, but the fate of the crew remained unknown until 1859, when a search mission sent by Franklin's wife found some skeletons and a written account of the expedition through April 25, 1848. The log indicated that the Franklin Expedition had become hopelessly mired in ice off King William Strait, about halfway between the Atlantic and Pacific oceans. Apparently, they abandoned the ships and attempted, in utter desperation, to *walk* back to the mainland, resorting to cannibalism along the way.

Just after midnight on August 16, we found ourselves locked in ice, unable to move so much as an inch, wryly aware that *Erebus* and *Terror* lay somewhere below. For two days, we were hostage to the paralytic grip of Arctic ice, and made light of the situation by staging an impromptu Arctic Follies, spreading beach chairs out on the ice floes—a large, flat mass of frozen seawater—the women crew members prancing about in bikinis worn over long-johns. We figured we would simply wait it out, until the winds changed and the ice floe moved ever so slightly, allowing us to push and probe our way forward.

Ice floes are a fascinating natural occurrence: a wild mish-mash of layered ice scrunched together by gale-force winds and piled one on top of the other. Over time—two, maybe three years—the salt in a floe filters through the ice and back into the water, leaving masses of frozen fresh water, often with an exquisite greenish-blue tint. We were quite content to enjoy the scenery and simply wait until nature decided it was time for us to move on. But providence interfered again.

We had been in regular contact with the Canadian Coast Guard (a matter of protocol since we were in Canadian waters) and learned that one of their ice breakers—coincidentally, and perhaps unnervingly, named the *Sir John Franklin*—was in the vicinity, passing through on its way to assist another ship. The Coast Guard was kind enough to swing by and, on the evening of August 17, the *Franklin* appeared out of the fog. Captain Paddy Chafe of Newfoundland, an officer in the Canadian Coast Guard, surveyed our predicament, proclaimed it hopeless, and instructed us to turn back and wait for the ice to break up later in the summer.

"With all due respect, Captain," I said, "I understand what you are saying, but this trip has been my dream for many years. We've thoroughly planned and prepared for the rigors of the Arctic and we understand the treacherousness of the ice and weather. But, we are here to try to complete our traverse and, if we fail, it is going to be because we failed, not because we quit. And so, if you could help us through this portion right here, to the open water forty miles north, that would be wonderful. But also understand that we are not turning back. We will follow you to hell, but hell is north."

The captain was adamant and advised us that he was going to report us to Ottawa unless we obeyed his directive. "Fine," I said, "and when you do, please give my best regards to Chretien."

"The prime minister? You know our prime minister?"

Jean Chretien, who was elected Canadian prime minister in October 1993, had been appointed president of the Canadian Treasury Board in 1974 and held that position when I was secretary of the treasury.

"Sure, I know him well from my days as secretary of the United States Treasury."

After some "discussion," and after I had signed a waiver absolving the Canadian government of any legal liability, we continued our northward trek with enthusiastic support from Ottawa. When Prime Minister Chretien learned of our journey, he wired a sincere message of encouragement to *Itasca*: "Understand you are trying the Northwest Passage. Bill, we're rooting for you. Anything we can do, you let us know. Good luck. Chretien."

Itasca proceeded in the wake of the *Franklin,* captained by a very irritated Paddy Chafe. The mammoth and powerful 420-foot *Franklin* would plow through the ice, cutting a hole while we followed behind for a stretch. But the "sailing" wasn't exactly smooth. As the *Franklin* crushed forward, we trailed behind, with enormous chunks of ice bouncing off the *Franklin* and ramming us with a vengeance. It felt as though we were bashing into buildings and we prayed that *Itasca*'s propeller would survive the wrath. It was rather obvious that Captain Chafe was attempting to punish us for what he clearly perceived as our impertinence by keeping just far enough ahead of us so that the ice pushed aside by the *Franklin* would close in just as we entered the swath. I wasn't sure how much more abuse *Itasca*'s screw could take, so I told my captain to pull up close to the *Franklin* and ride in her wake.

"Allan," I said, "pull up within twenty-five yards."

We immediately received communication from the *Franklin,* asking us to back off and expressing concern that we would ram her should she make a sudden stop. Sudden stop? Not likely. Even if there was a problem, I knew we could simply veer off into the ice. We kept on Chafe's tail, which alleviated some, but not all, of the pounding. And after thirteen hours of navigating through shrieking, crunching, and banging ice, made all the more difficult by dense fog, we broke into clear waters, and bade farewell to the *Franklin*. Captain Jouning and his crew were exhausted, utterly spent.

"Well, since you got through that, you can get through anything," Captain Chafe's voice crackled over the radio. "I never thought you would make it."

It was evident at that point that our Canadian friends had gone from thinking we were, in John Bockstoce's words, "a bunch of useless, toffee-nosed yachtsmen" to a "grudging respect for the maneuvering skills of our helmsmen and the strength of our ship." Respect has to be earned, and we had earned it. Although the icebreaker was helpful, we would have made it without the assistance of the *Franklin*.

On August 26, 1994, we sailed into the record books. *Itasca* and her crew did what had never before been done, and it had done so in an incredible twenty-three days. During our celebration that night, the Aurora Borealis, or Northern Lights, exploded into life, providing us with a dazzling display of natural fireworks, and a fitting tribute to a triumphant voyage!

———

JOHN LORET, EXECUTIVE DIRECTOR OF THE SCIENCE MUSEUM OF LONG ISLAND AND PRESIDENT EMERITUS OF THE EXPLORERS CLUB, SEPTEMBER 1, 1999

I served on an icebreaker in the Arctic when we tried the Northwest Passage back in 1948 and couldn't make it. The ice was too heavy. Bill didn't have an icebreaker, so our voyage was a real challenge. The Itasca wasn't even as powerful as the icebreaker I was on in the '40s. But I wasn't worried. I know Bill; nothing bothers him. We got stuck a couple of times, and some people would be running around the bridge going nuts. Not Bill. He was cool. He thinks clearly, makes decisions, and sticks by them.

The essence of an explorer is to try to do something that hasn't been done before, to do what other people haven't done and also to make a contribution. Bill wanted to do this because he is an explorer and an adventurer, but he also felt he could make a contribution with this voyage.

A TIME TO GIVE

In a pensive period following President Ford's defeat in 1976, I became alarmed over the statist, anti-freedom philosophy that was growing like a cancer through the very marrow of this country. I felt that our political officials (with the notable exception of President Ford and a few others who were on their way out) were philosophically bankrupt. And the sight of so-called "leaders" of business and industry sheepishly capitulating to the philosophy of big government left me utterly disgusted. We were surrendering the battle of ideas and ideals that were so central to our founding and our freedom. For the first and only time in my life, I genuinely feared for the future of my country.

It was clear that something had to be done to balance the ideological field of battle if conservatives were going to make any progress in promoting free market policies—but what? I was already working on the book that would become *A Time for Truth*, but I was eager to do something more, something direct and practical and concrete.

It was then that I was approached by John M. Olin. John and I had been casual acquaintances for a few years as we both owned homes in East Hampton and knew each other mainly by reputation.

A 1913 chemical engineering graduate of Cornell University, John Olin's life was one of research, study, discovery, and productivity. He began his business career in 1914 with Western Cartridge, a family concern in East Alton, Illinois, that evolved under his leadership into the Olin Corporation, a major manufacturer with interests in brass, pharmaceuticals, chemicals, paper, cellophane, munitions, sporting goods, and home building. By the time he retired in 1957, John Olin had amassed twenty-four patents for his scientific inventions, was a leader in conservation and wildlife preservation, and created a fortune and a philanthropic foundation that touched the lives of thousands.

Toward the end of 1976, John approached me with his concerns over the state of the nation, concerns that mirrored my own. John knew that human freedom is an indispensable ingredient in the advancement of the human race. He knew that economic freedom and human rights are inseparable; you can't have political and social freedom unless individuals are free to engage in the peaceful exchange of goods and services and ideas. He knew that collectivism is the antithesis of freedom, and that it always leads to stagnation, decline, and the stifling of the human spirit. He was resolute about using the resources at his disposal to advance the cause of freedom in the battlefield of ideas, and about using his foundation to fight encroachments on our basic liberties.

John, then eighty-five years old, told me of his plan to develop a new, private foundation to advance his ideals. He explained how he planned to dedicate the bulk of his estate to the foundation, but said he needed someone to firmly take the reins and make sure that his money would be spent on programs and activities consistent with his philosophy. Over the next several weeks, John and I had numerous long and philosophic discussions on the need to support programs that promote free enterprise and a strong American defense, and ways that personal philanthropy could contribute to those objectives. John asked if I would be willing to work with him to develop a mission for his foundation, hire a staff to execute that mission, and preside over it after his death. After leaving government in January 1977, I accepted the honor gratefully and enthusiastically.

In 1977, we established the general mission of the John M. Olin Foundation as follows: to provide support for projects that reflect or are intended to strengthen the economic, political, and cultural institutions upon which the American heritage of constitutional government and private enterprise is based. Before long, we were off and running, planting the seeds that would enable the John M. Olin Foundation to grow into the major philanthropic and philosophical force that it is today.

―――

JAMES E. PIERESON, EXECUTIVE DIRECTOR OF THE JOHN M. OLIN
FOUNDATION, AUGUST 17, 1998

John Olin was very impressed with what Bill had done in government as a conservative, outspoken, bold advocate of free markets. Bill is very interested in the ideas that animate the conservative movement. He wants to promote an understanding of free markets and the constitution and the rule of law. When he went into the government, he saw . . . what a [problem] the government had become and saw how important it was to make a case for free markets, limited government, a stricter interpretation of the Constitution. He got involved in the John M. Olin Foundation because it was an outgrowth of his political activities. We have tried to make an intelligent case for conservatism and free markets over these twenty years with Bill at the helm.

―――

John had already laid the groundwork by assembling a highly accomplished board of trustees and stellar staff.[1] Frank O'Connell, a retired labor lawyer and counsel for the Olin Corporation, was appointed the first director of the foundation. Frank retired in 1979 and was replaced by Michael Joyce. Mike had served as director of the Institute for Educational Affairs (IEA), which advised corporations on philanthropy and provided small grants to scholars. Through IEA, Mike had worked with such luminaries as one-time leftist Irving Kristol, who had become a leading conservative intellectual. (Irving always reminded me of Winston Churchill's famous quip: "If at twenty you are not a Liberal, you have no heart. If at forty, you are not a Conservative, you have no mind.")

As such, Mike was perfectly situated to begin building a network of scholars that would form the core of our "counter-intelligencia," as I had proposed in A Time for Truth. He was eager to bring in some experts on public policy and hired an exceptional political scientist from the University of Pennsylvania, James Piereson, in 1981 to work with the grantees. When Mike left in 1985 to take the helm of the fledgling Bradley Foundation in Milwaukee, Jim took over at the Olin Foundation.

When John Olin died in 1982, he left an extraordinarily strong foundation from which to continue his vision. John donated half his estate to the foundation, bringing its assets to $60 million. With sound investing, we were able to steadily increase the foundation's assets (and, concurrently, its philanthropic giving). When John's wife, Evelyn, passed away in 1993, the remainder of the estate—valued at $95 million—was transferred to the foundation. By the late 1990s, our assets totaled roughly $120 million. We were able to make grants of roughly $20 million annually while still sowing the seed John had left us.

On a broad scale, our endowment was not particularly large when compared with, say, the Ford Foundation, the W. K. Kellogg Foundation, or the Lilly Foundation—all of which have assets well into the billions. However, from the beginning, we made up for our relatively modest resources by establishing a clear and focused mandate and mission, centered on the goal of creating a principled, credible conservative challenge to the overwhelmingly liberal ideological monopoly in academia. In short, we strove from day one to get the greatest return on our investment. We further broadened our impact by spending far in excess of the paltry 5 percent of assets that foundations are required to spend each year. This not only gave us a presence much greater than our assets would suggest, but also set us on a course for extinction—a centerpiece of John Olin's vision for the foundation.

Foundations started by capitalists like Andrew Carnegie, Henry Ford, and John D. MacArthur veered to the left after their deaths and financed institutions and endeavors that work not for capitalism and freedom, but against it. Indeed, the Ford Foundation's slide into collectivism caused Henry Ford II to sever all ties to the organization. In his statement announcing his resignation in 1977, Henry Ford II said, "The foundation is a creation of capitalism [but] it is hard to discern recognition of this fact in anything the foundation does. It is ever more difficult to find an understanding of this in many of the institutions, particularly the universities, that are the beneficiaries of the foundation's grant program." I called Mr. Ford after reading of his resignation in the newspapers and asked him to explain what had happened. He answered: "I tried for thirty years to change it from within to no avail."

John Olin was adamant that the same would not happen to his foundation. Consequently, the assets of the Olin Foundation will be spent during the lifetimes of the current trustees, while those who knew John Olin and respect his views and wishes control the fund. Milton Friedman has made the point many times that businessmen ought to take as much care in their charitable contributions as they do in their business investment decisions. If, in the name of philanthropy, they thoughtlessly turn over their fortunes to foundations and institutions dedicated—whether by foolishness or design—to destroying the free economy, they are merely collaborating in their own extermination. Consistent with John's wishes, the Olin Foundation seeks to support scholars oriented toward freedom. The aim is to educate, not indoctrinate. We are abundantly confident that reason, and therefore freedom, will prevail in the free marketplace of ideas.

To that end, the John M. Olin Foundation focuses its grants in four general areas: Public Policy Research, which provides support for the formulation, implementation, and evaluation of public policy in the social and economic fields; American Institutions, which promote understanding of the moral, cultural, and institutional underpinnings of a free government; Law and the Legal System, which seeks to deepen the understanding of the American judicial system and to preserve the rule of law as a bedrock of the American constitutional government; and Strategic and International Studies, which includes studies of national security affairs, strategic issues, American foreign policy, and the international economy.

I became president of the Olin Foundation in 1977, and Irving Kristol and I started the Institute for Educational Affairs (IEA) the following year. A few years later, the Olin Foundation, along with a handful of other donors, began providing support through the IEA for conservative newspapers on college campuses across the country.

The first of these was the *Dartmouth Review*, a lively and irreverent publication that challenged the liberal and left-wing orthodoxy that had a stranglehold on the campus. The Dartmouth administration coddled the leftists and immediately caved in to their every demand. Given that situation, the *Review*, with its iconoclastic view of political and campus issues, was bound to upset the administration and faculty. That it did so proves only that it fulfilled its function as a newspaper in a free society—and in this instance exposed the excesses of the far Left by documenting the growing politicization of the Dartmouth curriculum and administration.

Although we did not necessarily agree with everything the *Dartmouth Review* published, we stood firmly behind the publication on principle as administrators repeatedly tried to silence, intimidate, and suppress the paper. It was astonishing to watch the Dartmouth faculty and administrators, who were perpetually extolling the virtues for "diversity," "dissenting viewpoints," and "free speech" attempt to suppress a campus publication solely because it had the temerity to challenge their precious dogmas.

Fortunately, the *Dartmouth Review* survived the attack, and continues to publish today. Many alumni of the paper moved on to notable careers in politics, business, and journalism. Equally significant, the *Review* spawned a forceful movement that has spread to campuses around the country. Conservative-oriented newspapers now exist on more than seventy-five campuses across the country, ranging from Harvard in the East to Michigan in the Midwest to the University of Oregon on the West coast. The John M. Olin Foundation has encouraged this movement with substantial annual grants that provide small operating subsidies for these newspapers, and by underwriting conferences at which student editors can compare notes and exchange ideas.

Our purpose in supporting this movement is twofold. First, we wanted to encourage the development of conservative opinion on campuses that have traditionally been one-dimensional. Second, we wanted to generate a network of young conservative writers and editors who might, at some point, go into journalism, and thus bring some balance to that profession. We have achieved considerable success on both fronts. Conservative papers are influential on many campuses, and many graduates of the program are now working in the field as editors, writers, and correspondents for major newspapers and television outlets.

Today, the Olin Foundation sponsors numerous "counter-intelligencia" efforts on numerous campuses (about half of our philanthropy has been earmarked for higher education). We have supported many magazines and journals over the years and were instrumental in starting two: *New Criterion*, a monthly magazine (now edited by former *New York Times* art critic Hilton Kramer) whose primary purpose, since its founding in 1982, has been to offer a rational alternative to the Left on matters of art and culture, and to restore to American cultural life a standard of criticism and a respect for tradition that are essential if the arts are to avoid becoming instruments of political dissuasion; and *The National Interest*, a journal of public affairs published by Irving Kristol. Together, these magazines provide an important outlet for conservatives to publish and effectively contribute to the intellectual "debate of ideas."

A distressing number of direct or indirect attacks on our basic liberties seem to come from intellectuals and scholars who should have a greater appreciation of the importance of a free society than anyone else. Certainly, if one looks at the kind of collectivist societies our leftist intellectuals find so attractive, one looks in vain for anything resembling academic freedom. Indeed, those whose paychecks are signed by a socialist state quickly find that they are intellectual prisoners of the state.

Today, there is a far greater appreciation for markets and the benefits of the free enterprise system. It is clear to me that the work of the John M. Olin Foundation and the scholars, writers, and thinkers we have supported are at least partly responsible for the change. While the battle for freedom is never-ending, the John M. Olin Foundation has stood as a solid sentry—a consistent, persistent voice for reason and against hypocrisy.

The foundation has done a great deal of good in creating John M. Olin Chairs at various universities and institutions around the country. It is our practice not to endow a chair into perpetuity, but to make relatively short-term grants in support of specific proposals involving specific individuals whose works promise to contribute significantly to the ongoing debate in the marketplace of ideas. We have tried to encourage the appreciation of conservative ideas in an intelligent way by supporting the best scholars and the strongest institutions whose ideas and programs have broad influence in our society. We have programs at most of the leading academic institutions and have supported many well-known scholars. Yet we have scrupulously avoided joining any of the sectarian battles over who or what is "real conservatism" and define our mandate broadly, consistent with our goal of educating rather than indoctrinating.

In addition to our work in higher education, we also strive to influence the intellectual climate that is the bedrock of law and economics. For instance, the Olin Foundation has invested around $50 million to bring to the law the principles of economics. Where some legal scholars view the law largely as a tool for shifting wealth between adversaries, we encourage them to consider the incentives fostered by their focus. Obviously, there is an economic nexus to, say, antitrust law. But in using the law as a tool of public policy, the consequences of those policies must be fully understood and appreciated. Our Law and Economics program has emerged as a powerful and influential antidote to statist mores, as well as something of a new check and balance on the often-unchecked power of the judiciary.

John Olin built a great industrial enterprise without ever losing sight of the fundamentals of a free society. When he endowed his foundation, he made it clear that its mission was to preserve our freedoms and strengthen our resolve in the unending battle we face. When he spoke to other businessmen, John unhesitatingly came down hard on the vital importance of preserving this system.

There are many able and conscientious foundation executives, like Mike Joyce and Jim Piereson. But for every Joyce and Piereson, there are dozens who practice the foundation equivalent of "pack journalism"—managers who, with aims far different from their foundations' creators, make a career of trying to awe their directors with some abstract vision of "public interest," a clouded "vision" of what freedom really means and what freedom requires. John Olin, and the philanthropic movement he inspired, played an immense role in the preservation of liberty in this wonderful country. Indeed, it is difficult to think of any major conservative initiative over the last twenty-five years that was not supported in some fashion by the Olin Foundation.

But those days are rapidly coming to an end. Around 2005, the sun will set on the Olin Foundation—just as John Olin insisted. It is absolutely vital that other visionary philanthropists take the baton that John left us, and run with it. I have tried to do that with my own foundation, and hope that I can inspire others to do the same.

Since the William E. Simon Foundation was established in 1967, I have carefully evaluated potential grant recipients, always ensuring that their aims are consistent with mine. When I die, various trusts will continue to fund the foundation, but it will not last beyond the lifetimes of my children. All seven of my children serve on the board, and I have groomed them to be as careful with charitable giving as I was in the business and governmental decisions. Under my direction, and eventually the leadership of my children, the William E. Simon Foundation will continue, as stated in the mission statement, to support programs "to strengthen the free-enterprise system and the moral and spiritual values on which it rests: individual freedom, initiative, thrift, self discipline, and faith in God."

The main purpose of my foundation is to help the needy by providing the means by which they may help themselves—in essence, the philosophy expressed by Andrew Carnegie in his essay, "The Gospel of Wealth." Carnegie wrote, "In bestowing charity, the main consideration should be to help those who will help themselves; to provide part of the means by which those who desire to improve may do so; to give those who desire to rise the aids by which they may rise; to assist, but rarely or never to do all."

———

JAMES E. PIERESON, AUGUST 17, 1998

There is an overlap of philosophy [with the John M. Olin and William E. Simon foundations] in the sense that the Olin Foundation wants to promote free markets, individual responsibility, and the private sector, and we do it by promoting ideas—universities, think tanks, books. The William E. Simon Foundation seeks to help needy people help themselves. The liberal version of philanthropy that you find in the Ford and Rockefeller and Carnegie foundations tends to be advocacy philanthropy, where they try to show why the government has to step in and help people. As a consequence, they have promoted welfare and other government programs to help people. Bill's philosophy is a lot different. Bill wants to help people help themselves. He does not want to promote more programs from the government.

———

While I certainly agree with Carnegie that the wealthy have an obligation to share their good fortune with the deserving less fortunate, and that no one should get an entirely free ride, monetary gifts cannot compare with corporal gifts of mercy. I have always devoted not only my money, but also my time to charitable endeavors. My children, and their children, have been brought up with the same, typically American values.

———

KATIE SIMON MORRIS, DAUGHTER, JULY 27, 1998

It was fostered in us by both our parents that we were so lucky that we should give back to the community, to those in need, to those in crisis, and that we were also so fortunate in our own lives that it was only fair to give something back.

I am involved in a couple of different charities in New Jersey. One is called Christmas in April, a national charity headquartered in Washington that rehabilitates homes for the handicapped, the elderly, and the needy; I'm on the board of directors of the Morris County chapter. The other charity I am involved with is the Jersey Battered Women's Shelter, a charity my mother was very involved in. I worked with children in crisis who were staying at the shelter.

It is easy to write a check, and hard to devote time. But it is so much more fulfilling to devote time. Writing a check is not emotionally fulfilling . . . Working hands-on is incredibly gratifying. It brings me out of myself. It helps me feel like I am contributing in some small way. I love to look on people's faces; they are just so grateful. And I am so lucky to begin with, so why not give back?

———

I so firmly believe in personal service to humanity that I have included in the William E. Simon Foundation's by-laws a stipulation that my children must perform charity work—hands-on work, not just writing a check—in order to keep their seats on the board and to earn the generous stipend that comes with the position. All of them are deeply involved in charity. I have taught my children to give of themselves, and they in turn share that sentiment, as do I, with the grandchildren. What better legacy for the Simon family?

———

AIMEE SIMON BLOOM, DAUGHTER, DECEMBER 15, 1998
I've always volunteered. I have volunteered everywhere I have ever lived. It is just something I love to do, and it is something my father loves. It is a sense of caring for other people. We took our children in to see [the Broadway musical] Lion King on Sunday. We walked by this homeless guy who was playing the saxophone. I gave my six-year-old son a couple of dollars and said, "Alex, put it in his case. That is how he makes his living." Alex looked at me, and said, "How

can he make a living on that change in his case?" All through Lion King, *he kept asking, "Mom, can we give him $300 if he is still there when we come out?" He was really bothered. When we left the theater, he was still there, and we gave him quite a bit of money. Alex handed him the money and the guy was incredulous. We just made his Christmas!*

A TIME FOR FAITH

I wish I could say my embrace of Christian principles was quick, clean, and complete. It was not. I did not experience a sudden flash or epiphany or conversion, nor was my "enlightenment" reminiscent of Voltaire's deathbed acceptance of the Church. Rather, my transformation was, and continues to be, a gradual journey toward spiritual awareness, appreciation, and love.

I can point to three distinct experiences which, collectively, put me on the path to becoming a more truly committed Christian and Catholic: volunteering at Covenant House, my pilgrimages to Lourdes and Medjugorje, and becoming a Eucharistic minister.

The idea for Covenant House was born on a snowy night in the late-1960s when a Franciscan priest named Father Bruce Ritter provided shelter for six young runaways in his tiny apartment on the east side of Manhattan. From that modest beginning, Covenant House has grown into an entity that provides support and shelter annually for tens of thousands of youngsters in cities across the nation and in countries around the globe. Its mission is to "serve the suffering children of the street, and to protect and safeguard all children ... with absolute respect and unconditional love."

I was introduced to Father Ritter by J. Peter Grace, chairman of W. R. Grace, and was immediately impressed with his commitment, genuine love, and respect for runaway and abandoned children. While talking with Father Ritter, it hit home, for the first time, that while my children and I have never known anything but a loving, nurturing home, there are countless youngsters to whom that blessing is entirely foreign. I eagerly accepted Father Ritter's invitation to spend some time at Covenant House in New York City.

Covenant House introduced me to children who have never known love and support, who had never had a father or mother or a Schatzie to nurture and guide them. I was deeply affected, as was Carol, and we made a financial, and far more important, a personal commitment to the children of Covenant House. We became regular volunteers. In time, it became an important holiday tradition for the Simon family to spend part of Christmas at Covenant House, where we served meals to the children and tried to bring a little joy and laughter.

Over time, I began to see how, for many unfortunate youths, Covenant House was the beginning of a spiritual discovery, and the first real opportunity to experience humanity and civility and God's love. Until coming to Covenant House, many youths simply had no idea of their abilities and potentials, no concept of the productive and joyful human beings they could become. They were understandably reluctant to accept love and put their trust in either man or God. Covenant House, however, proved to be their sanctuary and salvation—and, in a different way, mine.

While Covenant House reintroduced me to the principles of Christian charity and love, my pilgrimages to Lourdes and Medjugorje brought me back to my spiritual roots. My first pilgrimage to Lourdes in 1993 changed my life dramatically and permanently. I saw the sick healed and the poor and downtrodden embraced with solace and hope. I wheeled the handicapped to the spring and to the chapels that have been erected in the vicinity of Our Lady's appearances, and felt that I had a glimpse of the Kingdom of God. Since then, I have made an annual pilgrimage to Lourdes, and each journey is more spiritually fulfilling than the last.

Lourdes brings me back to my roots, and serves as a reminder of my mortality and of the more important concerns in this finite life. It awakens my spirit and fosters a feeling of closeness to God that remains in my heart long after the visit has ended. Every year at Lourdes, I pray that God will take me while I am right there, for I know that at Lourdes, Bill Simon is as close to a state of grace as he can possibly be.

———

J. PETER GRACE, INDUSTRIALIST, MAY 18, 1994[1]

[Bill Simon] took a liking to me, although I don't know why because I am very different from him. One day we were having lunch—I really like him—and I said, "You've got maybe the best mind in the United States. You are filthy rich. You've got seven of the greatest children. You've got good health. You've got everything. If something happens to you and you go before God and he asks you what have you done for the least of your brethren, what the hell are you going to say? God would say, I gave you everything—money, children, wife, success, brains—and what have you done for anybody?"

He went hog wild. He is very spiritual in many ways. He went for the first time [to Lourdes] last year and told me a number of times that it had the greatest effect on his life than anything he has ever done. When you go over there, you see all these sick people being rolled around by volunteers . . . You just see thousands of people praying at the Grotto, going to Mass, saying the Rosary in candle-lit ceremonies, putting sick people in the bath and taking care of them. It is a tremendous experience to see that, to see the caliber of the people from Italy, Germany, France, Belgium, Holland, England...praying at the grotto to Mary, the mother of Jesus. I was surprised it affected him so greatly, but it did. It had a tremendous effect on him.

At Medjugorje, I was actually the recipient of a miracle. Medjugorje ("between the hills") is a small village in Bosnia-Herzogovinia (formerly Yugoslavia) where, since 1981, the Blessed Mother has been appearing and giving messages to the world, mainly through six young people. Since the first apparitions in 1984, millions of people of all faiths have visited Medjugorje. Countless have been healed and converted.

After our first Mass at Medjugorje, I remember telling my son Billy, "That is the closest I've ever felt to heaven on earth." I then pulled out the old, inexpensive rosary beads that I had bought about ten years earlier, and noticed that the chain was glittering in the sun. That was strange. The chain was just some cheap, dull alloy, yet it suddenly appeared radiant and golden and vibrant and remained so. I wasn't quite sure what to make of it, and upon my return brought the rosary to a jeweler for an appraisal. He confirmed that the chain, inexplicably, had turned to solid gold. I can't explain the transformation, either of the rosary or of my own life, except as a sign of divine intervention, and accept it as such.

During one of the Lourdes pilgrimages, I received my third revelation through a conversation with Cissie Ix, an incredible human being and a wonderful woman. Cissie serves God as a member of the Dames of Malta, a religious order of the Catholic laity and an affiliate of the Knights of Malta, a group that I had joined in the early 1970s but in which I had not been particularly active. Partly through Cissie's influence I became more involved in my Church, in both spiritual and nonspiritual ways. Cissie had mentioned to me that for many years she had been participating as a Eucharistic minister at Memorial Sloan-Kettering Hospital in Manhattan, where she and the Dames spiritually and physically assist the sick and dying. She told me how they actually bring the Blessed Sacrament to the ill.

The Sacrament of Holy Communion is a central element of Catholicism. The distribution of the consecrated bread and wine is a privilege afforded only ordained priests and Eucharistic ministers, laity who, through training and prayer, are allowed to join in this special celebration and distribute the Body and Blood of Christ. When I was a child the privilege of touching the host was reserved solely for ordained priests. But times have changed, and the Holy Father has afforded the faithful laity the opportunity to actually administer the Holy Eucharist, the same charge that Christ gave to his apostles nearly 2,000 years ago.

I deeply wanted to share this experience and, after undergoing extensive educational and spiritual training, became a Eucharistic minister. I perform my ministry at four hospitals in New York, New Jersey, and California.

At Cardinal Cooke Health Center in Harlem, I work with the AIDS patients. Often, these were people who have had tragic lives, many of whom never knew a father or benefited from an education; many of them were brought up on the streets with predictably tragic results: drugs, venereal diseases, jail, AIDS. They want to be talked to, and they want to be listened to. They want to visit. They wish to pray.

I spend time with these people who are on the doorstep of death, trying to comfort and console them, and let them know that a friend is by their side. I give them Holy Water from Lourdes and rosary beads blessed there. They are, without exception, overjoyed, and many cry as I pour water on their bodies. I pray with them and for them, asking the Lord to embrace them with the special peace that comes from knowing that salvation awaits and that the pain and grief of this world is fleeting and nothing more than a rite of passage. And I offer them the Holy Eucharist, an experience that is at least as meaningful for me as it for them.

There are many times when I have walked out of a hospital room with tears in my eyes, and I find myself wondering if I have given the sick and infirm half of what I have taken away from them. I am humbled by the faith that they demonstrate, and deeply grateful for the challenges these people have given me in defining my own faith.

One patient who comes to mind is Eddie, a man in his early forties, whom I encountered at the Cardinal Cooke Health Care Center. Eddie had AIDS and had lost over half his body weight. He was too weak to move. His legs were the circumference of my wrist, and he would weep as I poured Lourdes water on his emaciated body. Over a period of two years, Eddie became a good friend, and I was able to help reconcile him with his family, who were very bitter about his disease and had not seen him in two years. Perhaps the good Lord kept him alive longer than his prognosis would have indicated so that this reconciliation could take place.

Once, after giving Eddie Holy Communion, he looked at me and said, "Bill, would you please do me a favor? I can't move over myself and I don't like to ask the wonderful people here to move me too often, because I know they feel a little uncomfortable touching my body with all its sores."

He went on to ask me if I would very carefully put my arms under his body and slide him over. I moved him as gently as I could and said: "Eddie, when you get to heaven, and you're sitting at the feet of Jesus and the Blessed Mother, would you throw down a rope and pull me up with you?"

He cracked a smile. "You got it, Bill!"

———

MARY PAT FORTIER, FORMER ASSISTANT, JANUARY 5, 1994

The Eucharistic ministry speaks to a side of Bill that is becoming more and more important to him. He enlisted me as his sidekick when he began his weekly visits to Sloan-Kettering in 1992. He's very humble when he spends time with these cancer patients and gives Communion to them. It gives him an inner peace, and shows a side of him that few people get to see—the kind side, the compassionate side, the faithful friend you can count on no matter what. There's little he won't do for you once he's made you part of his life.

———

Redemption is not only a biblical tradition, but an American one. I had an awakening experience with Charles Colson, one of the many casualties of Watergate, who founded an organization called Prison Fellow Ministries after serving his own term. Chuck, former special counsel to President Nixon, is one of the inventors of "faith-based" charities—which start with the premise that religious faith is a vital element in motivating people to change their lives. Chuck found that the most effective way to break the cycle of crime is to change the hearts and minds of the people convicted of crimes. He does this by bringing the message of God's love to the inmates of our prisons.

In early 1999, Chuck invited me to minister with him, to actually go behind the prison walls and reach through the bars to pray with men serving long sentences or counting their days on death row.

At the first prison we visited, Jester II, we met an inmate named Ron Flowers, who had been convicted of murdering a young woman. Until completing one of the Prison Ministry's intensive accountability programs, Ron had never acknowledged his crime, and the victim's unforgiving mother had vowed he would never get out of prison while she was alive. After going through the program, Ron confessed. I was there the day the mother of the victim and the murderer faced each other. I was standing only three feet away when the mother walked up to Ron and hugged him, tears streaming down her face. Imagine a woman hugging and embracing a man who had cruelly murdered her daughter. I have never seen a more perfect example of pure forgiveness.

We also went to the death row prison in Huntsville, Texas. With 450 condemned inmates, Hunstville is the largest death row prison in the world. As I walked through the cell blocks, I prayed with convicted murders who were just days away from meeting their Maker. I knelt on the steel floor and put my hands through the bars. They knelt on the other side. I gave them rosary beads. I poured Lourdes water on their heads, and I prayed with them. I gave them Holy Communion. Their eyes beseeched me and they begged me to pray for them, and I did.

——

FATHER JOHN P. MCGUIRE, O.P., DIRECTOR OF CATHOLIC CAMPUS MINISTRY AT NEW YORK UNIVERSITY, MARCH 9, 2000

Bill really does see people as his brothers and sisters and he really does empathize with them, even though quite often they are of very humble origins. Many of the AIDS patients have a lifestyle that he wouldn't approve of, but disapproval of what may have caused the

AIDS doesn't factor into his care for them. He really sees them, in a very real way, as Christ living and suffering among us. He's told me that, and he means it. Tears come to his eyes when he says it. I am very touched by this.

I suspect Bill has always had a very deep personal piety that has bloomed as he has grown older. We've talked about what it means to commune with Christ, and he feels he can touch Christ through his ministry. Christ said: "When I was hungry you fed me. When I was in prison you visited me. When I was sick you cared for me." Bill takes that literally. He has a very, very real commitment to the needs of the sick and the poor. He has shared his means and his heart with people all over the world, always with the focus on people in need, never in self-aggrandizement. Often the beneficiaries are people who will never even know his name, but whose life will be entirely changed by his personal and financial care....

Bill is a very good churchman in other ways, as well. He has a very modern notion of the relationship between the laity and the hierarchy. He is not afraid to disagree with our national hierarchy on various issues, and I think that is a mature view of the role of the laity. In the past, typically, the laity would be told what to do and would do it. But Bill is not shy about saying, respectfully, if he doesn't agree with the hierarchy's positions on political or economic matters.

———

Each of us must find our own way to honor God and the path that He has set for us. But while I am a lamb of the Lord, I am no sheep, and there are times when the biblical admonition to "turn the other cheek" is best unheeded.

In the early 1980s, I and other conservative Catholics were growing increasingly concerned over the Church's leftward drift. I discussed my concerns with Catholic theologian Michael Novak. Michael is a fascinating man. Once a left-leaning seminarian, Michael left the seminary just short of ordination and engaged on an intellectual journey that ultimately brought him to the conservative American Enterprise Institute. In March of 1984, we began working together to seek out a representative group of lay Catholics to study Catholic social teaching and its relation to the economy.

Within months, we had established the Lay Commission on Catholic Social Teaching and the U.S. Economy. We viewed the commission as a modern version of an 1889 organization, the First National Lay Congress, which met in Baltimore and examined the spiritual requirements of Catholicism vis-a-vis American capitalism.

One of our first missions was to counter, at the invitation of the bishops, a critique of the U.S. economy. The bishops' pastoral letter— "Economic Justice for All"— called for a renewed commitment to assist and heal the suffering in our society, an initiative which I supported fully. However, the letter made a gargantuan leap and concluded that the American economic system is in direct conflict with morally responsible behavior—a conclusion that flies in the face of history and common sense. Experience shows that economies dedicated to freedom, individual opportunity, and economic growth do far more to alleviate poverty and suffering than all the schemes of the social engineers and commissars of history.

For many years, the Church had a well-defined body of social thought, erected upon sound and timeless principles. The bishops paid respect to those key principles, appropriately, but then veered off into socialist political theory where, in my opinion, they were out of their element. They demanded aggressive "redistribution" of wealth, with little regard for who it is that is expected to create the wealth that they would have governments redistribute. They argued that the American system is in conflict with the demands of morality and justice. We were exhorted to practice charity toward the poor, and then told that those with wealth are inherently greedy and covetous and their wealth must be confiscated by the state.

As an active lay member of the Church whose life had been spent mainly in the world of business, I gladly deferred to the bishops' deeper knowledge of spiritual concerns. Certainly, they are far better equipped than I to address the mysteries of the Trinity and the Latin liturgies.

On the other hand, it escaped me how one can practice Christian compassion to the poor merely by submitting to the demands of

Caesar's tax gatherers to avoid going to Leavenworth. History shows that compulsory charity—a contradiction in terms—tends to prolong and intensify the very problem it purports to address: poverty.

Only a free economic system can support a dynamic production of wealth for the benefit of all, and only in a land of luxury does poverty become a moral issue. A free economic system gives the poor an opportunity to work, invest, prosper, and, yes, to become rich, so that they can help others. The moral values underlying a free economy motivate the rich to bestow much of their wealth on works of charity and compassion to the needy. Consequently, there is no fundamental conflict between the goals of the Church and the principles of a free and just economic system—and the Lay Commission said so in a thoughtful 120-page statement entitled *Toward the Future: Catholic Social Thought and the U.S. Economy.*

In the statement, we resisted linking Christianity to any particular political system or set of economic policies, but noted that Catholic social teaching and American politics have a great deal in common: Both seek to liberate people from tyranny and poverty; both encourage people to reach their full potential through the exercise of personal responsibility and free, common association.

In an encyclical seven years later, Centesimus Annus (The Centenary), Pope John Paul II, recognized with greater clarity than any other religious leader the superior capacity of the free market to meet the needs and aspirations of people everywhere. Reflecting on the collapse of socialism and the lessons to be learned,[2] Pope John Paul's epitaph for socialism condemned the modern welfare state for its tendency to promote class warfare and suppress fundamental human rights, as well as its inability to fulfill basic needs. In sum, the pope said that the state should not take over the responsibilities which we, as Christians, have toward our fellow man.

Although I do not suggest that the Lay Commission directly influenced a papal encyclical, some twenty formulations in the encyclical were similar to passages in *Toward the Future*. Perhaps we were able to bring another credible voice to the debate.

MOST REVEREND EDWARD M. EGAN, ARCHBISHOP (NOW CARDINAL) OF
NEW YORK, JUNE 8, 2000

Bill Simon was a man who knew that for which he stood. Many
years ago, when I was an auxiliary bishop in the Archdiocese of New
York, I had the pleasure of meeting him and coming to be his friend.
Immediately, we found ourselves in agreement on many, many issues
facing both the Church and the nation.

Bill did not believe that the message of the Gospel was terribly
complicated. He understood that all of us are held to be persons of
honor, justice, and charity. For him, however, charity was to express
itself not just in giving assistance but also, and especially, in providing inspiration. The help he gave people in need was regularly aimed
at helping them to help themselves.

The theological basis for all of this was quite clear in Bill's mind.
We are images of God who have intellects and wills, he would insist.
The Lord is given glory when we use these two splendid faculties for
our own good, the good of others, and the good of our communi-
ties. Many need assistance. But assistance must lead to initiative and
self-reliance.

All of this explain's Bill's deep commitment to education, especially
for the poor. When I told him of the needs of an inner-city high school
in Bridgeport, where I served for eleven years as bishop, he asked some
very pointed questions: Were the youngsters in that school truly poor?
Would their education inspire them to work and achieve on their own?
Were they being taught the Catholic Faith in its entirety? And, of
course, was the school utilizing its funds properly? When I was able to
document affirmative answers to all of his questions, his charity followed without hesitation. He lived and gave on the basis of principle.

Knowing Bill Simon was a singular grace. He insisted on clear
thinking, precise language, and total honesty. All of these were part
and parcel of his life, and he expected to find them in everyone whom
he was counseling or supporting. It was a delight to converse with
him, to learn from him, and even at times to bring him around to a
point of view he had not held before.

Another facet of the Bill Simon character that made him especially *admirable was his deep-seated concern for the suffering of others. His hours in hospitals and prisons, conversing with persons who were hurting, illustrate this wonderful quality most tellingly. Confident, demanding, exact, and intolerant of nonsense—all of this he certainly was. However, his ability to feel the hurt of his fellow human beings and his irresistible urge to alleviate that hurt made him a truly noble gentleman. I count it a privilege to have been his friend.*

——

As Americans, many of us tend to think of our heritage primarily in political terms—in the context of the basic freedoms and rights that most other societies around the world have never been able to achieve or, in some sad instances, contemplate. But underlying our political freedoms, and providing a moral basis without which they would be meaningless, lies our religious heritage.

Some pundits claim that familiar institutions of family, church, schools, and the democratic political process are no longer pertinent in today's atmosphere of change. To the contrary, they are even more important than ever and represent our only real hope of overcoming the confusion and cynicism that pervade every layer of our society.

Liberals and totalitarian governments are hostile to faith and family, and for good reason: advocates of government control want, indeed need, to destroy competing sources of loyalty—in particular, voluntary sources of loyalty. When all institutions that were neither created nor controlled by the state are gone, the options left will be chaos—or government.

——

Bill Donohue, president, Catholic League for Religious and Civil Rights, April 20, 1998

Catholics have been, as individuals, far more passive than other segments of the population . . . when there is bigotry and defamation aimed at the Catholic Church. The assaults on the institutional Church are mounting, and this is where we need the support of lay people.

Bill has a Catholic outrage at some biased reporting, bigoted tele-

vision shows and movies that defame the Catholic Church. He does seem to be very attentive to the fact that other groups are treated better in the media than are Catholics and the Catholic Church....

There are two things that strike me about Bill Simon. Number one: There is nothing half-hearted in his comments; he speaks from the soul; he feels things very deeply, very passionately; he is a man of strong conviction. Number two: He takes the initiative. Something will hit him in the gut and he'll want to discuss it with me, want to know what we're doing about it and how he can be of assistance. His initiative and strong convictions make him stand out. He has certainly been a source of great advice and enthusiasm for me.

———

Religion has a very definite place in our free society and, despite what some courts say, religion does indeed have a place in our public schools. In an environment where condoms are dispensed freely and family values are shunned as old-fashioned, a little spirituality wouldn't hurt a bit.

A Time to Mourn;
A Time to Heal

It was a classic case of benign neglect of our marriage vows. Perhaps I was resentful that Carol's objections had played a role in my decision to get out of politics and not to return to Washington. Perhaps she was bitter that I was so rarely home. Maybe after so many years of marriage, we were both suffering a "mid-life crisis" or a marital "burnout," to borrow a couple of bromides from pop psychology. In any case, I left Carol in 1991 and moved to California. But I was neither willing nor able to truly sever our relationship, nor renounce the sacrament of marriage.

Throughout our separation, I called Carol frequently, probably four days a week, and did my best to maintain relationships with my children. However, even grown children with children of their own are, understandably, unsettled by a separation of their parents. And despite their efforts not to take sides, it was inevitable that some of the children would feel resentment toward me for leaving. I could hardly blame them; at times, I resented myself. There were few days, and in fact few moments, when I was not haunted by guilt.

MARY SIMON STREEP, DAUGHTER, MAY 16, 1994

It doesn't matter if you are ten years old or thirty-seven, it still hurts when you see your parents in such turmoil. You want your parents to always be the perfect parents you always envisioned them to be. And when something like this happens, it sort of brings your world to a halt and makes you realize that life goes on. You just have to pick up the pieces and sort of figure out what happened. It was particularly hard because I think the two of them were really hurting, and coming to us for support. We wanted to be there to support them, obviously. . . . It was very, very hard.

―――

Carol and I had been married for more than forty years. I loved her and always would. I think everyone—including myself, Carol, and all seven children—knew I'd eventually return. When I left, my daughter-in-law, Janet, Pete's wife, said to Carol, "Get on the plane, Mom, and take him by the ear and bring him home!" If she had, I would have returned on the spot. I longed to return and needed only some sign from Carol that she would have me back, that she wanted me. Carol, however, was frightfully stubborn (sharing a trait I've been accused of possessing). Perhaps she knew that I had to find my own way home at my own pace, as I eventually did.

After I had been in California for about a year and a half, Carol fell and broke her shoulder while she was on an Outward Bound hike in Colorado. The x-ray revealed more than a broken bone; the cancer had returned, with a vengeance. I packed my bags and returned home immediately.

Carol welcomed me more readily and more charitably than perhaps I deserved, but that was her nature. She knew my conscience had inflicted, and would continue to inflict, sufficient punishment and there was no purpose in dwelling on the issue of my departure or rubbing salt in our wounds. There were few words spoken about my time on the West coast; we had a more immediate problem to address. Carol was determined, once more, to prevail over cancer. I did my best to remain cheerful and upbeat; it was important to support Carol with my love, not burden her with my concerns. But I had lost my father to cancer, and I knew that a recurrence of a disease we thought we had beaten fifteen years earlier would most likely have dire consequences. Indeed, the doctors gave her little hope, and we had another episode of "I-don't-want-chemotherapy-because-I-will-lose-my-hair." Again, she relented to reality and consented to chemo.

For most of the next eighteen months, Carol seemed, outwardly anyhow, reasonably well, reasonably comfortable. She tolerated the chemo and radiation without complaint. Aside from the usual nausea and exhaustion that would follow her treatments, Carol was generally able to go about her life, doting on the grandchildren, volunteering for various philanthropic causes, and refusing even to consider the possibility that the disease could kill her. This was a demonstration of her incredible inner resolve and toughness, a degree of denial and, above all, a deep and abiding faith.

———

DR. KEN ADLER, CAROL SIMON'S ONCOLOGIST, APRIL 24, 2000

Carol took the news [that cancer had returned] with tremendous grace and stoicism and a positive attitude. She had a lot of faith in herself, her God, and her family; I think that sustained her in dealing with the treatments.

Bill, I think, was stunned at first. Then, after the initial shock, he was supportive as a husband and would come to the office with Carol, both for her visits and treatment. He would be by her side and give her support while she was getting intravenous chemotherapy. He also offered her spiritual support. They both had a lot of faith in God. While Carol was sick, they went to Lourdes and brought Holy Water back for my other patients.

But Carol did not allow cancer to interfere with her day-to-day life. She just sort of integrated the treatment into her life and lived with it. She went about her life, took care of her children and grandchildren, and what was amazing to me was her continued involvement with philanthropy. She was very involved with the battered women's program, and did a great deal for cancer patients in our community.

Carol just wasn't going to let cancer get the better part of her, to over-take her. She maintained a remarkably positive attitude throughout her illness because she didn't want to burden her family. At the end, though, she knew she was dying.

―――

It was always hard to read Carol's emotions; she internalized pain, both physical and psychological, and rarely offered any indication of what she was feeling or thinking. Once, in early 1995, though, I found her sitting in front of the mirror, a forlorn expression on her face, as she observed how the disease and the treatment had altered her appearance, seemingly adding a decade or more to her age.

―――

AIMEE SIMON BLOOM, DAUGHTER, DECEMBER 15, 1998
I was really happy that he came back, and that is what my mother wanted, for them to get back together. He was really there for my mother, and he did the right thing, looking after her through her ill-ness. She always had an attitude that she was going to beat it. He was with her day and night...He is always there when you really, really need him. If a crisis comes up, he will be there.

Growing up he was very much a father, very much there for us. He was a wonderful role model. He is very kind; there is a very sweet side to him. On one side, he has this horrible temper and flies off the han-dle, but five seconds later he forgets everything. He is very forgiving. He is very happy-go-lucky.

―――

It was clear to me, and down deep it must have been clear to Carol, that she was losing this war. I arranged a month-long sojourn to our home in Maui, and brought along Carol's physician and gynecologist. Although weak and frail, Carol delighted in playing the perfect host-ess, proudly showing off the home she had so elegantly decorated, eager to attend to the needs of the guests who were there to tend to hers. I couldn't help but think back to the time a few years back when I bought the Maui home.

Hawaii had long held a special attraction. I saw the islands first from the deck of a troop ship, as a twenty-year-old army private returning from Japan, and fell in love with its tropical beauty. By the 1990s, I had visited Hawaii at least fifty times. Viewing the islands as a Pacific bridge, the main conduit for business between Asia and North America, I decided to buy a home on Maui.

The estate I found, "Haiku House," was simply stunning: adorned by forty acres, trees imported from all over the world, a swimming pool, and a tennis court. Carol, however, was less than delighted—particularly since I bought it without telling her. However, after going to town on a major remodeling effort, including the addition of a beautiful bedroom for us, she grew to love our corner of paradise as much as I did and even made plans to live there permanently.

We had intended to spend the entire month of March 1995 at Haiku House. But after three weeks, Carol was simply too weak and ill and I decided, along with Carol's physician, Ames Filippone, to bring her home to New Jersey.

––––

DR. AMES FILIPPONE, RETIRED CHIEF OF SURGERY AT MORRISTOWN MEMORIAL HOSPITAL, APRIL 12, 2000

Carol knew from the moment that we determined the cancer had spread to her bones that her chances were slim. But she really held up a brave front and was as upbeat as you could expect. She was deeply religious. The family was very, very supportive. Every time she came to the office there were three or four of the children with her. Bill was very attentive and spent a lot of time with Carol....

As we left Hawaii and got into a station wagon to go to the plane, Carol turned and looked back and said, "Good-bye Haiku." My wife, Barbara, who was sitting next to her, almost broke into tears. It was quite evident that Carol knew she would never see her home in Hawaii again.

––––

During the next three months, Carol faded rapidly as the cancer ravaged her body. There was nothing left that anyone could do. In early

June, we admitted Carol to Morristown Memorial Hospital, suspecting that it was her final stop. Morristown Memorial occupied a special place in Carol's heart and, if she had to be in the hospital, it was the most appropriate one.

For years, Carol, a very private person who preferred anonymity to celebrity, had sent flowers (with an unsigned card) weekly to cancer patients at the hospital. She obtained the names of the patients from the hospital administrators, only a couple of whom, sworn to secrecy, knew the identity of the "unknown angel," as the nurses called her. In early June, an observant nurse at the hospital thought it strange that Carol had not received flowers from the anonymous benefactor, and questioned her. Carol's bright grin confirmed everything the nurse had guessed.

I stayed by Carol's side night and day, praying the Rosary, reflecting on the life we had led, begging God for her salvation (and mine), and reminiscing about the wonderful times we had shared and imagining the wonderful place where we would someday meet again. After several days, Carol lapsed into a coma. She died peacefully in her sleep on the evening of Sunday, June 18, 1995—Father's Day—with all of our children present. Carol's death was a devastating loss for the children, the grandchildren, and me.

We celebrated the funeral Mass at Christ the King Church, our home parish in New Vernon. All of the children and many of the grandchildren participated with readings or reflections, and Dr. Filippone delivered one of the eulogies, recalling Carol's valiant struggle and celebrating her love of life. I paid my final respects at the cemetery, where I left Carol a note at her gravestone: "Dear Carol, I love you. Please help me to come there with you."

———

JULIE SIMON MUNRO, DAUGHTER, JUNE 1995 (REMARKS AT CAROL'S FUNERAL MASS)

Not long ago, a family friend who had recently been diagnosed with cancer called my mother for advice. I heard her say, "My secret is that never for one instant do I believe that this thing is going to beat me—not ever!" Throughout her long battle with cancer she never complained and always stayed positive. Each incremental piece of bad news was dispatched in the same matter-of-fact way: "It's just a little spot. I'll get this one, too. I feel good today. How is everything with you?" In the hospital when my sister Aimee cried and said, "It's not fair!" my mother responded without hesitation, "Don't say that. I'm going to get better. I just need to rest and get nutrition." Her courage and her perseverance inspired so many people with their own struggles, whatever they were. She was a role model to all.

Service to the community was very important to both of my parents. Service helped her and made her feel a sense of gratitude for the good things in life. She loved her volunteer work; every Monday she would bring flowers to patients at the hospital to cheer them up ... She believed in the power of prayer ... She believed in miracles ... She was a good person in the old-fashioned sense—decent, kind, honest, and fair. She was a friend to many and she treasured what those friendships gave in return. ...

My sister Leigh told me last night about a lunch she had with my mom about two months ago. Mom had woken up the night before with the most incredible vision. She got out of bed and walked throughout the house in tears. She said she had an overwhelming feeling of gratitude for her family, friends, and the exceptional life she had been able to live.

——

Carol was only sixty-four years old. It was too soon for her to leave, and too soon for me to lose her. Like most married couples, we'd had our difficulties. But when viewed in the context of the joys we shared, the wonderful children we raised, the beautiful relationship that we had over the course of a lifetime, the difficult times seem inconsequential and irrelevant. I thank the Lord that I returned from California prior to her death. If Carol had died suddenly, perhaps in a car accident, and I had never had the chance to make amends, I don't know how I would have lived with myself. Those final months, as painful as they were, reaffirmed the love, respect, and devotion that had been the hallmark of our long marriage.

MARY ELLEN SIMON WHITE, SISTER, JULY 18, 1994

As they say, behind every successful man, there's a good woman, and Carol is a perfect example. She allowed Bill to be free. She is intuitive, very bright, gentle, and fair. She has a lot of strength. She has had difficult experiences that she's had to handle, and she's done them so well. She's just naturally a very graceful and gracious person. Carol's main interest was her family... She had seven children and a big house, and she managed it all. She was strict. They were a very close family. Their father definitely was very much a part of it, and they worked well together, but a mother is really the heart of a home. She's given him the freedom to do his work.

————

September 9, 1995, would have marked our forty-fifth wedding anniversary and that was the day our daughter, Katie, had scheduled her marriage. Carol knew she might not last to the wedding, and knew that without her such a significant event on our anniversary would be extremely painful for the entire family. Should we postpone the wedding? Should we select another date? In the hospital, Carol expressed her preference clearly: "Under no circumstances do I want you to postpone the wedding. Under *no* circumstances."

When the time came to make a decision, I was of a mixed mind. But the decision wasn't mine to make, and I left it up to Katie. We had a long heart-to-heart talk.

"Dad," Katie said, "Mom insisted that she wants me to get married, and that's what I am going to do. And you know what? We are going to have the greatest wedding you ever saw!"

My eyes filled with tears and I endorsed her decision wholeheartedly. I know that's what Carol would have wanted. She adored Katie's fiancé and was very much looking forward to the wedding. In fact, Carol left behind both a shower present and a wedding gift. Katie had two matrons of honor, her sisters Aimee and Julie, and at the dinner they gave her a set of dinner plates, each inscribed with a memorable sentiment and signed on the back by one of her sisters or bridesmaids.

But there was an extra plate. That one was inscribed, "God saved the best for last. Love, Mom." There wasn't a dry eye in the room.

The wedding day started off somewhat somber, with all of us consumed by memories and very much grieving Carol's absence. How she would have enjoyed her youngest child's wedding day! But in short order, serenity seemed to pass gently over all of us as we simultaneously came to accept the unfortunate fact of Carol's passing and the wonderful addition of Michael Morris to our family. If Carol could have sent us a sign that everything was going to be OK, she would have done so. And perhaps she did.

There is, as Ecclesiastes tells us, "a season and a time for every matter under heaven: a time to be born, and a time to die...A time to weep, and a time to laugh."[1] It was Katie's time, and our time, to move forward with our lives, and we did so together, as a family should. September 9, 1995, marked the beginning of one union, and the anniversary of another.

Meanwhile, I moved forward as well.

MOVING ON

For two decades, Carol and I had been friends with Tonia Adams Donnelley, a lovely and sensitive woman whose family vacationed with ours occasionally in Palm Beach. Toni was divorced and living in California, where I returned after Carol passed away. Our relationship matured quickly and we decided to marry.

Toni and I summoned the whole clan for a wedding atop a mountain on my Santa Barbara ranch and on July 2, 1996, all of my seven children and Toni's three children were in attendance as Father Maurice Chase conferred on us the sacrament of marriage. After the ceremony, the guests all hiked back down the mountain for a country western celebration and barbecue as Toni and I began our married life together.

———

TONI SIMON, WIFE, DECEMBER 9, 1998

About twenty years ago, a friend in Palm Beach called my husband and me to play tennis at the Bath & Tennis Club with him and a house guest. He said his house guest was not a very good tennis player, but we could pass him around. His house guest was Bill Simon.

He certainly was not very good at tennis, but he was good fun! If someone had told me I'd be married to him one day, I'd have told them they were crazy! We had dinner with his family that night, and over the following years we would see the Simons once each summer in East Hampton and once each winter if they came to Florida.

My marriage ended in divorce after fourteen years and shortly thereafter I moved to California where I lived for three years. Eventually, our paths came together in California. I fell in love with a man who has been described as strong, forceful, temperamental, bright, patriotic, and philanthropic. But I fell in love with the flip side of Bill Simon, the private side. He is kind, sensitive, and very childlike. This may sound odd, but he can be a very insecure man. I loved his insecurities, as they made me feel very needed.

On July 2, 1996, we were married on our beloved T-Bill Ranch. We had both our families and a few very close friends who hiked up the mountain to what we had named "Wedding Hill." I jokingly told Bill he had to ride up in the truck with the priest who was going to marry us. After all, I wanted that ring on my finger before Bill did any serious hiking!

It was a glorious day. Chuy and Kayla Perez, our wonderful caretakers, had taken up bales of hay for everyone to sit on. They set up a bar with a red-checked cloth with pails of iced champagne and beer. Chuy had hand-chipped our initials—WS and TD—and the date on the side of a huge rock which served as our altar. With Lake Cachuma, the Santa Ynez Valley and the three mountain ranges in the distance, Bill said it had to be God's church. We started with a friend playing "Ave Maria" on his guitar. A simple ceremony was performed by Father Maury, a remarkable man and most importantly, our friend, to which we added our own very special vows. Our hearts were overflowing with love! We then ended the ceremony standing and singing "America the Beautiful"—exactly what we were looking at. I will never forget that moment!

We have been on a honeymoon ever since.

My life with Toni is wonderful. Her friends are my friends, my friends are her friends, and the large family of ten children and two dozen (and counting) grandchildren is ours to share and enjoy together. We travel frequently, occasionally sail on *Itasca*, spend our time in our various homes in Santa Barbara, Hawaii, Manhattan, and East Hampton, and attend the Olympics together. We are perpetually surrounded by family and friends. Who could ask for more?

Neither Toni nor I are quite ready for the rocking chair, and I can't imagine we ever will be. Toni's a terrific athlete and a great tennis player, so she is able to keep up with my hyperactive schedule (most of the time!). She's a wonderful companion and friend, and I'm blessed to have her for a wife. Toni brought fun and laughter into my life at a time when I could have been mired in my ongoing grief over Carol's death. Although I never will "get over" losing Carol, I feel that with Toni I've been given yet another life to live—an *itasca*, "true beginning," so to speak. How, I often ask myself, could any one person be as fortunate as I?

———

ALEX DONNELLEY LAMM, STEP-DAUGHTER/ACTRESS,[1] JANUARY 31, 2000

It was and is a wonderful experience to become part of the Simon family, to be an insider and to see how everyone interacts and gets along. There was not one person in the Simon family who was not wonderful and welcoming and warm to me. They could not have been more inclusive....

I remember when Mom and Bill were beginning to spend a little time together, and getting to know the kids. I was concerned because my children were little and I wanted them to be polite and quiet. We were at his apartment when all of a sudden I heard my kids shrieking and laughing and running through the house. Mom looked over at me with this "Oh-my-God!" look of panic. Then, around the corner comes Bill Simon with two flowers pushed up his nose, his hands over his head like monster claws and growling. I turned to my mom and said, "OK, I'll get my kids to behave when you get him to behave!"

That was my intro to "Bill the Grandpa."

––––

Although I became a senior citizen a few years back, I continue to be intimately involved in business matters with William E. Simon & Sons, in philanthropy through the John M. Olin Foundation, my own foundation, and hands-on ministries. I plan to remain as active as I can for as long as I can, with Toni by my side every step of the way.

Sooner or later, a branch block in my heart, detected a few years ago, or the pulmonary fibrosis which more recently has afflicted my lungs, will probably do me in. Although I'd love to live forever, I am ready to go whenever the good Lord calls, but until then I intend to continue living life to the fullest.

––––

DR. O. WAYNE ISOM, SURGEON (NEW YORK HOSPITAL-CORNELL MEDICAL CENTER), AUGUST 20, 1999

I operated on Bill about ten years ago, replacing his aortic valve. He had reached a point where he could drop dead. He just zoomed right through the operation. He had a real positive attitude and recuperated very quickly. About three weeks after the surgery, my secretary pulls out this Time *magazine article with a picture of Bill Simon scuba diving off the South Pacific at 100 and some odd feet. I thought, "My God!" When he came back, I said, "Bill, what the hell were you thinking?"*

He said, "You told me I could resume my normal activities, and that's one of them." That kind of summarizes what I've known about Bill, about his lust for life and his determination to go all-out and get things done.

Another example: He's been pretty sick with idiopathic pulmonary fibrosis. Idiopathic means we don't know what causes it; pulmonary fibrosis is scarring of the lungs. Six or eight weeks ago, he was at an acute phase, a phase where it can be lethal. His doctors in Santa Barbara, who did a great job, were very aggressive, but initially it didn't look like he was doing very well. They did a biopsy of his lung and his lung collapsed and they had to put a chest tube in to expand the lung. It looked like he would be confined to oxygen constantly and he was told that he could never fly again....

Knowing Bill as I do, I said, "Well, Bill, you are doing better!" He paused and said, "What the hell do you mean I'm doing better?" I said, "With what you've got, you either die or you get better, and you're not dead. What you've got to do is just make up your mind that you are going to start exercising and get your strength back."

Two days later I called and Toni, his wife, said, "I don't know what you told him, but I can't stop him from going around the swimming pool. He keeps walking around and around and around and just finished twenty-five laps!"

He is very focused. Once he decides what the problem is, he goes after it. He has made an almost unbelievable recovery, almost unbelievable.

———

Jonathan Swift once said, "May you live all the days of your life." Certainly, I have, I truly have, and my life has been full of joy and achievement, of adventure, of perpetual personal renaissance, and, on occasion, of sorrow and regret. But mostly, it has been a story of freedom and risk-taking.

The Lord has richly graced me with the four pillars of a good life—faith, family, friends, and freedom—and, reflecting on a lifetime and with the benefit of hindsight, I am grateful beyond measure for the blessings with which I have been bestowed, and with the incredibly good fortune to have been born an American.

America is only two hundred years old, quite young when compared to the longevity of ancient Egypt, which reigned for some 3,000 years, and Rome, which lasted ten centuries. Yet in those brief two centuries, we have significantly changed the world through the contributions of our scientists, our investors, our artists, our laborers, and all those who have dedicated their lives to serving the public good. I believe we are on the verge of even greater things and see no limit to the potential of America and Americans. Our philosophical wealth and our unique sense of life were eloquently captured by Alexis de Tocqueville: "The incredible American believes that if something has not been accomplished, it is because he has not yet attempted it." That has always been my attitude, and that of many of my contemporaries. I hope that generations to come inherit that uniquely American can-do confidence.

My generation alone has witnessed a tremendous sweep of history. We saw the rise and fall of communism and the Berlin Wall, held our breath during the Cuban Missile Crisis, and grieved when a young president was cut down in his prime. We saw America conquer space and send a man to the moon, then became ensnared in the jungles of Vietnam. We heard our leaders tell us that we could afford guns and butter, even as they sowed the seeds of an inflationary nightmare. We watched our economy lurch from inflation to recession and back to inflation, and from price controls to the energy crisis, followed by Watergate.

We have emerged stronger and more prosperous than ever, as has been the history of the American people. The resolve and basic goodness of our people has enabled the American Dream to survive for another generation. We have traded soaring inflation, staggering unemployment, and an ever-expanding bureaucracy for price stability, millions of new jobs, and the beginning of the end of big government. Just imagine all that we can create in another two hundred years if we retain our freedom. I literally get goose bumps when I think of the opportunities that should await my children and grandchildren as this new millennium unfolds. What a wonderful time to be alive!

The enemies of capitalism—enemies of freedom, achievement, and the philosophical foundation of the most prosperous and moral nation in the history of the universe—find it inconsistent or contradictory that a man such as myself—a financier, an adventurer in spirit and in fact, an individualist, and occasionally a fun-loving hell-raiser—has strong religious convictions, makes an annual pilgrimage to Lourdes, spends countless hours personally caring for troubled children and distributing Communion to AIDS patients, and provides numerous minority scholarship funds. They assume that I am attempting to assuage some horrible guilt, or perhaps buy my way into heaven, by giving away millions of dollars to charitable and educational causes.

What they refuse to acknowledge is that my beliefs and actions—my values—are entirely consistent with the laws of nature, the nature of a free man, and the commandments of God. As a businessman, I trade value for value. As an adventurer, I adhere to natural law—the same law that governs the marketplace and the realm of faith. As a lay clergyman and life-long member of the Roman Catholic Church, I embrace the Christian spirit and faith, although I recognize that I am a sinner rather than a saint.

I would say to those who characterize the fight for liberty as "reactionary" that in the context of history, coercion is clearly reactionary and liberty is progressive. I would tell them that the twin ideas of human liberty and the free market were born only yesterday. I would note that allowing millions upon millions of individuals to pursue their material interests, with minimal interference from the state, has unleashed an incredible and orderly outpouring of inventiveness and wealth. And I would remind them how our ancestors sacrificed their lives to establish and defend the principles on which America rests, the brightest light ever to appear in the long night of tyranny and privation that is the history of the human race.

Now, in my eighth decade, I remain an unapologetic, indeed exuberant, believer in the American Dream—the dream of an America that doesn't punish success, the dream of an America that doesn't pit rich against poor, the dream of an America that says whoever you are and from wherever you came you can succeed on these shores. That is the American ideal, the American Dream.

I frequently tell my children and grandchildren the story of the wise man in Damascus who could answer any riddle in life.

One day, a young boy decided to play a trick on the old man. The boy said to himself: "I will capture a bird, hold it cupped in my hand, and ask the old man if it is dead or alive. If he says dead, I shall let it fly away, but if he says alive, I shall crush it in my hands. The old man shall certainly give me the wrong answer." So, the young boy caught a bird and went to the wise old man. "Is the bird dead or alive?" he asked.

"My son," said the old man, "the answer to that question is in your hands."

Shall freedom reign? The answer is in our hands. Long live America. Long live the American Dream. And long, long live freedom.

POSTSCRIPT

by John M. Caher

On the morning of June 8, 2000, the great doors of St. Patrick's Cathedral in Manhattan swung open and a flag-draped coffin[1] carrying William Edward Simon led approximately two thousand mourners out to the sun-swept streets of Manhattan. It was the perfect setting for Bill Simon's funeral Mass.

St. Patrick's is the largest Gothic cathedral in the United States and a recognized center of Catholic life in this country. Its awesome calm stands in contrast to the frenetic activity and enterprise of the bustling city outside. Serenity in the midst of chaos, chaos in the midst of serenity—that was Bill Simon.

Among the mourners were statesmen, Olympians, leaders of business and industry and public figures such as Gerald Ford, Henry Kissinger, Alexander Haig, Jack Kemp, Rudolph Giuliani, and Donna de Varona. Also among the mourners were scores upon scores of obscure private citizens—the young man in overalls pushing a baby carriage and the elderly woman silently praying on her rosary beads—whose lives were touched in one way or another by Bill.

Bill Simon had passed away five days earlier. Although he was dancing up a storm at a barbecue just a week before, his death wasn't a total surprise. Nearly a year earlier, he collapsed in Rome during an incident precipitated by pulmonary fibrosis, an idiopathic lung disorder. All of us—Bill's family, friends, and employees—feared we might lose him. We prayed for Bill, and selfishly dreaded the absence of such an extraordinary figure from our own lives. We were all too aware how lucky we were to have encountered such a unique man.

But Bill, ever the fighter, made a remarkable, death-defying recovery. He just couldn't do it twice. When it was clear that the end was near, Toni got word to all the children. Toni also called Edward Egan, an old friend of Bill's who had been a bishop in Connecticut and had just been elevated to archbishop-designate of the Archdiocese of New York. Although Bill was too weak to converse, he listened intently to the soon-to-be-cardinal. The words left Bill at ease and fully accepting. Bill died quietly and peacefully, with the serenity of a true believer.

Bill's death made news around the globe, and the varied focal points of the obituaries and tributes illustrate the impact he had in so many different areas, from business to government to philanthropy to philosophy to sports. Some of the articles focused on Bill's leadership during the energy crisis, when he calmed a panicked nation. Others highlighted his service to the Olympic Movement. (A *Newsday* story was headlined: "How Simon Saved the Games: The Late Former President of USOC Left a Legacy as a Creative Renegade.")[2]

Syndicated columnist Richard Reeves penned a column explaining how Bill's brilliantly articulated philosophy changed the parameters of this nation's political debate. "Next to Ronald Reagan, Simon was the most important figure in the rise of the political right in the 1980s and '90s."[3]

Heritage Foundation President Edwin J. Feulner, in a commentary in the *Washington Times*, wrote eloquently of Bill's spiritual side and his literal adherence to Andrew Carnegie's "Gospel of Wealth." "For years, he used to get up early on Christmas morning and drive to Covenant House, a runaway youth shelter in New York. When his children were old enough, he brought them along, too. They worked in the kitchen. They served meals. Afterward, they distributed presents and spent time with teenagers and unwed mothers—young people who had hit rock bottom," Mr. Feulner wrote.[4]

Leslie Lenkowsky, in a tribute printed in the *Chronicle of Philanthropy*, credited Bill with making the case "for philanthropy that identified progress with the growth of enterprise rather than of government." "What Mr. Simon did," wrote Mr. Lenkowsky, professor of philanthropic studies and public policy at the Indiana University Center on Philanthropy, "was to show how 'conservative'—or as he probably would have preferred, 'classical liberal'—ideas could be translated into serious grant making...If not well appreciated in his own time, Bill Simon's legacy—like that of his philanthropic hero, Andrew Carnegie—is likely to grow steadily in the future."[5]

———

JAMES E. PIERESON, AUGUST 17, 1998

Bill is a person with tremendous energy. He does not like to sit still. He wants to be involved in many different things. He is not the type of person to get involved in one thing and spend all his time on it. I don't think any one thing can absorb his attention. He has incredibly high standards to make sure that everything he does is done right.... When it is all summed up, I think people will realize he was one of the most important figures of the last third of the twentieth century. When you consider his success on Wall Street, his political success, his books, the John M. Olin Foundation, the leveraged buyout work, the Olympics, the philanthropy, I think it will be seen that he was a trailblazer in a whole host of different fields and, at least on the political/intellectual side, one can look back and say he was on the winning side . . . with the demise of communism and the admission that socialism doesn't work. Bill was one of the people who was raising that flag back in the mid-1970s. When you sum it all up, you see a tremendously important figure.

———

In his homily, Archbishop-designate Egan spoke of Jesus' sermon at Galilee, when Christ delivered "what is perhaps the most celebrated religious discourse in all of history." Jesus articulated a message that was truly revolutionary, and seemingly contradictory: the poor will have a kingdom, the humble will inherit the earth, and the persecuted will be rewarded. It was a sermon that Bill Simon took to heart, and one that he took literally.

"I did not know Bill Simon when he was Energy czar," Archbishop-designate Egan told mourners. "I did not know Bill Simon when he was secretary of the treasury. I did not know Bill Simon when he was an incredibly successful and famous investment banker...I knew Bill Simon as a man who was striving to live out that sermon in Galilee....

"Last year I took [a] trip with Bill Simon...to Rome where he was to receive two honorary doctorates from ancient Roman universities, the Gregorian and the Angelicum. Bill was not feeling at all well. Nonetheless, he decided that the trip would not be a delightful tour, but a religious pilgrimage...He arranged for us to stay in a monastery on the Aventine hill, a beautiful monastery, but a monastery, without any of the ordinary amenities that we Americans expect. As Bill became sicker, we called the doctor and after a little talk with the doctor, I decided I'd have a little talk with Bill.

" 'We need to move to a hotel,' I insisted....

" 'I'm staying right here,' he replied. 'I came here to do this thing the right way. I came to Rome to pray and this is where I belong. This is no pleasure trip, Bishop. I am here to tell the Lord about all the wonderful suffering people to whom I bring Communion in the hospital. He will hear me better here.'

"To anyone who knew Bill Simon over the past ten to twelve years, you will recognize that nothing gave him so much joy and spiritual pleasure as bringing the Eucharist to the sick in the hospitals. He told me he brought his spiritual sons and daughters with him in his heart. He was a pilgrim in Rome for himself and for them. There would be no compromise; he would hunger and thirst for justice and holiness, and he would have his fill. We stayed in the monastery."

After the Bible readings, the grandchildren brought their gifts to the altar. There were six eulogies, all beautiful and unique in their own way, and collectively representing a blend of Bill's public and private lives.

"Anyone who met Bill for the first time was impressed by his brain. Anyone who *knew* Bill was moved by his heart," President Ford told the congregation. "He was a Wall Street wizard turned Eucharistic minister—an economic statesman, equally at home in the gilt-edged corridors of power and comforting AIDS patients in an East Harlem hospital."

Olympic gold medalist Donna de Varona reflected on Bill's olympian spirit. "He believed in working hard and, thank goodness for all of us, playing hard," she said. "Whether he was advocating for Olympic athletes, ministering to AIDS patients, solving the energy crisis, or making huge sums of money, and then diligently giving it away, he believed in competing with his whole heart and soul, but always in fairness. There were never any hidden agendas with Bill Simon."

Grandson Jonathan Streep, nineteen, recalled Bill's playful, fanciful side, a side which some of those with whom he battled in business and government never saw but which his family knew intimately. "Santa Claus represents almost every aspect of our grandfather," Jonathan told the mourners. "Imagine a child's delight when their grandfather tells them he would write them notes excusing them from school to go out and get ice cream, or when he would toss us around the pool, spitting water in our faces every chance he got. Or when he would drive his Rolls Royce like a maniac all over his front lawn, chasing the geese in all directions. This was our grandfather."

Granddaughter Cary Simon read a poem she had written in which she compared her beloved "Pa" to the stars in the heavens—infinite, spinning in their own orbit, and providing the light of the world.

Daughter Julie Simon Munro shared her final conversation with her dad, when he was hospitalized and she was aboard *Itasca* in the Fiji islands. She spoke to her father from an island called Musket Cove, on the west side of Fiji. "So there he was, desperately ill in the hospital, and there I was out in the middle of the ocean. And yet, I felt as close to his spirit as I could be...."

Julie revealed her difficulties in conceiving a child, and Bill's willingness to leave the matter in God's hands. "When the doctors told me they couldn't help me, and that I was unlikely to bear children of my own, my father just wouldn't believe it. He insisted we travel to Lourdes together in order to volunteer with the sick, and to pray for a baby. A year later, our daughter Gigi was born, which strengthened his faith and completely changed my life... I was able to tell him two weeks ago that we were expecting another grandchild... He was so thrilled, you would have thought it was his first."

And finally, it was the turn of Bill's oldest child, William E. Simon, Jr. "Some people become identified with one word: Abraham Lincoln—honesty; Winston Churchill—determination... For Dad, it was freedom. He made mention of it in practically every article he wrote, every speech he delivered," Bill Jr. told the mourners. "Did this focus on freedom flower in his youth, where he yearned to be his own person? Or, was it later, where his brilliant success on Wall Street became less about acquiring material wealth than developing his God-given potential—in a word, to be free in the fullest possible sense? Or was it later still, when he became one of the early and most forceful leaders of the conservative movement, which was premised on individual freedoms?"

Bill described his father as "a man who loved his family more than words could ever say... a man who fought for freedom every day of his life, and a man who introduced God to those who needed Him most.... He never once stopped trying to learn or stopped caring about those four pillars in his life—family, faith, friends, and freedom—and his legacy will be a beacon for generations to come."

That is indeed his legacy. This book, virtually completed at the time of his death and the last of his myriad obsessions, is his epitaph.

To me, Bill Simon was the quintessential American—a patriot in spirit and in fact; a man whose basic goodness radiated through his hands-on philanthropy; a person of devout and abiding faith; a relentless competitor who fought hard but fair; a fiercely loyal friend to anyone who earned his friendship; a frighteningly formidable foe to anyone who crossed him; a multimillionaire aristocrat who never forgot his Depression-era roots; a defender of the underdog for whom few sins were worse than kicking a person when they were down; a cheerful and infectious optimist who really and truly thought every day in America was wonderful and the next day would be even better; and a bit of a rascal who never quite shed the mischievous spirit that precipitated his not-always-by-choice departure from a number of high schools. He was Uncle Sam, Horatio Alger, and Tom Sawyer, all blended into one exquisite portrait painted by Norman Rockwell.

The three years during which I worked so closely on these memoirs with Bill were among the most professionally satisfying and personally enlightening of my career and life. As a journalist for over twenty years, I have interviewed presidential candidates, cabinet members, governors, astronauts, professional athletes, legal titans, brilliant artists, leaders of industry, and various figures of historic significance. I am not easily star-struck or impressed by celebrity. But I knew from the beginning that Bill Simon was something special, something unique, one of the very few truly larger-than-life figures I would encounter in my life. His passion was something to behold and, at times, endure. ("Life is NOT a dress rehearsal!" he admonished time and again.) His success in so many endeavors in so many different fields was an inspiration and a reminder of all that is possible in this remarkable country, so long as we remain free.

Personally, Bill helped me reconnect with my own patriotism and faith, although I doubt he had any idea he was doing so. Certainly, I had not become unpatriotic to the nation and national values that I cherish, or hostile to the Roman Catholic roots that are as ingrained in my being as my Irish-American heritage. Far from it. But I had grown complacent and those essential elements of my life were tucked away in a mental and moral closet, somewhat forgotten and neglected, but neither discarded nor abandoned. Bill, through the blunt nature of his personality, and the object lesson that was his life, blew apart the closet door and helped me rediscover this intellectual and spiritual treasure trove, and I am profoundly grateful.

That we succeeded in posthumously completing this book, embodying all the hope and spirit of Bill and his beloved country, is my way of saying "thanks" to the giant and the legend that was William E. Simon.

ACKNOWLEDGMENTS

by William E. Simon, Jr.

My father's final project was to document his incredible life story, so that his family and country might fully and completely understand where he came from, where he went, and why he was so passionately, fervently, obsessively devoted to the cause of freedom—both as an abstract ideal and a pragmatic means to ensuring a just and fair society.

Unfortunately, Dad died before his memoirs could be published. Fortunately, he had already reviewed and approved a nearly completed version of this book, and left dozens of audio and video tapes in which he eloquently articulated his thoughts, beliefs, and recollections. While there were certainly some loose ends to tie up, the thoughts, observations, and opinions are strictly and solely those of my father.

Autobiographies are all too frequently self-indulgent and all too rarely objective. Dad, who hardly ever did anything in a conventional manner, avoided those normal pitfalls by retaining researchers (culminating with John Caher, a professional journalist) whose job it was to candidly interview dozens of people with whom he had dealt over the years. There were no restrictions on what they could ask, and no restrictions on what they could be told. They were directed only to seek the truth. Throughout this book, the comments of friends, associates, family, and acquaintances appear as "other voices," and their observations add unique dimensions and perspectives to this portrait of my father and his historic life and times.

I know I convey Dad's sentiments in expressing sincere appreciation to all those who supported and assisted this initiative, especially President Gerald R. Ford and Secretary George P. Shultz. President Ford and Secretary Shultz not only submitted to interviews, but wrote separate introductions to this book. Dad would have been absolutely delighted, and profoundly moved, by the friendship and loyalty so publicly displayed through the efforts and kind words of President Ford and Secretary Shultz.

In addition, several of my father's colleagues and acquaintances graciously volunteered their expertise on various topics to ensure the accuracy of this book.

John Bockstoce and Captain Allan W.C. Jouning shared their technical knowledge on the Northwest Passage and their journey through it on an expedition Dad initiated; Olympian Michael Lenard offered insight into the Olympic Games; William Salomon, Robert MacDonald, and John Fitterer assisted with the Wall Street chapter; David Bradford provided keen insight into economic matters; Robin Jones and Roy Doumaini reviewed the chapter on the savings and loan initiative; and Ben Elliott helped put the finishing touches on the final chapter following my father's death.

Literary agent Anne Hawkins, of John Hawkins & Associates of Manhattan, provided invaluable editorial advice and was an immense help in preparing the manuscript for final delivery to our publisher, Regnery Publishing. Our editor at Regnery, Xiaochin Yan, offered invaluable insight and advice.

Additionally, I would like to thank our "go-to man," Chris LeMessurier, and our "go-to woman," Caroline M. Hemphill. Chris's official responsibility was to tape interviews with my father and others, and the audio and video tapes he produced should prove a valuable resource for future historians. But Chris did so much more—from tracking down old photographs to driving John Caher to interviews to cheerfully completing any number of tasks. Cary, director of special programs and assistant secretary-treasurer of the John M. Olin Foundation, was always there to do whatever needed to be done, and a whole lot needed to be done.

I know Dad would have reserved a very special and heart-felt "thank you" for his dear friend and confidante, Jim Piereson, the superb executive director of the John M. Olin Foundation. Jim was involved from start to finish. His wisdom, attention to detail, incredible memory for historic facts, impeccable judgment and good taste, and his commitment to Dad and what he stood for is evident on every single page of this book. I know, firsthand, how much Jim put into this book, and I also know, firsthand, how deeply appreciative Dad was of his efforts.

Finally, this book never would have been completed without the able assistance of John Caher. John labored mightily with Dad, Jim, and myself for a number of years, conducted numerous interviews, and did an extraordinary amount of legwork to cover the diverse areas of Dad's life.

——

William E. Simon, Jr.
December 2003

ENDNOTES

CHAPTER 1: SHIRTSLEEVES TO SHIRTSLEEVES

1. Sociology, my favorite course, was fascinating. Economics was a bloody bore, probably because of the professor, who himself was a bloody bore. Frankly, nothing I learned about economics at Lafayette helped me a bit on Wall Street (and, in fact, a quip I once made suggesting that the only advice I would seek from an economist was directions to the men's room was typical of the attitude on the Street). My real education in economics didn't come for another twenty years, when I went to Washington as deputy secretary of the treasury and learned first hand from the likes of George Shultz and Ezra Solomon and studied the works of Milton Friedman and George Stigler. There is no better modern book on economic freedom, by the way, than Milton Friedman's, *Capitalism and Freedom* (The University of Chicago Press, Chicago, 1962).

CHAPTER 2: OUT ON THE "STREET"

1. In 1987, my charitable foundation established funding for the Timothy Charles Simon Wing of the Morristown Memorial Hospital.

CHAPTER 3: AT SALOMON BROTHERS

1. The firm retained Morton Hutzler's name until 1970, but for years everyone knew the company only as Salomon Brothers.
2. Robert Sobel, *Salomon Brothers 1910-1985: Advancing to Leadership* (copyrighted by Salomon Brothers in 1986), 103.

3. Rudy Smutny later became a partner in the firm of duPont, Glore Forgan, which in 1970 became a major backer for an up-and-coming computer services magnate: H. Ross Perot. See Martin Mayer, *Nightmare on Wall Street* (Simon & Schuster, New York: 1993), 39.

4. Even by the late 1960s, Salomon Brothers' partners were paid a salary of about $35,000, plus 5 percent on their capital and the payment of taxes by the firm.

5. At the same time, Morton Hutzler's was dropped from the firm name.

CHAPTER 4: INSIDE THE BELTWAY

1. One of the great joys of my life was being able to call Jesse Owens my friend. Jesse was not only a great champion, but also a man of incredible character, courage and integrity. The son of a cotton picker and grandson of slaves, Jesse Owens overcame incredible adversity to become, in my opinion, the greatest athlete of the twentieth century. His four gold medals at the 1936 Olympic Games in Berlin disproved the racist ranting of Adolph Hitler and gave all freedom-loving people—black and white—a hero for all times. President Ford honored Jesse in 1976 with the Presidential Medal of Freedom, and in 1979 President Carter awarded him the Living Legends Award.

2. Willie Davenport, after giving up smoking, qualified for the 1976 Games, and won a bronze medal in the 110-meter hurdles in Montreal, the same event in which he had won the gold medal in 1968. In all, Willie, who was inducted into the Olympic Hall of Fame in 1991, the same year as I, competed in five Olympic games—the 1964, 1968, 1972, and 1976 games as a member of the track and field team, and the 1980 games as a member of the U.S. bobsled team.

3. Fred Malek went on to become president of Mariott Corp., the hotel chain, and Northwest Airlines.

4. Salomon Brothers generally required partners to leave their bonus capital with the firm, and even held onto those assets for five years after a partner retired or resigned. However, since I was going to government, and therefore needed to place my assets in a blind trust, I was able to leave the firm with a nest egg of about $5 million.

CHAPTER 5: THE ENERGY CZAR

1. The eight largest oil companies were: Exxon, Texaco, Gulf, Mobil, Standard of California, Standard of Indiana, Shell, and Atlantic Richfield.

2. On April 28, 1974, John Mitchell and Maurice Stans were acquitted of all

fifteen counts in a criminal conspiracy case involving campaign contributions not connected to Watergate. Peter Fleming, Carol's old boyfriend, represented Mitchell in a trial that would mark the first time in our nation's history that two cabinet members were jointly tried on charges connected to their official and political duties. Later, Mitchell, Haldeman, and Ehrlichman—three of the president's closest advisors—were charged (and ultimately convicted) with Watergate-related infractions.

3. It was not publicly known at the time, nor was I aware, that the grand jury had named Richard Nixon as an unindicted coconspirator.

4. For the record, I liked and respected both Haldeman and Ehrlichman and never witnessed any dishonesty on the part of either.

5. John Dean was a despicable back stabber who, a short while later, displayed his vindictiveness and cost Earl L. Butz his job as secretary of agriculture. Earl made the mistake of making an off-color joke to Dean during a private discussion aboard an airplane. Dean promptly reported Earl Butz's quip in *Rolling Stone* magazine. Classy guy.

6. "An Interview with William Simon," *The Today Show*, July 9, 1973.

7. We did in fact have dinner at the White House on Thursday, March 7, 1974, with President and Mrs. Nixon. Despite her public image as cold and aloof, Pat Nixon was a gracious and delightful woman, and a great comfort to the president during all his trials and tribulations. He truly valued her judgment, and Carol and I valued her friendship. I remember once when Carol had a small lunch at our home for the subcabinet, and the First Lady went out of her way to attend. That's the kind of person she was, thoughtful and sincere.

CHAPTER 6: SUCCESSOR TO HAMILTON

1. At the time President Nixon imposed wage and price controls, he severed the last link between the dollar and gold, a link that had existed, in diminishing degrees, since 1792. The gold standard had, certainly by the 1970s and probably much earlier, outlived its usefulness and was neither practical nor sensible in the modern economy.

2. My first undersecretary for monetary affairs was Paul Volcker who, of course, went on to serve as chairman of the Federal Reserve. Paul, however, did not stay long and was replaced by Jack Bennett, a tremendous man whose father had once held that very position.

3. Terry Falk Lenzner, an Exeter and Harvard-trained lawyer, was deputy counsel for the Senate Watergate Committee. Terry was an intriguing character, whose legal career ranged from combatting organized crime as an assistant U.S. attorney in New York to defending the antiwar activist

Philip Berrigan on charges of plotting to kidnap Henry Kissinger. In 1998, Lenzner was a private investigator working for President Clinton's lawyers when the president was under investigation for various alleged legal and moral indiscretions.

4. Gerald R. Ford, *A Time to Heal* (New York: Harper & Row, 1979), 21.

CHAPTER 7: IN THE CENTER OF THE STORM

1. Donald Rumsfeld, of course, returned to Washington as President George W. Bush's secretary of defense.

2. "Blueprints" had an impact not only during the Ford administration, but on subsequent administrations as well. It provided the basis for Ronald Reagan's tax initiatives in 1981 and, in December 1992, Secretary of the Treasury Nicholas Brady issued a similar call for fundamental reform. Even now, "Blueprints" is considered required reading for anyone considering major tax reform and its implications.

CHAPTER 8: THE FORD PRESIDENCY

1. Martin Mayer, "Default at the *New York Times*," *Columbia Journalism Review*, January/February 1976.

CHAPTER 9: A TIME FOR TRUTH

1. In 1991, Salomon Brothers admitted having submitted phony bids in auctions of Treasury securities, an offense which cost the firm $290 million in fines to settle a complaint brought by the Securities and Exchange Commission, and effectively—and wrongly—ended John Gutfreund's career.

2. Richard Allen was at the time the top foreign policy advisor to Governor Reagan. He had previously served as deputy national security advisor to President Nixon, and later served as President Reagan's national security advisor.

3. The committee consisted of George Shultz, as chairman, myself, and Arthur Burns, Milton Friedman, Alan Greenspan, Paul McCracken, Charls [CQ]Walker, Michael Halbouty, Rep. Jack Kemp, James Lynn, Murray Weidenbaum, Caspar Weinberger, and Walter Wriston.

CHAPTER 10: JIMMY CARTER'S OLYMPIC BOYCOTT

1. Jesse Owens died of lung cancer in Tucson, Arizona, on March 31, 1980. The last line of the inscription on his grave marker sums up my thoughts of this great man: "His faith in America inspired countless others to do their best for themselves and their country."

2. Donna de Varona, who at the age of thirteen was the youngest member of the Olympic swimming team to compete at the 1960 Olympics in Rome, broke eighteen world swimming records and won two gold medals in Tokyo in 1964.

3. Article IX of the USOC Constitution states: "No member of the USOC may deny, or threaten to deny, any amateur athlete the opportunity to compete in the Olympic Games."

4. Many of our staunchest allies, however, did not honor the boycott. France, Italy, Switzerland, Belgium, and even Puerto Rico, a U.S. territory, participated in the 1980 Games. Although Margaret Thatcher reluctantly asked British athletes to boycott, most of them ignored her request and went to Moscow.

Chapter 11: USOC Presidency

1. The gold medal for the pentathlon was given to Hugo Wieslander of Sweden, while Ferdinand Bie of Norway was awarded the gold medal for the decathlon. However, the medals, meaningless to Wieslander and Bie, who knew they rightly belonged to Thorpe, were lost.

2. Jim Thorpe tragically died an alcoholic in 1953, twenty-nine years before his athletic redemption.

3. Jack Kelly, who succeeded me as USOC president, had an unusual perspective on the amateurism debate. His father, Jack Sr., a tremendous oarsman from Philadelphia, won the singles and doubles competitions at the 1920 Games in Antwerp. The elder Kelly, however, was denied an opportunity to row in the Royal Henley Regatta in England because he was a workingman, a laborer. I always thought it was delicious irony that his daughter, a beautiful and talented actress named Grace Kelly, became royalty when she married Prince Rainier of Monaco in 1956.

4. By the 1992 Barcelona Games, the Olympic community had accepted "open" competition. Not surprisingly, many of those who were most opposed reversed their position—and then took credit when sanity finally prevailed!

5. Two months after my term as president ended, and Robert Helmick, an Iowa lawyer and friend of Horst Dassler, took over, the USOC signed a contract with ISL. A month after that, the International Olympic Committee anointed Bob Helmick as the new U.S. representative on the IOC, over the protestations of the USOC. Helmick resigned under pressure in 1991 after press reports that he earned at least $127,000 in 1990 from clients involved with the Olympic movement.

6. AT&T had committed itself, way back on September 29, 1982, to sponsor the relay.

7. William E. Simon, "Olympics for Olympians," *New York Times*, Sunday, July 29, 1984, E-23.

8. In 1976, two days before the Montreal Games were to begin, twenty-four countries pulled out in protest of the inclusion of New Zealand, which had sent a rugby team on tour of South Africa in violation of an international sports ban on South Africa for its official policy of racial segregation. In 1980, the United States and many of its allies boycotted, followed by the Soviet withdrawal in 1984.

9. The ten Olympians who carried the flag, which had been presented to me by President Reagan on June 14, were: Bruce Jenner, John Naber, Billy Mills, Sammy Lee, Pat McCormick, Mack Robinson, Wyomia Tyus, Richard Sandoval, William "Parry" O'Brien, and Al Oerter.

10. Figure skater Tonya Harding was implicated in 1994 in an attack on another athlete, Nancy Kerrigan, in an apparent effort to eliminate Ms. Harding's prime competition by injuring her rival. Bill Hybl, who had previously served as interim president of the USOC and who ran a large foundation, El Pomar, which provided crucial support for the USOC's move to Colorado Springs, was asked to lead the ethics investigation. Ms. Harding eventually pleaded guilty to a conspiracy charge for her role in the attack on Ms. Kerrigan. Bill became USOC president in 1996.

11. Throughout 1999, the news was filled with reports of officials with the Salt Lake City Organizing Committee essentially bribing IOC members with gifts and perks to secure rights to host the 2002 Winter Games.

12. U.S. Olympic Hall of Fame members are selected by the National Sportscasters and Sportswriters Association (NSSA), the USOC Board of Directors, and Hall of Fame members. The first Olympic Hall of Fame class was inducted in 1983 in Chicago. That charter class includes Jesse Owens, Muhammed Ali, Al Oerter, Wilma Rudolph, and Jim Thorpe.

13. I was immensely honored to receive the General Douglas MacArthur Award from the USOC in September 1999. The award, named after a former president of the USOC and one of America's greatest heroes, had at that time been bestowed only on two members of the 1936 U.S. Olympic track and field team, Marty Glickman and Sam Stoller.

CHAPTER 12: LEVERAGED BUYOUTS

1. Henry Kravis, of course, went on to make an incredible fortune in leveraged buyouts and orchestrated the biggest LBO in history—the $25 billion deal for RJR Nabisco in 1988.

Chapter 13: California, Here I Come!

1. It's important to understand and appreciate the difference between a merchant bank and an investment bank. A merchant bank is an entity that invests in and owns assets. It is an investor as opposed to a consultant. An investment bank, regardless of its name, is really not an investor. Rather, it primarily serves as an advisory capacity, similar to the way a real estate broker serves as an advisor or consultant or conduit. We set up WSGP— a merchant bank—as a vehicle to buy commercial banks, savings and loans, and real estate.

2. Larry Thrall died March 2, 1998, of complications following abdominal surgery. He was only fifty-six years old and left behind a wife and three children—a casualty, I'm afraid, of the acrimony and stress that resulted from the California initiative and the thrift crisis.

3. The worldwide stock market crash of October 1987, however, scuttled Ariadne's ambitions and put Bruce Judge out of business. We later bought Ariadne out of its real estate investments. When the bottom fell out on the real estate market, the property was worth considerably less than the $32 million we paid for it.

4. The initial purpose of William E. Simon & Sons was, and is, to prudently manage the Simon family capital. Eventually, WES & Sons opened offices in Morristown and Los Angeles and accepted institutional monies. Then, and now, William E. Simon & Sons is a risk-taking firm. We put our own money up every single day, and we risk our own money every single day. In addition, we more recently began to manage third-party capital, and today our assets under management total approximately $1 billion.

5. See 12 U.S.C. s1464 (t) (2) (A).

6. The Bishop Estate, along with our investor group, made a substantial profit by investing in the First Interstate Bank of Hawaii, a commercial bank that WSGP sold in 1990.

7. In 1992, we sold HonFed to BankAmerica Corp. for $157 million, a sum that more than tripled our investment and made $25 million for the Bishop Estate.

8. *U.S. v. Winstar Corp.*, 518 U.S. 839 (1996).

9. The case was continuing its slow journey through the courts long after Mr. Simon's death, but culminated in an extremely favorable ruling in March 2003 when Judge Emily C. Hewitt of the United States Court of Federal Claims ordered the government to pay $305 million in damages to Westfed Holdings Inc. Following Judge Hewitt's decision, Chief Judge

Lawrence M. Baskir (who, in May 2002, adopted the opinion of another judge who accused the government of "ignoring or misrepresenting the law" and opined that the "United States has not acted in a manner worthy of the great just nation it is") said that over the lengthy life of this protracted litigation "the government's tactics have not improved," that there is no question the government breached its contract, and refused the government's request to dismiss the action. The Simon family and the investor group were entirely vindicated.

CHAPTER 14: CONQUERING THE NORTHWEST PASSAGE

1. I met Captain Jouning through my friend William F. Buckley. Bill had retained Captain Jouning on various excursions and spoke highly of his seamanship and good fellowship.

CHAPTER 15: A TIME TO GIVE

1. Among the great Americans on the board were: John J. McCloy, president of Chase Manhattan Bank, undersecretary of war under President Roosevelt, high commissioner to Germany in the Truman administration, and advisor to several presidents; investment banker John W. Hanes, a senior partner in Charles D. Barney & Company; Eugene F. Williams, Jr., president of Centerre Trust Co. in St. Louis; Walter O'Connell, vice chairman of the Peat Marwick accounting firm; and George J. Gillespie III, a partner at the law firm of Cravath, Swaine & Moore, and John's personal attorney, and, later, mine as well. Later, when McCloy, Hanes, and O'Connell retired or died, they were replaced by: Richard Furlaud, a chairman of Squibb Corp; Charles Knight, chairman of Emerson Electric; and Peter Flanigan, a longtime friend of mine and colleague from the Nixon administration and partner at Dillon, Read, and Co.

CHAPTER 16: A TIME FOR FAITH

1. Peter Grace died of cancer in April 1995.
2. A century earlier, in *Rerum Novarum*—which, for one hundred years, remained the Church's premier statement on social and economic affairs—Pope Leo XIII rejected what was then a growing socialist movement as "futile" and "unjust," and even "evil."

CHAPTER 17: A TIME TO MOURN; A TIME TO HEAL

1. Ecclesiastes 3:1-2, 4.

CHAPTER 18: MOVING ON

1. Alex Donnelley Lamm, Toni's daughter, is a regular on the long-running television soap opera, *The Young and the Restless*. Professionally, she uses her maiden name, Alex Donnelley.

POSTSCRIPT

1. There were seventeen honorary pallbearers: Ettore Barbatelli, Raymond G. Chambers, Richard F. Chapdelaine, George J. Gillespie III, Theodore E. Gordon, George W. Gowen, O. Wayne Isom, Allan W.C. Jouning, William M. Kearns Jr., Henry A. Kissinger, William C. Maloney, James E. Piereson, William R. Salomon, John B. Schulte, James P. Shenfield, George P. Shultz, and William B. Tutt.

2. John Jeansonne, "How Simon Saved the Games: The Late Former President of the USOC Left a Legacy as Creative Renegade," *Newsday*, June 15, 2000, A-84.

3. Richard Reeves, "The Man Who 'Righted' Journalism," *Denver Post*, June 11, 2000, I-3.

4. Edwin J. Feulner, "Private Side of a Public Figure," *Washington Times*, June 9, 2000, A18.

5. Leslie Lenkowsky, "William Simon's Legacy to Philanthropy," *The Chronicle of Philanthropy*, June 15, 2000, 55.

INDEX